Table of Contents

Introduction ....

Main Dish Recipes..16
   Cauliflower Soup 16
   Chicken and Delicious Sauce 16
   Different Lasagna...17
   Delicious Pork Chops..17
   Chili Bowl...18
   Chicken and Squash Spaghetti 18
   Easy Pork Roast 19
   Broccoli Soup 19
   Pork Chops and Gravy 20
   Pork Bowls..20
   Beef Meatloaf 21
   Pork and Veggies 21
   Chicken and Tasty Cauliflower Rice 22
   Chicken Curry...22
   Shrimp and Zucchini Spaghetti 23
   Fish and Carrot Soup 23
   Trout Fillet and Sauce 24
   Shrimp and Mushrooms 24
   Lemon and Garlic Shrimp 25
   Haddock and Mayonnaise..25
   Chicken and Mushrooms 26
   Chicken and Salsa..26
   Salsa Chicken Soup 27
   Hot Beef Stew 27
   Leg of Lamb and Spinach Salad..28
   Lamb Stew 28
   Beef and Mushroom Stew 29
   Pomegranate and Walnuts Chicken 29
   Sausages and Mashed Celeriac..30
   Seafood Summer Mix...30
   Mexican Chicken Soup 31
   Okra and Beef Stew 31
   Beef and Cabbage Stew 32
   Lamb Shanks and Carrots 32
   Pork with Lemon Sauce 33

Meatballs and Sauce 33

Salmon and Veggies 34

Shrimp and Turnips 34

Squid and Veggies 35

Artichokes and Sauce 35

Squash and Chicken Cream 36

Veggie Soup 36

Cabbage and Carrot Soup 37

Asparagus Cream 37

Fresh Fennel and Leek Soup 38

Chicken Stew 38

Turkey Stew 39

Mushroom Stew 39

Stuffed Bell Peppers 40

Crab Legs 40

Snacks and Appetizer Recipes 41

Cranberry Dip 41

Chili Dip 41

Zucchini Dip 42

Beets and Squash Dip 42

Cheese and Sausage Dip 43

Creamy Mushroom Dip 43

Cauliflower Dip 44

Spicy Mango Dip 44

Tomato Dip 45

Mustard and Mushrooms Dip 45

Artichoke Dip 46

Asparagus and Prosciutto Appetizer 46

Salmon Patties 47

Cod Puddings 47

Mussels Appetizer 48

Italian Mussels Appetizer 48

Spicy Mussels 49

Mussels Bowls 49

Clams and Mussels 50

Stuffed Clams 50

Shrimp and Sausage Appetizer Bowls 51

Asian Shrimp Appetizer 51

Mediterranean Octopus Appetizer 52

Chinese Squid Appetizer 52

Simple Artichokes...53

Cajun Shrimp..53

French Endives..54

Endives and Ham Appetizer 54

Eggplant Spread 55

Okra Bowls...55

Easy Leeks Platter...56

Tomatoes Appetizer...56

Cinnamon and Pumpkin Muffins 57

Spicy Chili Balls 57

Italian Dip..58

Avocado Dip...58

Minty Shrimp Appetizer 59

Zucchini Appetizer Salad 59

Zucchini Hummus 60

Crab and Cheese Dip...60

Spinach Dip..61

Stuffed Mushrooms 61

Turkey Meatballs 62

Italian Chicken Wings..62

Zucchini Rolls 63

Spicy Salsa...63

Salmon Balls...64

Delicious Oysters 64

Tuna Patties...65

Worcestershire Shrimp...65

Side Dish Recipes 66

Napa Cabbage Side Salad 66

Asian Brussels Sprouts 66

Cauliflower and Parmesan 67

Swiss Chard and Garlic 67

Mushroom and Arugula Side Dish 68

Red Chard and Olives 68

Kale and Almonds 69

Green Cabbage and Paprika 69

Coconut Cream and Sausage Gravy 70

Vietnamese Eggplant Side Dish...70

Baby Mushrooms Sauté 71

Cauliflower and Eggs Salad 71

Asparagus and Cheese Side Dish 72

Sprouts and Apple Side Dish 72

Radishes and Chives...73

Hot Radishes with Bacon and Cheese 73

Avocado Side Salad 74

Swiss Chard and Pine Nuts 74

Spinach and Chard Mix 75

Cherry Tomatoes and Parmesan Mix 75

Almond Cauliflower Rice 76

Saffron Cauliflower Rice 76

Hot Cauliflower Rice and Avocado 77

Celery and Rosemary Side Dish 77

Lemon Cauliflower Rice 78

Spinach Cauliflower Rice 78

Squash Puree 79

Celeriac Fries 79

Green Beans Side Dish 80

Cauliflower and Pineapple Risotto 80

Parsnips Mash...81

Cauliflower Mash...81

Turnips Puree 82

Carrot Mash 82

Carrots with Thyme and Dill 83

Lemon Broccoli 83

Poached Fennel 84

Mixed Bell Peppers Side Dish 84

Beet and Garlic...85

Green Beans and Tomatoes..85

Bok Choy and Garlic 86

Red Cabbage and Applesauce 86

Beets and Capers 87

Beet and Arugula Side Salad 87

Tomato and Beet Side Salad 88

Broccoli and Garlic...88

Brussels Sprouts and Dill 89

Savoy Cabbage and Bacon 89

Sweet Cabbage..90

Collard Greens and Tomato Sauce 90

Dessert Recipes 91

   Raspberry Dessert 91

   Blueberries and Strawberries Cream 91

   Lemon Cream 92

   Cream Cheese Bars 92

   Cocoa Pudding 93

   Avocado Pudding 93

   Peppermint Pudding 94

   Coconut Pudding 94

   Orange Cake 95

   Walnuts Cream 95

   Lemon Cream 96

   Chocolate Cream 96

   Berry Cream 97

   Strawberry Cream 97

   Caramel Pudding 98

   Peanut and Chia Pudding 98

   Pumpkin Cream 99

   Chia Jam 99

   Melon Cream 100

   Peach Cream 100

   Peaches and Sweet Sauce 101

   Chestnut Cream 101

   Cheesecake 102

   Banana Cake 102

   Pumpkin Cake 103

   Apple Cake 103

   Upside Down Cake 104

   Almond Cake 104

   French Coconut Cream 105

   Flavored Pears 105

   Pumpkin Pudding 106

   Strawberries and Cranberries Marmalade 106

   Pear Marmalade 107

   Peach Marmalade 107

   Strawberries Compote 108

   Sweet Peaches 108

   Simple Peach Compote 109

   Apple Cobbler 109

Zucchini Cake 110

Pineapple and Cauliflower Pudding...110

Chocolate Pudding 111

Strawberries Compote 111

Carrot, Pecans and Raisins Cake 112

Fresh Figs 112

Sweet Carrots 113

Pear Pudding..113

Winter Fruit Cobbler 114

Pumpkin Granola...114

Carrot and Chia Seed Pudding 115

Cinnamon Rice Pudding...115

Breakfast Recipes...116

Colored Cauliflower and Eggs Breakfast 116

Simple Breakfast Hash Browns 116

Delicious Breakfast Meatloaf 117

Cajun Breakfast Hash Browns...117

Eggs and Chives...118

Eggs and Cheese Breakfast...118

Breakfast Blueberry Cake 119

Egg Casserole 119

Breakfast Pancake 120

Tomato and Spinach Eggs 120

Breakfast Frittata 121

Mexican Breakfast Casserole 121

Burrito Casserole 122

Breakfast Oatmeal..122

Chocolate Oatmeal 123

Blueberry and Yogurt Bowl...123

Breakfast Cauliflower Pudding...124

Scotch Eggs 124

Celeriac and Bacon Breakfast..125

Meat Quiche 125

Cinnamon Oatmeal..126

Cauliflower Congee 126

Breakfast Avocado Cups...127

Smoked Salmon and Shrimp Breakfast..127

Beef Breakfast Pie 128

Delicious Breakfast Skillet..128

6

Pork Sausage Quiche 129

Sausage, Leeks and Eggs Casserole 129

Almond Porridge 130

Almond and Chia Breakfast..130

Nuts Bowl 131

Kale and Prosciutto Muffins..131

Bacon Muffins 132

Cheddar and Parmesan Muffins 132

Eggs and Turkey..133

Chia Pudding 133

Pumpkin Spread..134

Mushroom, Tomatoes and Zucchini Mix 134

Okra and Zucchinis Breakfast 135

Squash and Cranberry Sauce 135

Beef and Radish Hash 136

Sweet Carrots Breakfast...136

Breakfast Omelet...137

Nuts, Squash and Apples Breakfast 137

Leek and Beef Breakfast Mix..138

Strawberries and Coconut Breakfast....................................138

Chorizo and Veggies Mix 139

Delicious Vanilla and Espresso Oatmeal 139

Coconut and Pomegranate Oatmeal 140

Cauliflower Rice Bowl 140

Conclusion...141

Introduction 143

Main Dish Recipes..144

Butternut And Chard Soup...144

Tender Pork Chops 144

Asian Style Salmon...145

Creamy Soup...145

Easy Tomato Soup..146

Carrot And Ginger Soup..146

Red Peppers Soup...147

Delicious Fish Stew 147

Chicken Stew 148

Veggie Stew..148

Special Pork And Sauce 149

Beef Stew 149

Cold Veggie Delight 150

Mushroom Stew 150

Different And Special Stew 151

Mexican Chicken Soup 151

Creamy Carrot Soup 152

Cauliflower Soup 152

Cod Fillets And Orange Sauce 153

Special Cod Dish 153

Light Salmon 154

Wonderful Salmon And Veggies 154

White Fish Delight 155

Healthy Mackerel 155

Fast Mussels 156

Simple Octopus 156

Easy Artichoke Soup 157

Incredible Beet Soup 157

Refreshing Fennel Soup..158

Unbelievable Chicken...158

Flavored And Delicious Chicken 159

Superb Stuffed Tomatoes..159

Sweet Potato Salad 160

Beef Soup 160

Rich Beef Stew 161

Perfect Chicken Stew..161

Turkey Stew 162

Special Turkey Wings 162

Flavored Chicken And Veggies...163

Crazy Carrots Casserole 163

Rich Cabbage Salad 164

Tomato Stew...164

Colored Tomato And Zucchini 165

Easy And Delicious Zucchini Pasta 165

Easy And Delicious Salad...166

Shrimp Delight 166

Easy Asparagus And Prosciutto Dish......................................167

Special Artichokes 167

Shrimp Surprise 168

Simple Artichoke Dish..168

Snacks And Appetizers Recipes 169

Special Party Spread 169

Red Pepper Spread..169

Onions Delight 170

Special And Delicious Snack...170

Carrot Snack 170

Crab Appetizer...171

Appetizer Meatballs 171

Chicken Appetizer 171

Fish Delight 173

Great Green Dip 173

Carrot Snack 174

Mushroom Appetizer 174

Zucchini Appetizer 175

Crazy And Unique Appetizer 175

Almonds Surprise 176

Sweet Potato Spread 176

Mint Dip 177

Popular Shrimp Appetizer 177

Incredible Scallops 178

Broiled Lobster Tails 178

Delightful Herring Appetizer...178

Salmon Patties 179

Clams And Mussels Appetizer...179

Special Shrimp Appetizer 180

Stuffed Squid 180

Exotic Anchovies 181

Appetizer Salad 181

Carrot Appetizer 182

Salmon Cakes...182

Simple Beef Party Patties..183

Hearty Eggplants Appetizer 183

Elegant Scallops Salad 184

Special Spinach Appetizer Salad 184

Textured Appetizer Salad...185

Incredible Chicken Appetizer 185

Special Bell Peppers Appetizer 186

Red Chard Wonder 186

Special Olives Snack 187

Tasty Turnip Sticks..187

Yummy Mushrooms Snack 188

Cauliflower Dip...188

Wrapped Shrimp 188

Refreshing Zucchini Snack 189

Turkey Appetizer Meatballs 189

Tuna Patties 189

Elegant Duck Appetizer 190

Summer Lamb Appetizer...190

Great Veggie Appetizer 191

Radish Snack...191

Spinach And Chard Appetizer Salad 191

Side Dish Recipes 192

Cauliflower Risotto And Artichokes...192

Cauliflower And Mushroom Risotto 192

Pumpkin And Cauliflower Rice 193

Special Veggie Side Dish 193

Simple Glazed Carrots 194

Great Broccoli Dish...194

Brussels Sprouts Delight 194

Special Sweet Potatoes 195

Tasty Cauliflower And Mint Rice..195

Special Collard Greens..196

Amazing Carrots Side Dish...196

Rich Beets Side Dish 197

Green Beans Side Dish 197

Sweet Potatoes Side Dish 198

Wonderful And Special Side Dish 198

Mashed Sweet Potatoes...199

Tasty Side Dish..199

Spinach Cauliflower Rice 200

Squash Puree...200

Healthy Mushrooms and Green Beans 201

Delicious Cauliflower Rice 201

Lovely Mash 201

Carrot Puree..202

Apple Mash 202

Simple Fennel Side Dish 202

Simple And Fast Side Dish 203

Mixed Veggies 203

Italian Side Dish..204

Artichokes Delight...204

Beets Side Dish..205

Tomato Side Salad 205

Broccoli Side Dish..206

Light Brussels Sprouts Side Dish 206

Perfect Side Dish..207

Unbelievable Cabbage Side Dish..207

Special Flavored Side Dish 208

Southern Side Dish...208

French Endives Side Dish 209

Fast Side Dish Delight 209

Delicious Okra..210

Kale And Carrots Side Dish...210

Sweet Potatoes 211

Classic Indian Side Dish 211

Delicious Pumpkin Side Dish..212

Healthy Broccoli Side Dish 212

Cauliflower And Leeks..213

Tasty Squash Side Dish...213

Special Carrots Side Dish..214

Nutritious Side Dish 214

Zucchini Side Dish 214

Dessert Recipes 215

Almond Cream Cheese Cake 215

Sweet Cauliflower Rice Pudding...215

Great Pears Dessert...216

Pears And Special Sauce...216

Tapioca Pudding 216

Sweet Apples 217

Amazing Chocolate Dessert..217

Simple And Delicious Cake..217

Carrot Cake..218

Simple Cobbler...218

Simple And Delicious Compote 219

Delightful Peaches Surprise 219

Carrots Dessert..219

Elegant Dessert 220

Special Lemon Cream...220

Delicious Carrot Dessert 220

Chocolate Cake 221

Simple And Delicious Compote 221

Special Pudding 222

Fast Dessert 222

Cool Pudding 223

Zucchini Dessert 223

Berry Compote 224

Refreshing Curd 224

The Best Jam Ever 224

Divine Pears 225

Berry Marmalade 225

Orange Delight 225

Simple Squash Pie 226

Winter Pudding 226

Banana Dessert 227

Apple Cake 227

Special Vanilla Dessert 228

Tasty And Amazing Pear Dessert 228

Cranberries Jam 228

Lemon Jam 229

Special Dessert 229

Superb Banana Dessert 229

Rhubarb Dessert 230

Plum Delight 230

Refreshing Fruits Dish 230

Dessert Stew 231

Original Fruits Dessert 231

Delicious Apples And Cinnamon...231

Crazy Delicious Pudding..232

Wonderful Berry Pudding 232

Winter Fruits Dessert..233

Different Dessert 233

Orange Dessert 234

Great Pumpkin Dessert..234

Breakfast Recipes 235

Eggplant Breakfast Spread 235

Chicken Liver Breakfast Spread..235

Mushroom Spread...236

Breakfast Chia Pudding 236

Breakfast Sweet Potatoes 237

Delicious Korean Eggs 237

Great French Eggs 238

Different Eggs Breakfast..238

Delicious Breakfast Casserole 239

Hearty Breakfast 239

Great Egg Casserole 240

Breakfast Quiche 240

Wonderful Frittata...241

Pumpkin and Apple Butter 241

Breakfast Spinach Delight 242

Delicious Breakfast Cobbler 242

Amazing Bacon And Sweet Potato Breakfast 243

Great Veggie Quiche 243

Tomato And Spinach Breakfast Mix 244

Special Breakfast Egg Muffins 244

Breakfast Scotch Eggs 245

Wonderful Breakfast Omelet...245

Superb Zucchini Breakfast..246

Poached Eggs...246

Delicious Breakfast Eggs And Sauce 247

Light Breakfast..247

Great Zucchini Spread 248

Great Butternut Squash Breakfast 248

Special Onion And Bacon Jam 249

Breakfast Apple Spread 249

Simple Breakfast Meatloaf..250

Summer Veggie Breakfast 250

Special Breakfast Butter..251

Zucchini And Carrots Delightful Breakfast 251

Bacon and Sweet Potatoes 252

Acorn Squash Breakfast Surprise 252

Tasty Zucchini And Squash...253

Breakfast Balls 253

Breakfast Muffins 254

Avocado Muffins..254

Chorizo Breakfast..255

Eggs, Ham And Mushroom Mix...255

Delicious Nuts And Fruits Breakfast 256

Leek and Kale Breakfast 256

Nuts Porridge 257

Simple Cherry Breakfast..257

Carrot Breakfast Dish 258

Cauliflower Rice Pudding..258

Breakfast Cauliflower Rice 259

Strawberries Breakfast 259

Conclusion...260

Recipe Index..261

Introduction

A Ketogenic diet is the best thing that could ever happen to you! Trust us! Millions of people all around the world have already discovered this special lifestyle and they all recommend it!
A Ketogenic diet will change you forever! It brings you so many health benefits and it helps you look and feel amazing!
This diet is easy to follow and it will soon show all its positive effects.

If you decided to start a Ketogenic diet, you should probably keep in mind some simple rules you need to follow!
You can consume a lot of veggies and fruits, organic meat, poultry, fish and seafood.
You can also consume nuts and seeds, cheese and healthy oils.
On the other hand, if you are on a Ketogenic diet you are not allowed to eat beans, grains, sugar and artificial ingredients!
Come on, it's not that complicated!

So, have you started a Ketogenic diet yet?
Perfect! Then, all you need now is to learn how to make the best Ketogenic dishes!
We've checked thousands of Ketogenic recipes and we find them all amazing but we thought you could be interested in discovering a new way to make keto meals.
We are talking about cooking keto meals using one of the best kitchen appliances ever: an instant pot!

We won't tell you more! It's time for you to discover the best keto dishes made in your instant pot!
Enjoy!

Main Dish Recipes

Cauliflower Soup

Preparation time: 10 minutes
Cooking time: 10 minutes
Servings: 4

Ingredients:

- 2 tablespoons olive oil
- 1 small yellow onion, chopped
- 1 cauliflower head, florets separated and chopped
- 3 cups chicken stock
- 1 teaspoon garlic powder
- 4 ounces cream cheese, cubed
- A pinch of salt and black pepper
- 1 cup cheddar cheese, shredded
- ½ cup coconut milk

Directions:

Set your instant pot on sauté mode, add oil, heat it up, add onion, stir and cook for 3 minutes. Add cauliflower, stir and cook for 1 minute more. Add stock, mil and garlic powder, stir, cover and cook on High for 6 minutes. Add cream cheese and pulse everything using an immersion blender. Add cheddar cheese, stir soup, ladle into bowls and serve. Enjoy!

Nutrition: calories 261, fat 4, fiber 4, carbs 7, protein 8

Chicken and Delicious Sauce

Preparation time: 1 hour and 10 minutes
Cooking time: 20 minutes
Servings: 4

Ingredients:

- 2 chicken breasts, skinless, boneless and chopped
- 1 tablespoon lemon juice
- 1 cup Greek yogurt
- 1 tablespoon garam masala
- ¼ teaspoon ginger, grated
- A pinch of salt and black pepper

For the sauce:

- 4 teaspoons garam masala
- 4 garlic cloves, minced
- 15 ounces canned tomato sauce
- ½ teaspoon paprika
- ½ teaspoon turmeric
- ¼ teaspoon cayenne

Directions:

In a bowl, mix chicken with lemon juice, yogurt, 1 tablespoon garam masala, ginger, salt and pepper, toss well and leave aside in the fridge for 1 hour. Set your instant pot on sauté mode, add chicken, stir and cook for 5 minutes. Add 4 teaspoons garam masala, garlic, tomato sauce, paprika, turmeric and cayenne, stir, cover the pot and cook on High for 10 minutes. Divide between plates and serve. Enjoy!

Nutrition: calories 452, fat 4, fiber 7, carbs 9, protein 12

Different Lasagna

Preparation time: 10 minutes
Cooking time: 25 minutes
Servings: 8

Ingredients:

- 2 garlic cloves, minced
- 1 pound beef, ground
- 1 yellow onion, chopped
- 1 egg
- ½ cup parmesan cheese, grated
- 1 and ½ cups ricotta cheese
- 20 ounces keto marinara sauce
- 8 ounces mozzarella, sliced

Directions:

Set your instant pot on sauté mode, add onion, garlic and beef, stir and sauté for 5 minutes. Add marinara sauce, stir and transfer half of this mix to a bowl. In another bowl, mix ricotta with parmesan and egg and whisk well. Add half of the mozzarella to your instant pot and spread. Add half of the ricotta mix and spread. Add the remaining beef and marinara mix, the rest of the mozzarella and the rest of the ricotta mix. Cover this with some tin foil, cover the pot and cook on High for 10 minutes. Slice lasagna, divide between plates and serve. Enjoy!

Nutrition: calories 339, fat 4, fiber 2, carbs 8, protein 36

Delicious Pork Chops

Preparation time: 10 minutes
Cooking time: 10 minutes
Servings: 4

Ingredients:

- 4 pork chops, boneless
- 1 tablespoon olive oil
- 3 tablespoons ghee, melted
- 1 cup chicken stock
- A pinch of salt and black pepper
- ¼ teaspoon sweet paprika

Directions:

Set your instant pot on sauté mode, add the oil, heat it up, add pork chops and brown for a few minutes on each side. Add ghee, salt, pepper, paprika and stock, stir, cover pot and cook on High for 5 minutes. Serve your pork chops with a keto side salad. Enjoy!

Nutrition: calories 362, fat 4, fiber 8, carbs 10, protein 19

Chili Bowl

Preparation time: 10 minutes
Cooking time: 15 minutes
Servings: 4

Ingredients:

- 2 pounds beef steak strips, cubed
- 1 teaspoon garlic, minced
- 1 tablespoon water
- 2 teaspoon lime juice
- ½ teaspoon chili powder
- 1 tablespoon olive oil
- A pinch of salt and black pepper
- 3 avocados, pitted, peeled and cubed

Directions:

Set your instant pot on sauté mode, add the oil, heat it up, add garlic, stir and cook for 1 minute. Add beef, stir and brown for 3 minutes more. Add water, lime juice, chili powder, salt and pepper, stir, cover the pot and cook on High for 10 minutes. Set the pot on sauté mode again, cook beef mix for a couple more minutes, divide into bowls and serve with avocados on top. Enjoy!

Nutrition: calories 300, fat 5, fiber 4, carbs 8, protein 17

Chicken and Squash Spaghetti

Preparation time: 10 minutes
Cooking time: 20 minutes
Servings: 4

Ingredients:

- 1 spaghetti squash, halved and seedless
- 1 cup water
- 1 cup keto marinara sauce
- 1 pound chicken, cooked and cubed
- 16 ounces mozzarella cheese, shredded

Directions:

Put 1 cup water in your instant pot, add the trivet, add squash, cover and cook on High for 20 minutes. Shred squash into spaghetti and transfer to a heatproof bowl. Add marinara sauce, chicken and mozzarella, toss, introduce in preheated broiler and cook for a few minutes. Divide into bowls and serve. Enjoy!

Nutrition: calories 329, fat 6, fiber 6, carbs 9, protein 10

Easy Pork Roast

Preparation time: 10 minutes
Cooking time: 45 minutes
Servings: 12

Ingredients:
- ½ cup beef stock
- 1 tablespoon olive oil
- ¼ cup keto Jamaican spice mix
- 4 pounds pork shoulder

Directions:
In a bowl, mix pork with oil and spice mix and rub well. Set your instant pot on sauté mode, add pork and brown for a few minutes on each side. Add stock, cover pot and cook pork shoulder on High for 40 minutes. Slice roast and serve. Enjoy!

Nutrition: calories 400, fat 6, fiber 7, carbs 10, protein 16

Broccoli Soup

Preparation time: 10 minutes
Cooking time: 10 minutes
Servings: 4

Ingredients:
- 1 broccoli head, florets separated and roughly chopped
- 4 cups chicken stock
- A pinch of salt and white pepper
- ¼ teaspoon garlic powder
- 1 cup carrots, chopped
- 2 tablespoons ghee, melted
- 1 yellow onion, chopped
- 2 cups cheddar cheese, shredded
- 1 cup coconut cream

Directions:
Set your instant pot on sauté mode, add ghee, heat it up, add onion, stir and cook for 2-3 minutes. Add carrots, broccoli, stock, garlic powder, salt and pepper, stir, cover and cook on High for 5 minutes. Add cream and cheese, stir, ladle into bowls and serve. Enjoy!

Nutrition: calories 320, fat 6, fiber 7, carbs 9, protein 12

Pork Chops and Gravy

Preparation time: 10 minutes
Cooking time: 25 minutes
Servings: 4

Ingredients:
- 3 bacon slices, chopped
- 3 garlic cloves, minced
- 1 tablespoon olive oil
- 1 small yellow onion, chopped
- 8 ounces mushrooms, sliced
- 4 pork chops, bone in
- 1 cup beef stock
- 1 teaspoon garlic powder
- 1 thyme sprigs, chopped
- 10 ounces cream of mushrooms
- 1 tablespoon parsley, chopped

Directions:

Set your instant pot on sauté mode, add oil, heat it up, add bacon, stir and cook for 2 minutes. Add garlic, onion and mushrooms, stir and cook for 3 minutes more. Add pork chops, garlic powder, stock and thyme, stir, cover and cook on High for 20 minutes. Add cream of mushrooms, stir, set the pot on simmer mode, cook for a few minutes and divide everything between plates. Sprinkle parsley on top and serve. Enjoy!

Nutrition: calories 400, fat 8, fiber 7, carbs 12, protein 17

Pork Bowls

Preparation time: 10 minutes
Cooking time: 45 minutes
Servings: 4

Ingredients:
- 2 pounds pork sirloin roast, cut into thick slices
- A pinch of salt and black pepper
- 2 teaspoons garlic powder
- 2 teaspoons cumin, ground
- 1 tablespoon olive oil
- 16 ounces keto green chili tomatillo salsa

Directions:

In a bowl, mix pork with cumin, salt, pepper and garlic powder and rub well. Set your instant pot on sauté mode, add the oil heat it up, add pork and brown on all sides. Add salsa, toss a bit, cover and cook on High for 45 minutes. Divide between plates and serve hot. Enjoy!

Nutrition: calories 400, fat 7, fiber 6, carbs 10, protein 14

Beef Meatloaf

Preparation time: 10 minutes
Cooking time: 20 minutes
Servings: 4

Ingredients:

- 2 pounds beef, ground
- ¼ cup parmesan, grated
- ¼ cup yellow onion, chopped
- 1 egg, whisked
- A pinch of salt and black pepper
- 1 tablespoon garlic, minced
- ½ teaspoon thyme, dried
- 1 tablespoon olive oil
- 1 yellow onion, chopped
- 1 cup keto ketchup
- ½ cup beef stock

Directions:

In a bowl, mix beef with cheese, ¼ cup onion, egg, thyme, salt and pepper and stir really well. Set your instant pot on sauté mode, add the oil, heat it up, and 1 yellow onion, stir and cook for 4 minutes. Add stock and ketchup, stir and cook for 1 minute more. Shape a round meatloaf out of the beef mix, add it to the pot, cover and cook on High for 15 minutes. Divide meatloaf on plates, drizzle the sauce from the pot all over and serve. Enjoy!

Nutrition: calories 363, fat 6, fiber 3, carbs 8, protein 14

Pork and Veggies

Preparation time: 10 minutes
Cooking time: 15 minutes
Servings: 6

Ingredients:

- 1 pound pork, ground
- 1 tablespoon olive oil
- ½ cup yellow onion, chopped
- 1 cup red bell peppers, chopped
- 2 garlic cloves, minced
- ½ cup parmesan, grated
- 4 cups baby spinach

Directions:

Set your instant pot on sauté mode, add the oil, heat it up, add pork, stir and brown for a couple of minutes. Add garlic, onion, spinach and bell peppers, stir, cover and cook on High for 3 minutes. Divide this into bowls, sprinkle cheese on top and serve. Enjoy!

Nutrition: calories 241, fat 10, fiber 2, carbs 5, protein 15

Chicken and Tasty Cauliflower Rice

Preparation time: 10 minutes
Cooking time: 28 minutes
Servings: 6

Ingredients:

- 3 bacon slices, chopped
- 3 carrots, chopped
- 3 pounds chicken thighs, boneless and skinless
- 1 rhubarb stalk, chopped
- 2 bay leaves
- ¼ cup red wine vinegar
- 4 garlic cloves, minced
- A pinch of salt and black pepper
- ¼ cup olive oil
- 1 tablespoon garlic powder
- 1 tablespoon Italian seasoning
- 24 ounces cauliflower rice
- 1 teaspoon turmeric powder
- 1 cup beef stock

Directions:

Set your instant pot on sauté mode, add bacon, carrots, onion, rhubarb and garlic, stir and cook for 8 minutes. Add chicken, stir and cook for 1 minute more. Add oil, vinegar, turmeric, Italian seasoning, garlic powder and bay leaves, stir, cover and cook on High for 20 minutes. Add cauliflower rice and stock, stir, cover and cook on Low for 3 minutes more. Divide into bowls and serve. Enjoy!

Nutrition: calories 310, fat 6, fiber 3, carbs 6, protein 10

Chicken Curry

Preparation time: 10 minutes
Cooking time: 30 minutes
Servings: 4

Ingredients:

- 3 tomatoes, chopped
- 2 pounds chicken thighs, skinless, boneless and cubed
- 2 tablespoons olive oil
- 1 cup chicken stock
- 14 ounces canned coconut milk
- 2 garlic cloves, minced
- 1 cup white onion, chopped
- 3 red chilies, chopped
- 1 tablespoon water
- 1 tablespoon ginger, grated
- 2 teaspoons coriander, ground
- 1 teaspoon cinnamon, ground
- 1 teaspoon turmeric, ground
- 1 teaspoon cumin, ground
- 1 teaspoon fennel seeds, ground
- 1 tablespoon lime juice
- Salt and black pepper

Directions:

In your food processor, mix white onion with garlic, chilies, water, ginger, coriander, cinnamon, turmeric, cumin, fennel and black pepper, blend until you obtain a paste and transfer to a bowl. Set your instant pot on sauté mode, add the oil, heat it up, add blended paste, stir and cook for 30 seconds. Add chicken, tomatoes and stock, stir, cover pot and cook on High for 15 minutes. Add coconut milk, stir, cover pot again and cook on High for 7 minutes more. Add lime juice, salt and pepper, stir, divide into bowls and serve. Enjoy!

Nutrition: calories 430, fat 16, fiber 4, carbs 7, protein 38

Shrimp and Zucchini Spaghetti

Preparation time: 10 minutes
Cooking time: 6 minutes
Servings: 4

Ingredients:

- 12 ounces zucchini, cut with a spiralizer
- 2 tablespoons veggie stock
- 2 tablespoons ghee
- 2 tablespoons olive oil
- Salt and black pepper to the taste
- 4 garlic cloves, minced
- 1 pound shrimp, raw, peeled and deveined
- Juice of ½ lemon
- ½ teaspoon sweet paprika
- A handful basil, chopped

Directions:

Set your instant pot on sauté mode, add ghee and olive oil, heat them up, add garlic, stir and cook for 1 minute. Add shrimp, stock and lemon juice and cook for 1 minute more. Add zucchini pasta, salt, pepper and paprika, stir, cover pot and cook on High for 3 minutes more. Divide this into bowls, sprinkle basil on top and serve. Enjoy!

Nutrition: calories 300, fat 20, fiber 6, carbs 3, protein 30

Fish and Carrot Soup

Preparation time: 10 minutes
Cooking time: 20 minutes
Servings: 4

Ingredients:

- 1 yellow onion, chopped
- 12 cups chicken stock
- 1 pound carrots, sliced
- 1 tablespoon coconut oil
- Salt and black pepper to the taste
- 2 tablespoons ginger, minced
- 1 cup water
- 1 pound halibut, skinless, boneless and cut into medium chunks

Directions:

Set your instant pot on sauté mode, add oil, heat it up, add onion, stir and cook for 4 minutes. Add water, stock, ginger and carrots, stir, cover and cook on High for 8 minutes. Blend soup using an immersion blender, add halibut pieces, salt and pepper, stir a bit, cover pot and cook on High for 6 minutes. Ladle into bowls and serve hot. Enjoy!

Nutrition: calories 170, fat 6, fiber 2, carbs 6, protein 12

Trout Fillet and Sauce

Preparation time: 10 minutes
Cooking time: 6 minutes
Servings: 4

Ingredients:

- 4 trout fillets, boneless
- Salt and black pepper to the taste
- 3 teaspoons lemon zest, grated
- 3 tablespoons chives, chopped
- 6 tablespoons ghee
- 2 tablespoons olive oil
- 2 teaspoons lemon juice

Directions:

Set your instant pot on sauté mode, add oil and ghee, heat them up, and fish, lemon zest, lemon juice, salt and pepper, stir, cover and cook on Low for 4 minutes. Divide fish and ghee sauce on plates, sprinkle chives on top and serve. Enjoy!

Nutrition: calories 320, fat 6, fiber 1, carbs 4, protein 18

Shrimp and Mushrooms

Preparation time: 10 minutes
Cooking time: 20 minutes
Servings: 4

Ingredients:

- 8 ounces mushrooms, chopped
- 1 pound shrimp, peeled and deveined
- 1 yellow onion, chopped
- 1 asparagus bunch, cut into medium pieces
- Salt and black pepper to the taste
- 1 spaghetti squash, cut into halves
- 2 tablespoons olive oil
- 2 teaspoons Italian seasoning
- 1 teaspoon red pepper flakes, crushed
- ¼ cup ghee
- 1 cup parmesan cheese, grated
- 2 garlic cloves, minced
- 1 cup coconut cream
- 2 cups water

Directions:

Put the water in your instant pot, add steamer basket, add spaghetti halves, cover, cook on High for 10 minutes, scoop insides and transfer them to a bowl. Add asparagus to the steamer basket, cover pot again, cook on High for 3 minutes, cool it down in a bowl filled with ice water, drain and leave aside. Clean your instant pot, set it on sauté mode, add oil and ghee, heat it up, add mushrooms and onion, stir and cook for 3-4 minutes. Add pepper flakes, Italian seasoning, salt, pepper, squash and asparagus, stir and cook for a few minutes more. Add coconut cream, parmesan, garlic and shrimp, cover pot and cook on High for 4 minutes. Divide everything between plates and serve. Enjoy!

Nutrition: calories 465, fat 6, fiber 2, carbs 5, protein 10

Lemon and Garlic Shrimp

Preparation time: 10 minutes
Cooking time: 3 minutes
Servings: 4

Ingredients:
- 2 tablespoons olive oil
- 1 tablespoon ghee
- 1 pound shrimp, peeled and deveined
- 2 tablespoons lemon juice
- 2 tablespoons garlic, minced
- 1 tablespoon lemon zest
- Salt and black pepper to the taste

Directions:
Set your instant pot on sauté mode, add oil and ghee, heat them up, add garlic, shrimp, lemon juice, lemon zest, salt and pepper, stir, cover and cook on High for 3 minutes. Divide everything between plates and serve. Enjoy!

Nutrition: calories 159, fat 1, fiber 3, carbs 5, protein 5

Haddock and Mayonnaise

Preparation time: 10 minutes
Cooking time: 7 minutes
Servings: 4

Ingredients:
- 1 pound haddock
- 2 tablespoons mayonnaise
- 3 teaspoons veggie stock
- 2 tablespoons lemon juice
- Salt and black pepper to the taste
- 1 teaspoon dill, chopped
- A drizzle of olive oil
- ¼ teaspoon old bay seasoning

Directions:
In your instant pot, mix haddock with stock, lemon juice, mayo, salt, pepper, dill, oil and old bay seasoning, toss a bit, cover and cook on High for 7 minutes. Divide everything between plates and serve. Enjoy!

Nutrition: calories 164, fat 12, fiber 1, carbs 6, protein 14

Chicken and Mushrooms

Preparation time: 10 minutes
Cooking time: 15 minutes
Servings: 4

Ingredients:

- 4 chicken thighs
- 2 cups mushrooms, sliced
- ¼ cup ghee
- Salt and black pepper to the taste
- ½ teaspoon onion powder
- ½ teaspoon garlic powder
- ½ cup water
- 1 teaspoon Dijon mustard
- 1 tablespoon tarragon, chopped

Directions:

Set your instant pot on sauté mode, add ghee, melt it, add chicken, salt, pepper, onion powder and garlic powder, stir, cook for 2 minutes on each side and transfer to a bowl. Add mushrooms to your instant pot, stir and sauté them for 2 minutes more. Return chicken to the pot, also add mustard and water, stir well, cover and cook on High for 10 minutes. Add tarragon, stir, divide between plates and serve right away. Enjoy!

Nutrition: calories 263, fat 16, fiber 4, carbs 6, protein 18

Chicken and Salsa

Preparation time: 10 minutes
Cooking time: 17 minutes
Servings: 6

Ingredients:

- 6 chicken breasts, skinless and boneless
- 2 cups jarred keto salsa
- Salt and black pepper to the taste
- 1 cup cheddar cheese, shredded
- A drizzle of olive oil

Directions:

Set your instant pot on sauté mode, add a drizzle of oil, heat it up, add chicken, stir and cook for 2 minutes on each side. Add salsa, stir, cover and cook on High for 7 minutes. Spread cheese all over, cover pot again and cook on High for 3 minutes more. Divide between plates and serve right away. Enjoy!

Nutrition: calories 220, fat 7, fiber 2, carbs 6, protein 12

Salsa Chicken Soup

Preparation time: 10 minutes
Cooking time: 15 minutes
Servings: 6

Ingredients:
- 1 and ½ pounds chicken tights, skinless, boneless and cubed
- 15 ounces chicken stock
- 15 ounces canned keto chunky salsa
- 8 ounces Monterey jack cheese, shredded

Directions:

In your instant pot, mix chicken with stock, salsa and cheese, stir, cover and cook on High for 15 minutes. Stir soup, ladle into bowls and serve. Enjoy!

Nutrition: calories 270, fat 16, fiber 3, carbs 5, protein 22

Hot Beef Stew

Preparation time: 10 minutes
Cooking time: 8 hours
Servings: 4

Ingredients:
- 1 yellow onion, chopped
- 2 and ½ pounds beef, ground
- 15 ounces canned tomatoes and green chilies, chopped
- 6 ounces tomato paste
- 2 jalapenos, chopped
- 4 tablespoons garlic, minced
- 3 celery ribs, chopped
- 2 tablespoons coconut aminos
- 4 tablespoons chili powder
- Salt and black pepper to the taste
- A pinch of cayenne pepper
- 1 bay leaf
- 2 tablespoons cumin, ground
- 1 teaspoon oregano, dried
- 1 teaspoon onion powder
- 1 teaspoon garlic powder

Directions:

Set your instant pot on sauté mode, add beef, onion, garlic, salt and pepper, stir and cook for 3-4 minutes. Add celery, jalapenos, tomatoes and chilies mix, tomato paste, tomatoes, aminos, cayenne, cumin, onion powder, garlic powder, bay leaf and oregano, stir, cover and cook on High for 15 minutes. Discard bay leaf, divide stew among bowls and serve. Enjoy!

Nutrition: calories 327, fat 7, fiber 2, carbs 5, protein 22

Leg of Lamb and Spinach Salad

Preparation time: 10 minutes
Cooking time: 40 minutes
Servings: 4

Ingredients:

- 1 tablespoon olive oil
- 2 garlic cloves, minced
- 2 cups veggie stock
- 3 pounds leg of lamb, bone discarded and butterflied
- Salt and black pepper to the taste
- 1 teaspoon cumin, ground
- ¼ teaspoon thyme, dried

For the salad:

- 4 ounces feta cheese, crumbled
- ½ cup pecans, toasted
- 2 cups spinach
- 1 and ½ tablespoons lemon juice
- ¼ cup olive oil
- 1 cup mint, chopped

Directions:

Rub lamb with salt, pepper, 1 tablespoon oil, thyme, cumin and garlic. Add the stock to your instant pot, add leg of lamb, cover and cook on High for 40 minutes. Leave leg of lamb aside to cool down, slice and divide between plates. Meanwhile, in a bowl, mix spinach with mint, feta cheese, ¼ cup olive oil, lemon juice, pecans, salt and pepper, toss and divide next to lamb slices. Serve right away. Enjoy!

Nutrition: calories 234, fat 20, fiber 3, carbs 5, protein 12

Lamb Stew

Preparation time: 10 minutes
Cooking time: 20 minutes
Servings: 4

Ingredients:

- 1 yellow onion, chopped
- 2 pounds lamb meat, cubed
- 2 tablespoons ghee
- 3 carrots, chopped
- 2 cups beef stock
- 1 tomato, chopped
- 1 garlic clove, minced
- Salt and black pepper to the taste
- 2 rosemary sprigs, chopped
- 1 teaspoon thyme, chopped

Directions:

Set your instant pot on sauté mode, add ghee, heat it up, add lamb meat and brown for 2 minutes on all sides. Add onion, stir and cook for 1 minute more. Add carrots, tomato, garlic, thyme, rosemary, salt, pepper and stock, stir, cover and cook on High for 15 minutes. Divide into bowls and serve. Enjoy!

Nutrition: calories 260, fat 12, fiber 6, carbs 10, protein 36

Beef and Mushroom Stew

Preparation time: 10 minutes
Cooking time: 20 minutes
Servings: 5

Ingredients:

- 2 pounds beef chuck roast, cubed
- 1 cup beef stock
- 1 cup water
- 2 yellow onions, chopped
- 15 ounces canned tomatoes, chopped
- 4 carrots, chopped
- Salt and black pepper to the taste
- ½ pound mushrooms, sliced
- 2 celery ribs, chopped
- 1 tablespoon thyme, chopped
- ½ teaspoon mustard powder
- 2 tablespoons coconut flour

Directions:

Set your instant pot on sauté mode, add beef, stir and brown for 2 minutes on each side. Add tomatoes, mushrooms, onions, carrots, celery, salt, pepper mustard, stock, flour and thyme, stir, cover and cook on High for 15 minutes. Divide into bowls and serve. Enjoy!

Nutrition: calories 275, fat 7, fiber 4, carbs 7, protein 28

Pomegranate and Walnuts Chicken

Preparation time: 10 minutes
Cooking time: 17 minutes
Servings: 6

Ingredients:

- 12 chicken thighs
- 2 cups walnuts, toasted and chopped
- Salt and black pepper to the taste
- 3 tablespoons olive oil
- 1 yellow onion, chopped
- Juice of ½ lemon
- ¼ teaspoon cardamom, ground
- ½ teaspoon cinnamon, ground
- 1 cup pomegranate molasses
- 2 tablespoons stevia

Directions:

Put walnuts in your food processor, blend and transfer to a bowl. Set your instant pot on sauté mode, add 2 tablespoons oil, heat it up, add chicken, salt and pepper, brown for a couple of minutes on each side and transfer to a bowl. Add the rest of the oil to your instant pot, heat it up, add onion, stir and cook for 3 minutes. Add cardamom, cinnamon, walnuts, pomegranate molasses, chicken, stevia and lemon juice, stir, cover and cook on High for 10 minutes. Divide everything between plates and serve. Enjoy!

Nutrition: calories 265, fat 6, fiber 6, carbs 14, protein 16

Sausages and Mashed Celeriac

Preparation time: 15 minutes
Cooking time: 15 minutes
Servings: 6

Ingredients:

For the mash

- 2 celeriac, peeled and cut into cubes
- Salt and black pepper to the taste
- 1 teaspoon mustard powder
- 1 tablespoon ghee, melted

- 4 ounces warm coconut milk
- 6 ounces water
- 1 tablespoon cheddar cheese, grated

For the sausages:

- 6 pork sausages
- 2 tablespoons olive oil
- ½ cup keto onion jam

- 2 ounces veggie stock
- 3 ounces water
- Salt and black pepper to the taste

Directions:

Put celeriac cubes in your instant pot, add 6 ounces water, salt and pepper, stir, cover, cook on High for 6 minutes, drain, transfer to a bowl and mash using a potato masher. Add mustard powder, ghee, milk and cheese, stir really well and leave aside for now. Set your instant pot on Sauté mode, add oil, heat it up, add sausages and brown them on all sides. Add onion jam, stock, 3 ounces water, salt and pepper, stir, cover and cook on High for 8 minutes. Divide sausages on plates, add mashed celeriac on the side and serve with some of the cooking juices from the pot drizzled all over. Enjoy!

Nutrition: calories 421, fat 12, fiber 4, carbs 7, protein 15

Seafood Summer Mix

Preparation time: 10 minutes
Cooking time: 15 minutes
Servings: 4

Ingredients:

- 12 shell clams
- 12 mussels
- 1 and ½ pounds shrimp, peeled and deveined
- 1 and ½ pounds fish fillets, cut into medium pieces
- 20 ounces canned tomatoes, chopped
- 5 tablespoons ghee, melted
- 3 garlic cloves, minced
- 2 yellow onions, chopped

- 4 tablespoons parsley, chopped
- 8 ounces clam juice
- 1 and ½ cups veggie stock
- 2 bay leaves
- ½ teaspoon marjoram, dried
- 1 tablespoon basil, dried
- Salt and black pepper to the taste

Directions:

Set your instant pot on Sauté mode, add ghee, heat it up, add onion and garlic, stir and cook for a couple of minutes. Add clam juice, tomatoes, stock, parsley, basil, bay leaves, marjoram, salt and pepper, stir, cover and cook on High for 10 minutes. Add clams and mussels, stir, set the pot on simmer mode and cook for 8 minutes. Add fish and shrimp, stir, cook for 4 minutes, ladle into bowls and serve. Enjoy!

Nutrition: calories 300, fat 10, fiber 7, carbs 10, protein 17

Mexican Chicken Soup

Preparation time: 10 minutes
Cooking time: 30 minutes
Servings: 4

Ingredients:

- 2 chicken breasts, boneless and skinless and cubed
- 1 and ¼ cup jarred keto enchilada sauce
- 3 cups chicken stock
- 16 ounces canned tomatoes, chopped
- 4 ounces canned green chilies, chopped
- Salt and black pepper to the taste
- 2 garlic cloves, minced
- 1 cup white onion, chopped
- 1 teaspoon cumin, ground
- 1 teaspoon oregano

For serving:

- Chopped cilantro
- Chopped red onion
- Shredded cheddar cheese

Directions:

In your instant pot, mix chicken with enchilada sauce, stock, tomatoes, green chilies, salt, pepper, garlic, onion, cumin and oregano, stir, cover and cook on Manual for 15 minutes. Ladle soup into bowls, serve with chopped cilantro, red onion, and shredded cheese sprinkled all over. Enjoy!

Nutrition: calories 312, fat 7, fiber 2, carbs 8, protein 14

Okra and Beef Stew

Preparation time: 10 minutes
Cooking time: 30 minutes
Servings: 4

Ingredients:

- 1 yellow onion, chopped
- 1 pound beef, cubed
- 1 garlic clove, minced
- 2 cups chicken stock
- 1 cardamom pod
- 14 ounces okra
- 12 ounces tomato sauce
- Salt and black pepper to the taste
- 5 tablespoons parsley, chopped
- A drizzle of olive oil
- Juice of ½ lemon

For the marinade:

- ½ teaspoon onion powder
- ½ teaspoon garlic powder
- A pinch of salt
- 1 tablespoon 7- spice mix

Directions:

In a bowl, mix meat with 7-spice, a pinch of salt, onion and garlic powder, toss to coat and leave aside. Set your instant pot on Sauté mode, add a drizzle of olive oil, heat it up, add onion, garlic and cardamom, stir and cook for 3 minutes. Add meat, stir, brown for 2 minutes and mix with okra, stock, tomato sauce, salt and pepper, stir, cover and cook on Low for 20 minutes. Add lemon juice and parsley, stir, divide into bowls and serve. Enjoy!

Nutrition: calories 273, fat 8, fiber 4, carbs 8, protein 17

Beef and Cabbage Stew

Preparation time: 10 minutes
Cooking time: 1 hour and 20 minutes
Servings: 6

Ingredients:

- 2 and ½ pounds beef brisket
- 2 bay leaves
- 4 cups water
- 4 carrots, chopped
- 3 garlic cloves, chopped
- 1 cabbage head, roughly shredded
- Salt and black pepper to the taste
- 3 turnips, cut into quarters
- Horseradish sauce for serving

Directions:

Put the beef brisket in your instant pot, add water, salt, pepper, garlic and bay leaves, cover and cook at High for 1 hour. Add carrots, cabbage and turnips, stir, cover the pot again and cook on High for 6 minutes. Divide stew among plates and serve with horseradish sauce on top. Enjoy!

Nutrition: calories 293, fat 8, fiber 3, carbs 10, protein 17

Lamb Shanks and Carrots

Preparation time: 10 minutes
Cooking time: 35 minutes
Servings: 4

Ingredients:

- 4 lamb shanks
- 2 tablespoons olive oil
- 2 tablespoons coconut flour
- 1 yellow onion, chopped
- 3 carrots, sliced
- 2 garlic cloves, minced
- 2 tablespoons tomato paste
- 1 teaspoon oregano, dried
- 1 tomato, chopped
- 2 tablespoons water
- 4 ounces beef stock
- Salt and black pepper to the taste

Directions:

In a bowl, mix lamb shanks with flour, salt and pepper and toss. Set your instant pot on Sauté mode, add oil, heat it up, add lamb, brown for a couple of minutes on each side and transfer to a bowl. Add onion, oregano, carrots and garlic to the pot, stir and sauté for 5 minutes. Add tomato, tomato paste, water, stock and return lamb to pot as well. Stir, cover, cook on High for 25 minutes, divide everything between plates and serve. Enjoy!

Nutrition: calories 400, fat 14, fiber 3, carbs 7, protein 30

Pork with Lemon Sauce

Preparation time: 10 minutes
Cooking time: 1 hour
Servings: 4

Ingredients:
- 1 and ½ pounds pork shoulder, chopped
- 3 garlic cloves, minced
- 1 cinnamon stick
- 2 cloves
- 1 yellow onion, chopped
- Juice of 1 lemon
- Salt and black pepper to the taste
- 1 tablespoon ginger, grated
- ½ cup water
- 1 teaspoon rosemary, dried
- 2 tablespoons stevia
- 2 tablespoons coconut aminos
- 1 tablespoon olive oil

Directions:
Set your instant pot on Sauté mode, add oil, heat it up, add pork, salt and pepper, stir, brown for 5 minutes on each side and transfer to a plate. Add onions, ginger, garlic, lemon juice, water, stevia, aminos, rosemary, cinnamon, cloves, pork, salt and pepper to the pot, stir, heat up, cover pot and cook on Manual for 50 minutes. Discard cloves and cinnamon, stir pork mix, divide everything between plates and serve. Enjoy!

Nutrition: calories 310, fat 4, fiber 2, carbs 12, protein 24

Meatballs and Sauce

Preparation time: 10 minutes
Cooking time: 15 minutes
Servings: 8

Ingredients:
- 1 and ½ pounds pork meat, ground
- 1 egg
- 2 tablespoons parsley, chopped
- 4 tablespoons coconut flour
- 2 garlic cloves, minced
- Salt and black pepper to the taste
- ¾ cup beef stock
- ½ teaspoon nutmeg, ground
- ½ teaspoon sweet paprika
- 2 tablespoons olive oil
- 2 carrots, chopped
- 1 celeriac, cubed
- 1 bay leaf

Directions:
In a bowl, mix ground meat with egg, salt, pepper, parsley, paprika, garlic, 1 tablespoon stock and nutmeg, stir well and dust them with the coconut flour. Set your instant pot on Sauté mode, add oil, heat it up, add meatballs and brown them on all sides. Add carrots, bay leaf, celeriac and stock, stir, cover the pot and cook on High for 8 minutes. Discard bay leaf, divide meatballs and sauce into bowls and serve. Enjoy!

Nutrition: calories 383, fat 10, fiber 6, carbs 10, protein 15

Salmon and Veggies

Preparation time: 10 minutes
Cooking time: 15 minutes
Servings: 4

Ingredients:

- 4 salmon fillets, boneless
- 2 cups water
- 3 tablespoons olive oil
- 1 lemon, sliced
- 1 white onion, chopped
- 3 tomatoes, sliced
- 4 thyme sprigs, chopped
- 4 parsley sprigs, chopped
- Salt and black pepper to the taste

Directions:

Drizzle the oil on a parchment paper. Add a layer of tomatoes, salt and pepper. Drizzle some oil again, add fish and season with salt and pepper. Drizzle some more oil, add thyme and parsley, onions, lemon slices, salt and pepper and wrap packet. Add the water to your instant pot, add the steamer basket, add packet inside, cover and cook on High for 15 minutes. Unwrap packet, divide fish and veggies between plates and serve. Enjoy!

Nutrition: calories 200, fat 5, fiber 7, carbs 10, protein 20

Shrimp and Turnips

Preparation time: 10 minutes
Cooking time: 15 minutes
Servings: 4

Ingredients:

- 2 pounds shrimp, peeled and deveined
- 1 pound tomatoes, peeled and chopped
- 1 cup water
- 3 turnips, cut into quarters
- 4 tablespoons olive oil
- 4 onions, chopped
- 1 teaspoon coriander, ground
- 1 teaspoon curry powder
- Juice of 1 lemon
- A pinch of salt and black pepper

Directions:

Put the water in your instant pot, add steamer basket, add turnips, cover pot, cook on High for 6 minutes, drain, transfer to a bowl and leave aside for now. Clean your instant pot, set it on sauté mode, add oil, heat it up, add onions, stir and cook for 5 minutes. Add salt, coriander, curry, tomatoes, lemon juice, shrimp and turnips, stir, cover and cook on High for 6 minutes more. Divide shrimp into bowls and serve. Enjoy!

Nutrition: calories 183, fat 4, fiber 1, carbs 7, protein 15

Squid and Veggies

Preparation time: 10 minutes
Cooking time: 27 minutes
Servings: 4

Ingredients:

- 1 pound squid, cleaned and chopped
- 10 garlic cloves, minced
- 2-inch ginger piece, grated
- 2 green chilies, chopped
- ½ tablespoon lemon juice
- 2 yellow onions, chopped
- 1 curry leaf
- 1 tablespoon coriander powder
- ¼ cup coconut, shredded
- ¾ tablespoon chili powder
- 1 teaspoon garam masala
- Salt and black pepper to the taste
- A pinch of turmeric
- 1 teaspoon mustard seeds
- ¾ cup water
- 3 tablespoons olive oil

Directions:

Set your instant pot on Sauté mode, add oil, heat it up, add mustard seeds and coconut, stir and cook for 2 minutes. Add ginger, onions, garlic, chilies, salt, pepper, curry leaf, coriander powder, chili powder, garam masala, turmeric, water, lemon juice and squid, stir, cover and cook on Low for 25 minutes. Divide into bowls and serve right away. Enjoy!

Nutrition: calories 193, fat 7, fiber 1, carbs 7, protein 19

Artichokes and Sauce

Preparation time: 10 minutes
Cooking time: 20 minutes
Servings: 4

Ingredients:

- 4 artichokes, trimmed
- 2 cups chicken stock
- 1 tablespoon tarragon, chopped
- 4 lemon slices
- Zest from 1 lemon, grated
- Pulp from 1 lemon
- 1 celery stalk, chopped
- ½ cup olive oil
- Salt to the taste

Directions:

Put artichokes in your instant pot, add lemon slices on top, add stock, cover, cook on High for 20 minutes and transfer them to a platter. Meanwhile, in your food processor, mix tarragon with lemon zest, lemon pulp, celery, salt and olive oil, pulse very well, drizzle this over artichokes and serve right away. Enjoy!

Nutrition: calories 192, fat 6, fiber 7, carbs 9, protein 7

Squash and Chicken Cream

Preparation time: 10 minutes
Cooking time: 16 minutes
Servings: 6

Ingredients:

- 1 and ½ pounds butternut squash, baked, peeled and cubed
- 1 cup chicken meat, cooked and shredded
- ½ cup green onions, chopped
- 3 tablespoons ghee
- 30 ounces chicken stock
- ½ cup carrots, chopped
- ½ cup celery, chopped
- 1 garlic clove, minced
- ½ teaspoon Italian seasoning
- 15 ounces canned tomatoes and their juice, chopped
- Salt and black pepper to the taste
- A pinch of red pepper flakes, dried
- A pinch of nutmeg, grated
- 1 and ½ cup coconut cream

Directions:

Set your instant pot on Sauté mode, add ghee, melt it, add celery, carrots and onions, stir and cook for 3 minutes. Add garlic, squash, tomatoes, stock, Italian seasoning, salt, pepper, pepper flakes and nutmeg, stir, cover and cook on High for 10 minutes. Blend soup using an immersion blender, add coconut cream and chicken, stir, set the pot on simmer mode and cook for 3 minutes more. Ladle into bowls and serve. Enjoy!

Nutrition: calories 182, fat 2, fiber 7, carbs 10, protein 7

Veggie Soup

Preparation time: 10 minutes
Cooking time: 12 minutes
Servings: 8

Ingredients:

- 1 tablespoon olive oil
- 1 celery stalk, chopped
- 3 pounds tomatoes, chopped
- 2 carrots, chopped
- 1 onion, chopped
- 1 zucchini, chopped
- 4 garlic cloves, minced
- 30 ounces canned chicken stock
- Salt and black pepper to the taste
- 1 teaspoon Italian seasoning
- 2 cups baby spinach
- 1 cup asiago cheese, grated
- 2 tablespoons basil, chopped

Directions:

Set your instant pot on Sauté mode, add oil, heat it up, add onion, stir and cook for 5 minutes. Add carrots, garlic, celery, zucchini, tomatoes, stock, Italian seasoning, salt and pepper, stir, cover and cook on High for 6 minutes. Add basil and spinach, stir, ladle into bowls and serve with cheese sprinkled on top. Enjoy!

Nutrition: calories 172, fat 4, fiber 4, carbs 10, protein 6

Cabbage and Carrot Soup

Preparation time: 10 minutes
Cooking time: 10 minutes
Servings: 4

Ingredients:

- 1 cabbage head, shredded
- 1 small yellow onion, chopped
- 12 ounces baby carrots
- 3 celery stalks, chopped
- 2 tablespoons olive oil
- 3 teaspoons garlic, minced
- ¼ cup cilantro, chopped
- 4 cups chicken stock
- Salt and black pepper to the taste

Directions:

In your instant pot, mix cabbage with celery, carrots, onion, stock, olive oil and garlic, stir, cover and cook on High for 8 minutes. Add salt, pepper and cilantro, stir well, ladle into soup bowls and serve. Enjoy!

Nutrition: calories 165, fat 4, fiber 3, carbs 9, protein 10

Asparagus Cream

Preparation time: 10 minutes
Cooking time: 25 minutes
Servings: 4

Ingredients:

- 2 pounds green asparagus, trimmed and cut into medium pieces
- 3 tablespoons ghee
- 6 cups chicken stock
- 1 yellow onion, chopped
-
- ¼ teaspoon lemon juice
- ½ cup coconut cream
- Salt and white pepper to the taste

Directions:

Set your instant pot on Sauté mode, add ghee, heat it up, add asparagus, onion, salt and pepper, stir and cook for 5 minutes. Add stock, cover pot, cook on Low for 15 minutes, transfer everything to your blender and pulse well. Return soup to pot, add coconut cream and lemon juice, stir, ladle into bowls and serve. Enjoy!

Nutrition: calories 100, fat 5, fiber 1, carbs 8, protein 7

Fresh Fennel and Leek Soup

Preparation time: 10 minutes
Cooking time: 15 minutes
Servings: 2

Ingredients:
- 1 fennel bulb, chopped
- 2 cups water
- 1 bay leaf
- 1 leek, chopped
- 1 tablespoon olive oil
- Salt and black pepper to the taste
- 2 teaspoons parmesan cheese, grated

Directions:

In your instant pot, mix fennel with leek, bay leaf, oil, water, salt and pepper, stir, cover and cook on High for 15 minutes. Add cheese, stir, ladle into bowls and serve. Enjoy!

Nutrition: calories 126, fat 3, fiber 3, carbs 6, protein 5

Chicken Stew

Preparation time: 10 minutes
Cooking time: 40 minutes
Servings: 6

Ingredients:
- 6 chicken thighs
- 1 teaspoon olive oil
- ¼ pound baby carrots
- Salt and black pepper to the taste
- 1 yellow onion, chopped
- 2 tablespoons tomato paste
- 1 celery stalk, chopped
- ½ teaspoon thyme, dried
- 2 and ½ cups chicken stock
- 15 ounces canned tomatoes, chopped

Directions:

Set your instant pot on Sauté mode, add oil, heat it up, add chicken, salt and pepper, brown for 4 minutes on each side and transfer to a plate. Add celery, onion, tomato paste, carrots, thyme, salt and pepper, stir and sauté them for 4 minutes more. Add stock, chicken and tomatoes; cover and cook on High for 25 minutes. Transfer chicken pieces to a cutting board, leave aside to cool down for a few minutes, discard bones, shred meat and return it to the stew. Stir, divide into bowls and serve hot. Enjoy!

Nutrition: calories 182, fat 4, fiber 4, carbs 7, protein 14

Turkey Stew

Preparation time: 10 minutes
Cooking time: 33 minutes
Servings: 4

Ingredients:
- 1 tablespoon avocado oil
- 1 yellow onion, chopped
- 1 teaspoon garlic, minced
- 3 celery stalks, chopped
- 2 carrots, chopped
- Salt and black pepper to the taste
- 3 cups turkey meat, already cooked and shredded
- 15 ounces canned tomatoes, chopped
- 5 cups turkey stock
- 1 tablespoon cranberry sauce

Directions:
Set your instant pot on Sauté mode, add oil, heat it up, add carrots, celery and onions, stir and cook for 3 minutes. Add tomatoes, stock, garlic, meat, cranberry sauce, salt and pepper, stir, cover, cook on Low for 30 minutes, divide into bowls and serve. Enjoy!

Nutrition: calories 200, fat 4, fiber 1, carbs 6, protein 16

Mushroom Stew

Preparation time: 10 minutes
Cooking time: 20 minutes
Servings: 6

Ingredients:
- 1 tablespoon olive oil
- 1 celery stalk, chopped
- 1 and ½ cups beef stock
- 1 red onion, chopped
- 2 pounds beef chuck, cubed
- 1 teaspoon rosemary, chopped
- Salt and black pepper to the taste
- 1 ounce porcini mushrooms, chopped
- 2 carrots, chopped
- 2 tablespoons coconut flour
- 2 tablespoons ghee

Directions:
Set your instant pot on Sauté mode, add oil, heat it up, add beef, stir and brown for 5 minutes. Add onion, celery, rosemary, salt, pepper, carrots, mushrooms and stock, stir, cover and cook on High for 15 minutes. Heat up a pan with the ghee over medium high heat, melt it, add flour and 3 tablespoons cooking juices from the stew, stir, add to stew, set the pot on simmer mode and cook everything for 4 minutes more. Divide into bowls and serve. Enjoy!

Nutrition: calories 283, fat 4, fiber 3, carbs 8, protein 18

Stuffed Bell Peppers

Preparation time: 10 minutes
Cooking time: 12 minutes
Servings: 4

Ingredients:

- 4 bell peppers, tops and seeds removed and blanched in hot water for 3 minutes
- Salt and black pepper to the taste
- 16 ounces beef meat, ground
- 1 egg
- ½ cup coconut milk
- 2 onions, chopped
- 8 ounces water
- 10 ounces keto tomato soup

Directions:

In a bowl, mix beef with salt, pepper, egg, milk and onions and stir very well. Stuff bell peppers with this mix, place them in your instant pot, add tomato soup and water, cover and cook on High for 12 minutes. Divide stuffed peppers between plates, drizzle cooking juices all over and serve. Enjoy!

Nutrition: calories 182, fat 2, fiber 3, carbs 7, protein 10

Crab Legs

Preparation time: 5 minutes
Cooking time: 3 minutes
Servings: 4

Ingredients:

- 4 pounds crab legs, halved
- 3 lemon wedges
- ¼ cup ghee
- 1 cup water

Directions:

Put the water in your instant pot, add steamer basket, add crab legs inside, cover and cook on High for 3 minutes. Transfer crab legs to a bowl, add melted ghee, toss and serve them with lemon wedges on the side. Enjoy!

Nutrition: calories 100, fat 4, fiber 1, carbs 2, protein 7

Snacks and Appetizer Recipes

Cranberry Dip

Preparation time: 10 minutes
Cooking time: 4 minutes
Servings: 4

Ingredients:
- 2 and ½ teaspoons lemon zest, grated
- 3 tablespoons lemon juice
- 12 ounces cranberries
- 4 tablespoons stevia

Directions:
In your instant pot, mix lemon juice with stevia, lemon zest and cranberries, stir, cover and cook on High for 2 minutes. Set the pot on simmer mode, stir your dip for a couple more minutes, transfer to a bowl and serve with some biscuits as a snack. Enjoy!

Nutrition: calories 73, fat 0, fiber 1, carbs 2, protein 2

Chili Dip

Preparation time: 10 minutes
Cooking time: 10 minutes
Servings: 8

Ingredients:
- 5 ancho chilies, dried and chopped
- 2 garlic cloves, minced
- Slat and black pepper to the taste
- 1 and ½ cups water
- 2 tablespoons balsamic vinegar
- 1 and ½ teaspoons stevia
- 1 tablespoon oregano, chopped
- ½ teaspoon cumin, ground

Directions:
In your instant pot mix water chilies, garlic, salt, pepper, stevia, cumin and oregano, stir, cover and cook on High for 8 minutes. Blend using an immersion blender, add vinegar, stir, set the pot on simmer mode and cook your chili dip until it thickens. Serve with veggie sticks on the side as a snack. Enjoy!

Nutrition: calories 85, fat 1, fiber 1, carbs 2, protein 2

Zucchini Dip

Preparation time: 10 minutes
Cooking time: 10 minutes
Servings: 4

Ingredients:
- 1 yellow onion, chopped
- 1 and ½ pounds zucchini, chopped
- 1 tablespoon olive oil
- 2 garlic cloves, minced
- Salt and white pepper to the taste
- ½ cup water
- 1 bunch basil, chopped

Directions:

Set your instant pot on Sauté mode, add oil, heat it up, add onion, stir and sauté for 3 minutes. Add zucchini, salt, pepper and water, stir, cover and cook on High for 3 minutes. Add garlic and basil, blend everything using an immersion blender, set the pot on simmer mode and cook your dip for a few more minutes until it thickens. Transfer to a bowl and serve as a tasty snack. Enjoy!

Nutrition: calories 100, fat 2, fiber 3, carbs 4, protein 2

Beets and Squash Dip

Preparation time: 10 minutes
Cooking time: 20 minutes
Servings: 8

Ingredients:
- 1 yellow onion, chopped
- 2 tablespoons olive oil
- 5 celery ribs
- 8 garlic cloves, minced
- 8 carrots, chopped
- 4 beets, peeled and chopped
- 1 butternut squash, peeled and chopped
- 1 cup veggie stock
- ¼ cup lemon juice
- 1 bunch basil, chopped
- 2 bay leaves
- Salt and black pepper to the taste

Directions:

Set your instant pot on Sauté mode, add oil, heat it up, add celery, carrots and onions, stir and cook for 3 minutes. Add beets, squash, garlic, stock, lemon juice, basil, bay leaves, salt and pepper, stir, cover and cook on High for 12 minutes. Discard bay leaves, blend dip using an immersion blender, transfer to a bowl and serve as a snack. Enjoy!

Nutrition: calories 83, fat 1, fiber 3, carbs 4, protein 3

Cheese and Sausage Dip

Preparation time: 10 minutes
Cooking time: 5 minutes
Servings: 4

Ingredients:

- 2 cups Mexican cheese, cut into chunks
- 1 cup Italian sausage, cooked and chopped
- 5 ounces canned tomatoes and green chilies, chopped
- 4 tablespoons water

Directions:

In your instant pot, mix sausage with cheese, tomatoes and chilies and water, stir, cover, cook on High for 5 minutes, blend a bit using an immersion blender, transfer to a bowl and serve as a dip. Enjoy!

Nutrition: calories 100, fat 3, fiber 2, carbs 6, protein 4

Creamy Mushroom Dip

Preparation time: 10 minutes
Cooking time: 35 minutes
Servings: 6

Ingredients:

- 1 yellow onion, chopped
- ¼ cup olive oil
- 1 tablespoon coconut flour
- 1 tablespoons thyme, chopped
- Salt and black pepper to the taste
- 3 garlic cloves, minced
- 1 and ¼ cup chicken stock
- 10 ounces shiitake mushrooms, chopped
- 10 ounces cremini mushrooms, chopped
- 10 ounces Portobello mushrooms, chopped
- 1 ounce parmesan cheese, grated
- ½ cup coconut cream
- 1 tablespoons parsley, chopped

Directions:

Set your instant pot on Sauté mode, add oil, heat it up, add onion, salt, pepper, flour, garlic and thyme, stir well and cook for 5 minutes. Add stock, shiitake, cremini and Portobello mushrooms, stir, cover and cook on High for 25 minutes. Add cream, cheese and parsley, stir, set the pot on Simmer mode, cook dip for 5 minutes more, transfer to bowls and serve as a dip. Enjoy!

Nutrition: calories 152, fat 5, fiber 4, carbs 10, protein 6

Cauliflower Dip

Preparation time: 10 minutes
Cooking time: 10 minutes
Servings: 6

Ingredients:

- 2 tablespoons ghee
- 8 garlic cloves, minced
- 7 cups veggie stock
- 6 cups cauliflower florets
- Salt and black pepper to the taste
- ½ cup coconut milk

Directions:

Set your instant pot on Sauté mode, add ghee, heat it up, add garlic, salt and pepper, stir and cook for 2 minutes. Add stock and cauliflower to the pot, heat up, cover and cook on High for 7 minutes. Transfer cauliflower and 1 cup stock to your blender, add milk and blend well for a few minutes. Transfer to a bowl and serve as a dip for veggies. Enjoy!

Nutrition: calories 100, fat 4, fiber 4, carbs 7, protein 7

Spicy Mango Dip

Preparation time: 10 minutes
Cooking time: 13 minutes
Servings: 4

Ingredients:

- 1 shallot, chopped
- 1 tablespoon coconut oil
- ¼ teaspoon cardamom powder
- 2 tablespoons ginger, minced
- ½ teaspoon cinnamon powder
- 2 mangos, peeled and chopped
- 2 red hot chilies, chopped
- 1 apple, cored and chopped
- ¼ cup raisins
- 5 tablespoons stevia
- 1 and ¼ apple cider vinegar

Directions:

Set your instant pot on Sauté mode, add oil, heat it up, add shallot and ginger, stir and cook for 3 minutes. Add cinnamon, hot peppers, cardamom, mangos, apple, raisins, stevia and cider, stir, cover and cook on High for 7 minutes. Set the pot on simmer mode, cook your dip for 6 minutes more, transfer to bowls and serve cold as a snack. Enjoy!

Nutrition: calories 100, fat 2, fiber 1, carbs 3, protein 1

Tomato Dip

Preparation time: 10 minutes
Cooking time: 15 minutes
Servings: 20

Ingredients:

- 2 pounds tomatoes, peeled and chopped
- 1 apple, cored and chopped
- 1 yellow onion, chopped
- 3 ounces dates chopped
- Salt to the taste
- 3 teaspoons whole spice
- ½ pint balsamic vinegar
- 4 tablespoons stevia

Directions:

Put tomatoes, apple, onion, dates, salt, whole spice and half of the vinegar in your instant pot, stir, cover and cook on High for 10 minutes. Set the pot on simmer mode, add the rest of the vinegar and stevia, stir, cook for a few minutes more until it thickens, transfer to bowls and serve as a snack. Enjoy!

Nutrition: calories 100, fat 3, fiber 3, carbs 6, protein 2

Mustard and Mushrooms Dip

Preparation time: 10 minutes
Cooking time: 10 minutes
Servings: 4

Ingredients:

- 6 ounces mushrooms, chopped
- 3 tablespoon olive oil
- 1 thyme sprigs
- 1 garlic clove, minced
- 4 ounces beef stock
- 1 tablespoon balsamic vinegar
- 1 tablespoon mustard
- 2 tablespoon coconut cream
- 2 tablespoons parsley, finely chopped

Directions:

Set your instant pot on Sauté mode, add oil, heat it up, add thyme, mushrooms and garlic, stir and sauté for 4 minutes. Add vinegar and stock, stir, cover, cook on High for 3 minutes, discard thyme, add mustard, coconut cream and parsley, stir, set the pot on simmer mode and cook for 3 minutes more. Divide into bowls and serve as a snack. Enjoy!

Nutrition: calories 100, fat 3, fiber 2, carbs 4, protein 3

Artichoke Dip

Preparation time: 10 minutes
Cooking time: 5 minutes
Servings: 6

Ingredients:

- 14 ounces canned artichoke hearts
- 8 ounces cream cheese
- 8 ounces mozzarella cheese, shredded
- 16 ounces parmesan cheese, grated
- 10 ounces spinach, torn
- 1 teaspoon onion powder
- ½ cup chicken stock
- ½ cup coconut cream
- 3 garlic cloves, minced
- ½ cup mayonnaise

Directions:

In your instant pot, mix artichokes with stock, garlic, spinach, cream cheese, coconut cream, onion powder and mayo, stir, cover and cook on High for 5 minutes. Add mozzarella and parmesan, stir well, transfer to a bowl and serve as a snack. Enjoy!

Nutrition: calories 200, fat 3, fiber 0, carbs 4, protein 7

Asparagus and Prosciutto Appetizer

Preparation time: 5 minutes
Cooking time: 4 minutes
Servings: 4

Ingredients:

- 8 asparagus spears
- 8 ounces prosciutto slices
- 2 cups water
- A pinch of salt

Directions:

Wrap asparagus spears in prosciutto slices and place them on a cutting board. Add the water to your instant pot, add a pinch of salt, add steamer basket, place asparagus inside, cover and cook on High for 4 minutes. Arrange asparagus on a platter and serve as an appetizer. Enjoy!

Nutrition: calories 83, fat 3, fiber 2, carbs 6, protein 3

Salmon Patties

Preparation time: 10 minutes
Cooking time: 7 minutes
Servings: 4

Ingredients:

- 1 teaspoon olive oil
- 1 egg, whisked
- 4 tablespoons coconut flour
- 1 pound salmon meat, minced
- 2 tablespoons lemon zest, grated
- Salt and black pepper to the taste
- Arugula leaves for serving

Directions:

Put salmon in your food processor, blend it, transfer to a bowl, add salt, pepper, lemon zest, coconut and egg, stir well and shape small patties out of this mix. Set your instant pot on sauté mode, add oil, heat it up, add patties and cook them for 3 minutes on each side. Arrange arugula on a platter, add salmon patties on top and serve as an appetizer. Enjoy!

Nutrition: calories 162, fat 3, fiber 2, carbs 6, protein 16

Cod Puddings

Preparation time: 10 minutes
Cooking time: 20 minutes
Servings: 4

Ingredients:

- 1 pound cod fillets, skinless, boneless cut into medium pieces
- 2 tablespoons parsley, chopped
- 4 ounces coconut flour
- 2 teaspoons lemon juice
- 2 eggs, whisked
- 2 ounces ghee, melted
- ½ pint coconut milk, hot
- ½ pint shrimp sauce
- Salt and black pepper to the taste
- ½ pint water

Directions:

In a bowl, mix fish with flour, lemon juice, shrimp sauce, parsley, eggs, salt and pepper and stir. Add milk and melted ghee, stir well and leave aside for a couple of minutes. Divide this mix greased ramekins. Add the water to your instant pot, add the steamer basket, add puddings inside, cover and cook on High for 15 minutes. Serve the warm. Enjoy!

Nutrition: calories 172, fat 3, fiber 2, carbs 5, protein 6

Mussels Appetizer

Preparation time: 10 minutes
Cooking time: 7 minutes
Servings: 4

Ingredients:

- 2 pounds mussels, cleaned and scrubbed
- 1 white onion, chopped
- ½ cup veggie stock
- 2 garlic cloves, minced
- ½ cup water
- A drizzle of extra virgin olive oil

Directions:

Set instant pot on Sauté mode, add oil, heat it up, garlic and onion, stir and cook for 4 minutes. Add stock, stir and cook for 1 minute. Add the steamer basket, add mussels inside, cover and cook on High for 2 minutes. Arrange mussels on a platter and serve with some of the cooking juices drizzled all over. Enjoy!

Nutrition: calories 82, fat 3, fiber 2, carbs 3, protein 2

Italian Mussels Appetizer

Preparation time: 10 minutes
Cooking time: 10 minutes
Servings: 4

Ingredients:

- 28 ounces canned tomatoes, chopped
- 2 pounds mussels, scrubbed
- 2 jalapeno peppers, chopped
- ½ cup white onion, chopped
- ¼ cup veggie stock
- ¼ cup olive oil
- ¼ cup balsamic vinegar
- 2 tablespoons red pepper flakes, crushed
- 2 garlic cloves, minced
- Salt to the taste
- ½ cup basil, chopped

Directions:

Set your instant pot on Sauté mode, add oil heat it up, add tomatoes, onion, jalapenos, stock, vinegar, garlic and pepper flakes, stir and cook for 5 minutes. Add mussels, stir, cover, cook on Low for 4 minutes, add salt and basil, stir, divide everything into small bowls and serve as an appetizer. Enjoy!

Nutrition: calories 82, fat 1, fiber 2, carbs 2, protein 6

Spicy Mussels

Preparation time: 10 minutes
Cooking time: 6 minutes
Servings: 4

Ingredients:

- 2 pounds mussels, scrubbed
- 2 tablespoons olive oil
- 1 yellow onion, chopped
- ½ cup chicken stock
- ½ teaspoon red pepper flakes
- 14 ounces tomatoes, chopped
- 2 teaspoons garlic, minced
- 2 teaspoons oregano, dried

Directions:

Set your instant pot on Sauté mode, add oil, heat it up, add onions, stir and sauté for 3 minutes. Add pepper flakes, garlic, stock, tomatoes, oregano and mussels, stir, cover and cook on Low for 3 minutes. Divide mussels into small bowls and serve as an appetizer. Enjoy!

Nutrition: calories 82, fat 1, fiber 2, carbs 3, protein 2

Mussels Bowls

Preparation time: 5 minutes
Cooking time: 7 minutes
Servings: 4

Ingredients:

- 2 pounds mussels, scrubbed
- 12 ounces veggie stock
- 1 tablespoon olive oil
- 1 yellow onion, chopped
- 8 ounces spicy sausage, chopped
- 1 tablespoon sweet paprika

Directions:

Set your instant pot on Sauté mode, add oil, heat it up, add onion and sausages, stir and cook for 5 minutes. Add stock, paprika and mussels, stir, cover, cook on Low for 2 minutes, divide into bowls and serve as an appetizer. Enjoy!

Nutrition: calories 112, fat 4, fiber 2, carbs 4, protein 10

Clams and Mussels

Preparation time: 10 minutes
Cooking time: 13 minutes
Servings: 4

Ingredients:
- 15 small clams
- 30 mussels, scrubbed
- 2 chorizo links, sliced
- 1 yellow onion, chopped
- 10 ounces veggie stock
- 2 tablespoons parsley, chopped
- 1 teaspoon olive oil
- Lemon wedges for serving

Directions:
Set your instant pot on Sauté mode, add oil, heat it up, add onion and chorizo, stir and cook for 3 minutes. Add clams, mussels and stock, stir, cover, cook on High for 10 minutes, add parsley, stir, divide into bowls and serve as an appetizer with lemon wedges on the side. Enjoy!

Nutrition: calories 172, fat 4, fiber 3, carbs 7, protein 12

Stuffed Clams

Preparation time: 10 minutes
Cooking time: 4 minutes
Servings: 4

Ingredients:
- 24 clams, shucked
- 3 garlic cloves, minced
- 4 tablespoons ghee
- ¼ cup parsley, chopped
- ¼ cup parmesan cheese, grated
- 1 teaspoon oregano, dried
- 1 cup almonds, crushed
- 2 cups water
- Lemon wedges

Directions:
In a bowl, mix crushed almonds with parmesan, oregano, parsley, butter and garlic, stir and divide this into exposed clams. Add the water to your instant pot, add steamer basket, add clams inside, cover and cook on High for 4 minutes. Arrange clams on a platter and serve them as an appetizer with lemon wedges on the side. Enjoy!

Nutrition: calories 92, fat 3, fiber 3, carbs 6, protein 5

Shrimp and Sausage Appetizer Bowls

Preparation time: 10 minutes
Cooking time: 5 minutes
Servings: 4

Ingredients:

- 1 and ½ pounds shrimp, heads removed
- 12 ounces sausage, cooked and chopped
- 1 tablespoon old bay seasoning
- 16 ounces chicken stock
- Salt and black pepper to the taste
- 1 teaspoon red pepper flakes, crushed
- 2 sweet onions, cut into wedges
- 8 garlic cloves, minced

Directions:

In your instant pot, mix stock with old bay seasoning, pepper flakes, salt, black pepper, onions, garlic, sausage and shrimp, stir, cover and cook on High for 5 minutes. Divide into small bowls and serve as an appetizer. Enjoy!

Nutrition: calories 251, fat 4, fiber 3, carbs 6, protein 7

Asian Shrimp Appetizer

Preparation time: 10 minutes
Cooking time: 4 minutes
Servings: 4

Ingredients:

- 1 pounds shrimp, peeled and deveined
- 2 tablespoons coconut aminos
- 3 tablespoons vinegar
- ¾ cup pineapple juice
- 1 cup chicken stock
- 3 tablespoons stevia

Directions:

Put shrimp, pineapple juice, stock, aminos and stevia in your instant pot, stir a bit, cover and cook on High for 4 minutes. Arrange shrimp on a platter, drizzle cooking juices all over and serve as an appetizer. Enjoy!

Nutrition: calories 172, fat 4, fiber 1, carbs 3, protein 20

Mediterranean Octopus Appetizer

Preparation time: 10 minutes
Cooking time: 16 minutes
Servings: 6

Ingredients:

- 1 octopus, cleaned and prepared
- 2 rosemary sprigs
- 2 teaspoons oregano, dried
- ½ yellow onion, chopped

- 4 thyme sprigs
- ½ lemon
- 1 teaspoon black peppercorns
- 3 tablespoons olive oil

For the marinade:

- ¼ cup extra virgin olive oil
- Juice of ½ lemon
- 4 garlic cloves, minced

- 2 thyme sprigs
- 1 rosemary sprigs
- Salt and black pepper to the taste

Directions:

Put the octopus in your instant pot, add oregano, 2 rosemary sprigs, 4 thyme sprigs, onion, lemon, 3 tablespoons olive oil, peppercorns and salt, stir, cover, cook on High for 10 minutes, transfer to a cutting board, cool it down, separate tentacles and transfer them to a bowl. Add ¼ cup olive oil, lemon juice, garlic, 1 rosemary sprigs, 2 thyme sprigs, salt and pepper, toss to coat and leave aside for 1 hour. Place octopus on preheated grill over medium high heat, cook for 3 minutes on each side, arrange on a platter and serve. Enjoy!

Nutrition: calories 162, fat 3, fiber 1, carbs 2, protein 7

Chinese Squid Appetizer

Preparation time: 10 minutes
Cooking time: 15 minutes
Servings: 4

Ingredients:

- 4 squid, tentacles from 1 squid separated and chopped
- 1 cup cauliflower rice
- 14 ounces fish stock

- 4 tablespoons coconut aminos
- 1 tablespoon mirin
- 2 tablespoons stevia

Directions:

In a bowl, mix chopped tentacles with cauliflower rice, stir well and stuff each squid with the mix. Place squid in your instant pot, add stock, aminos, mirin and stevia, stir, cover and cook on High for 15 minutes. Arrange stuffed squid on a platter and serve as an appetizer. Enjoy!

Nutrition: calories 162, fat 2, fiber 2, carbs 3, protein 10

Simple Artichokes

Preparation time: 10 minutes
Cooking time: 15 minutes
Servings: 4

Ingredients:
- 4 big artichokes, trimmed
- Salt and black pepper to the taste
- 2 tablespoons lemon juice
- ¼ cup olive oil
- 2 teaspoons balsamic vinegar
- 1 teaspoon oregano, dried
- 2 garlic cloves, minced
- 2 cups water

Directions:
Add the water to your instant pot, add the steamer basket, add artichokes inside, cover and cook on High for 8 minutes. In a bowl, mix lemon juice with vinegar, oil, salt, pepper, garlic and oregano and stir very well. Cut artichokes in halves, add them to lemon and vinegar mix, toss well, place them on preheated grill over medium high heat, cook for 3 minutes on each side, arrange them on a platter and serve as an appetizer. Enjoy!

Nutrition: calories 162, fat 4, fiber 2, carbs 3, protein 5

Cajun Shrimp

Preparation time: 4 minutes
Cooking time: 3 minutes
Servings: 4

Ingredients:
- 1 cup water
- 1 pound shrimp, peeled and deveined
- ½ tablespoon Cajun seasoning
- 1 teaspoon extra virgin olive oil
- 1 bunch asparagus, trimmed

Directions:
Put the water in your instant pot, add steamer basket, add shrimp and asparagus inside, drizzle Cajun seasoning and oil over them, toss a bit, cover pot and cook on High for 3 minutes. Arrange on appetizer plates and serve as an appetizer. Enjoy!

Nutrition: calories 152, fat 2, fiber 3, carbs 8, protein 15

French Endives

Preparation time: 10 minutes
Cooking time: 7 minutes
Servings: 4

Ingredients:
- 4 endives, trimmed and halved
- Salt and black pepper to the taste
- 1 tablespoon lemon juice
- 1 tablespoon ghee

Directions:

Set your instant pot on Sauté mode, add ghee, heat it up, add endives, season with salt and pepper, drizzle lemon juice, cover pot and cook them on High for 7 minutes. Arrange endives on a platter, drizzle some of the cooking juice over them and serve as an appetizer. Enjoy!

Nutrition: calories 100, fat 3, fiber 2, carbs 7, protein 2

Endives and Ham Appetizer

Preparation time: 10 minutes
Cooking time: 20 minutes
Servings: 4

Ingredients:
- 4 endives, trimmed
- 1 cup water
- Salt and black pepper to the taste
- 1 tablespoon coconut flour
- 2 tablespoons ghee
- 4 slices ham
- ½ teaspoon nutmeg, ground
- 14 ounces coconut milk

Directions:

Add the water to your instant pot, add steamer basket, add endives inside, cover, cook them on High for 10 minutes, wrap them in ham and transfer them to a baking dish. Clean your instant pot, set it on simmer mode, add the ghee, heat it up, add coconut flour, milk, salt, pepper and nutmeg, stir and cook for 7 minutes. Pour milk and nutmeg mix over endives, introduce them in preheated broiler and broil for 10 minutes. Arrange on a platter and serve as an appetizer. Enjoy!

Nutrition: calories 152, fat 3, fiber 3, carbs 6, protein 12

Eggplant Spread

Preparation time: 10 minutes
Cooking time: 10 minutes
Servings: 6

Ingredients:
- 2 pounds eggplant, peeled and cut into medium chunks
- Salt and black pepper to the taste
- ¼ cup olive oil
- 4 garlic cloves, minced
- ½ cup water
- 3 olives, pitted and sliced
- ¼ cup lemon juice
- 1 bunch thyme, chopped
- 1 tablespoon sesame seed paste

Directions:
Set your instant pot on sauté mode, add oil, heat it up, add eggplant pieces, stir and cook for 5 minutes. Add garlic, water, salt and pepper, stir, cover, cook on High for 3 minutes, transfer to a blender, add sesame seed paste, lemon juice and thyme, stir and pulse really well. Transfer to bowls, sprinkle olive slices on top and serve as an appetizer. Enjoy!

Nutrition: calories 87, fat 4, fiber 2, carbs 6, protein 2

Okra Bowls

Preparation time: 10 minutes
Cooking time: 15 minutes
Servings: 6

Ingredients:
- 1 pound okra, trimmed
- 6 scallions, chopped
- 3 green bell peppers, chopped
- Salt and black pepper to the taste
- 2 tablespoons olive oil
- 1 teaspoon stevia
- 28 ounces canned tomatoes, chopped

Directions:
Set your instant pot on Sauté mode, add oil, heat it up, add scallions and bell peppers, stir and cook for 5 minutes. Add okra, salt, pepper, stevia and tomatoes, stir, cover, cook on High for 10 minutes, divide into small bowls and serve as an appetizer salad. Enjoy!

Nutrition: calories 121, fat 3, fiber 3, carbs 6, protein 4

Easy Leeks Platter

Preparation time: 10 minutes
Cooking time: 10 minutes
Servings: 4

Ingredients:
- 4 leeks, washed, roots and ends cut off
- Salt and black pepper to the taste
- 1/3 cup water
- 1 tablespoon ghee

Directions:
Put leeks in your instant pot, add water, ghee, salt and pepper, stir, cover and cook on High for 5 minutes. Set the pot on sauté mode, cook leeks for a couple more minutes, arrange them on a platter and serve as an appetizer. Enjoy!

Nutrition: calories 73, fat 3, fiber 4, carbs 9, protein 7

Tomatoes Appetizer

Preparation time: 10 minutes
Cooking time: 10 minutes
Servings: 4

Ingredients:
- 4 tomatoes, tops cut off and pulp scooped
- ½ cup water
- Salt and black pepper to the taste
- 1 yellow onion, chopped
- 1 tablespoon ghee
- 2 tablespoons celery, chopped
- ½ cup mushrooms, chopped
- 1 cup cottage cheese
- ¼ teaspoon caraway seeds
- 1 tablespoon parsley, chopped

Directions:
Set your instant pot on sauté mode, add ghee, heat it up, add onion and celery, stir and cook for 3 minutes. Add tomato pulp, mushrooms, salt, pepper, cheese, parsley and caraway seeds, stir, cook for 3 minutes more and stuff tomatoes with this mix. Add the water to your instant pot, add the steamer basket, and stuffed tomatoes inside, cover and cook on High for 4 minutes. Arrange tomatoes on a platter and serve as an appetizer. Enjoy!

Nutrition: calories 152, fat 2, fiber 4, carbs 6, protein 7

Cinnamon and Pumpkin Muffins

Preparation time: 10 minutes
Cooking time: 20 minutes
Servings: 18

Ingredients:

- 4 tablespoons ghee
- ¾ cup pumpkin puree
- 2 tablespoons flaxseed meal
- ¼ cup coconut flour
- ½ cup erythritol
- ½ teaspoon nutmeg, ground
- 1 teaspoon cinnamon powder
- ½ teaspoon baking powder
- ½ teaspoon baking soda
- 1 and ½ cups water
- 1 egg

Directions:

In a bowl, mix ghee with pumpkin puree, egg, flaxseed meal, coconut flour, erythritol, baking soda, baking powder, nutmeg and cinnamon, stir well and divide into a greased muffin pan. Add the water to your instant pot, add the steamer basket, add muffin pan inside, cover pot and cook on High for 20 minutes. Arrange muffins on a platter and serve as a snack.

Nutrition: calories 50, fat 3, fiber 1, carbs 2, protein 2

Spicy Chili Balls

Preparation time: 10 minutes
Cooking time: 5 minutes
Servings: 3

Ingredients:

- 3 bacon slices
- 1 cup water
- 3 ounces cream cheese
- ¼ teaspoon onion powder
- Salt and black pepper to the taste
- 2 jalapeno peppers, chopped
- ½ teaspoon parsley, dried
- ¼ teaspoon garlic powder

Directions:

Set your instant pot on sauté mode, add bacon, cook for a couple of minutes, transfer to paper towels drain grease and crumble it. In a bowl, mix cream cheese with jalapenos, bacon, onion, garlic powder, parsley, salt and pepper, stir well and shape balls out of this mix. Clean the pot, add the water, and the steamer basket, add spicy balls inside, cover and cook on High for 2 minutes. Arrange balls on a platter and serve as an appetizer. Enjoy!

Nutrition: calories 150, fat 5, fiber 1, carbs 2, protein 5

Italian Dip

Preparation time: 10 minutes
Cooking time: 20 minutes
Servings: 4

Ingredients:

- 4 ounces cream cheese, soft
- ½ cup mozzarella cheese
- ¼ cup coconut cream
- Salt and black pepper to the taste
- 1/2 cup tomato sauce
- 4 black olives, pitted and chopped
- ¼ cup mayonnaise
- ¼ cup parmesan cheese, grated
- 1 tablespoon green bell pepper, chopped
- 6 pepperoni slices, chopped
- ½ teaspoon Italian seasoning
- 2 cups water

Directions:

In a bowl, mix cream cheese with mozzarella, coconut cream, mayo, salt and pepper, stir and divide this into 4 ramekins. Layer tomato sauce, parmesan cheese, bell pepper, pepperoni, Italian seasoning and black olives on top, Add the water to your instant pot, add the steamer basket, add ramekins inside, cover and cook on High for 20 minutes. Serve this dip warm with veggie sticks on the side. Enjoy!

Nutrition: calories 250, fat 15, fiber 4, carbs 4, protein 12

Avocado Dip

Preparation time: 10 minutes
Cooking time: 2 minutes
Servings: 4

Ingredients:

- ¼ cup erythritol powder
- 1 cup water
- ½ cup cilantro, chopped
- 2 avocados, pitted, peeled and halved
- ¼ teaspoon stevia
- Juice from 2 limes
- Zest of 2 limes, grated
- 1 cup coconut milk

Directions:

Add the water to your instant pot, add the steamer basket, add avocado halves, cover and cook on High for 2 minutes. Transfer to your blender, add lime juice and cilantro and pulse well. Add coconut milk, lime zest, stevia and erythritol powder, pulse again, divide into bowls and serve. Enjoy!

Nutrition: calories 150, fat 6, fiber 2, carbs 4, protein 2

Minty Shrimp Appetizer

Preparation time: 10 minutes
Cooking time: 20 minutes
Servings: 16

Ingredients:
- 2 tablespoons olive oil
- 10 ounces shrimp, cooked, peeled and deveined
- 1 tablespoons mint, chopped
- 2 tablespoons erythritol
- 1/3 cup blackberries, ground
- 11 prosciutto slices
- 1/3 cup veggie stock.

Directions:
Wrap each shrimp in prosciutto slices and drizzle oil over them. In your instant pot, mix blackberries with mint, stock and erythritol, stir, set on simmer mode and cook for 2 minutes. Add steamer basket, and wrapped shrimp, cover pot and cook on High for 2 minutes. Arrange wrapped shrimp on a platter, drizzle mint sauce all over and serve. Enjoy!

Nutrition: calories 175, fat 6, fiber 2, carbs 1, protein 8

Zucchini Appetizer Salad

Preparation time: 10 minutes
Cooking time: 6 minutes
Servings: 4

Ingredients:
- 1 cup mozzarella, shredded
- ¼ cup tomato sauce
- 1 zucchini, roughly sliced
- Salt and black pepper to the taste
- A pinch of cumin, ground
- A drizzle of olive oil

Directions:
In your instant pot, mix zucchini with oil, tomato sauce, salt, pepper and cumin, toss a bit, cover and cook on High for 6 minutes. Divide between appetizer plates and serve right away. Enjoy!

Nutrition: calories 130, fat 4, fiber 2, carbs 4, protein 3

Zucchini Hummus

Preparation time: 10 minutes
Cooking time: 6 minutes
Servings: 4

Ingredients:
- 4 cups zucchini, chopped
- 3 tablespoons veggie stock
- ¼ cup olive oil
- Salt and black pepper to the taste
- 4 garlic cloves, minced
- ¾ cup sesame seeds paste
- ½ cup lemon juice
- 1 tablespoon cumin, ground

Directions:
Set your instant pot on sauté mode, add half of the oil, heat it up, add zucchini and garlic, stir and cook for 2 minutes. Add stock, salt and pepper, cover pot and cook on High for 4 minutes more. Transfer zucchini to your blender, add the rest of the oil, sesame seeds paste, lemon juice and cumin, pulse well, transfer to bowls and serve as a snack. Enjoy!

Nutrition: calories 80, fat 5, fiber 3, carbs 6, protein 7

Crab and Cheese Dip

Preparation time: 10 minutes
Cooking time: 20 minutes
Servings: 8

Ingredients:
- 8 bacon strips, sliced
- 12 ounces crab meat
- ½ cup mayonnaise
- ½ cup coconut cream
- 8 ounces cream cheese
- 2 poblano pepper, chopped
- 2 tablespoons lemon juice
- Salt and black pepper to the taste
- 4 garlic cloves, minced
- 4 green onions, minced
- 1 cup parmesan cheese, grated

Directions:
Set your instant pot on sauté mode, add bacon, cook until it's crispy, transfer to paper towels, drain grease and leave aside. In a bowl, mix coconut cream with cream cheese, mayo, half of the parmesan, poblano peppers, garlic, lemon juice, green onions, salt, pepper, crab meat and bacon and stir really well. Clean your instant pot, add crab mix, spread the rest of the parmesan on top, cover and cook on High for 14 minutes. Divide into bowls and serve as a snack. Enjoy!

Nutrition: calories 200, fat 2, fiber 2, carbs 4, protein 3

Spinach Dip

Preparation time: 10 minutes
Cooking time: 20 minutes
Servings: 6

Ingredients:

- 6 bacon slices, cooked and crumbled
- A drizzle of olive oil
- 1 tablespoon garlic, minced
- 5 ounces spinach
- 1 and ½ cups water
- ½ cup coconut cream
- 8 ounces cream cheese, soft
- 1 and ½ tablespoons parsley, chopped
- 2.5 ounces parmesan, grated
- 1 tablespoon lemon juice
- Salt and black pepper to the taste

Directions:

Set your instant pot on sauté mode, add oil heat it up, add spinach, stir, cook for 1 minute and transfer to a bowl. Add cream cheese, garlic, salt, pepper, coconut cream, parsley, bacon, lemon juice and parmesan, stir well and divide this into 6 ramekins. Add the water to your instant pot, add steamer basket, add ramekins inside, cover and cook on High for 15 minutes. Introduce in a preheated broiler for 4 minutes and serve right away. Enjoy!

Nutrition: calories 255, fat 7, fiber 3, carbs 5, protein 7

Stuffed Mushrooms

Preparation time: 10 minutes
Cooking time: 15 minutes
Servings: 5

Ingredients:

- ¼ cup mayo
- 1 teaspoon garlic powder
- 1 small yellow onion, chopped
- 24 ounces white mushroom caps
- 1 and ½ cups water
- Salt and black pepper to the taste
- 1 teaspoon curry powder
- 4 ounces cream cheese, soft
- ¼ cup coconut cream
- ½ cup Mexican cheese, shredded
- 1 cup shrimp, cooked, peeled, deveined and chopped

Directions:

In a bowl, mix mayo with garlic powder, onion, curry powder, cream cheese, cream, Mexican cheese, shrimp, salt and pepper, stir and stuff mushrooms with this mix. Add the water to your instant pot, add steamer basket, add mushrooms inside, cover pot and cook on High for 14 minutes. Arrange mushrooms on a platter and serve as an appetizer. Enjoy!

Nutrition: calories 244, fat 16, fiber 3, carbs 7, protein 12

Turkey Meatballs

Preparation time: 10 minutes
Cooking time: 6 minutes
Servings: 16

Ingredients:

- 1 egg
- Salt and black pepper to the taste
- ¼ cup coconut flour
- 2 tablespoons sun-dried tomatoes, chopped
- 1 pound turkey meat, ground
- ½ teaspoon garlic powder
- ½ cup mozzarella cheese, shredded
- 2 tablespoons olive oil
- ¼ cup tomato paste
- 2 tablespoon basil, chopped

Directions:

In a bowl, mix turkey with salt, pepper, egg, flour, garlic powder, sun-dried tomatoes, mozzarella and basil, stir well and shape 12 meatballs out of this mix. Set your instant pot on sauté mode, add oil, heat it up, add meatballs, stir and brown for 2 minutes on each side. Add tomato paste over them, toss a bit, cover and cook on High for 8 minutes. Arrange meatballs on a platter and serve them right away. Enjoy!

Nutrition: calories 100, fat 6, fiber 3, carbs 5, protein 3

Italian Chicken Wings

Preparation time: 10 minutes
Cooking time: 27 minutes
Servings: 6

Ingredients:

- 6-pound chicken wings, cut into halves
- 2 cups water
- Salt and black pepper to the taste
- ½ teaspoon Italian seasoning
- 2 tablespoons ghee
- ½ cup parmesan cheese, grated
- A pinch of red pepper flakes, crushed
- 1 teaspoon garlic powder
- 1 egg

Directions:

Put the water in your instant pot, add the trivet, add chicken wings, cover and cook on High for 7 minutes. Meanwhile, in your blender, mix ghee with cheese, egg, salt, pepper, pepper flakes, garlic powder and Italian seasoning and blend very well. Arrange chicken wings on a lined baking sheet, pour cheese sauce over them, introduce in preheated broiler and broil for 5 minutes. Flip and broil for 5 minutes more, arrange them all on a platter and serve. Enjoy!

Nutrition: calories 134, fat 5, fiber 1, carbs 2, protein 7

Zucchini Rolls

Preparation time: 10 minutes
Cooking time: 7 minutes
Servings: 24

Ingredients:

- 2 tablespoons olive oil
- 3 zucchinis, thinly sliced
- 24 basil leaves
- 2 tablespoons mint, chopped
- 1 and ½ cups water
- 1 and 1/3 cup ricotta cheese
- Salt and black pepper to the taste
- ¼ cup basil, chopped
- Tomato sauce for serving

Directions:

Set your instant pot on sauté mode, add zucchini slices, drizzle the oil over them, season with salt and pepper, cook for 2 minutes on each side and transfer to a plate. In a bowl, mix ricotta with chopped basil, mint, salt and pepper, stir, divide this into zucchini slices and roll them. Add the water to your instant pot, add steamer basket, add zucchini rolls inside, cover and cook on High for 3 minutes. Arrange on a platter and serve with tomato sauce on the side. Enjoy!

Nutrition: calories 70, fat 3, fiber 1, carbs 2, protein 4

Spicy Salsa

Preparation time: 10 minutes
Cooking time: 3 minutes
Servings: 4

Ingredients:

- 1 red onion, chopped
- 2 tablespoons lime juice
- 2 avocados, pitted, peeled and chopped
- 3 jalapeno pepper, chopped
- Salt and black pepper to the taste
- 2 tablespoons cumin powder
- ½ tomato, chopped

Directions:

In your instant pot, mix onion with avocados, peppers, salt, black pepper, cumin, lime juice and tomato, stir, cover and cook on Low for 3 minutes. Divide into bowls and serve. Enjoy!

Nutrition: calories 120, fat 2, fiber 2, carbs 5, protein 4

Salmon Balls

Preparation time: 10 minutes
Cooking time: 10 minutes
Servings: 4

Ingredients:

- 2 tablespoons ghee
- 2 garlic cloves, minced
- 1/3 cup onion, chopped
- 1 pound wild salmon, boneless, skinless and minced
- ¼ cup chives, chopped

- 1 egg
- 2 tablespoons Dijon mustard
- 1 tablespoon coconut flour
- Salt and black pepper to the taste

For the coconut sauce:

- 4 garlic cloves, minced
- 2 tablespoons ghee
- 2 tablespoons Dijon mustard

- Juice and zest of 1 lemon
- 2 cups coconut cream
- 2 tablespoons chives, chopped

Directions:

Set your instant pot on sauté mode, add 2 tablespoons ghee, heat it up, add onion and 2 garlic cloves, stir, cook for 3 minutes and transfer to a bowl. Add salmon, chives, coconut flour, salt, pepper, 2 tablespoons mustard and egg, stir and shape medium balls out of this mix. Set the pot on sauté mode again, add 2 tablespoons ghee, heat it up, add 4 garlic cloves, stir and cook for 1 minute. Add coconut cream, 2 tablespoons Dijon mustard, lemon juice and zest and chives, stir, drop salmon balls into this sauce, cover pot, cook on High for 6 minutes, arrange on a platter and serve. Enjoy!

Nutrition: calories 171, fat 5, fiber 1, carbs 6, protein 23

Delicious Oysters

Preparation time: 10 minutes
Cooking time: 6 minutes
Servings: 3

Ingredients:

- 6 big oysters, shucked
- 1 and ½ cups water
- 3 garlic cloves, minced
- 1 lemon cut into wedges

- 1 tablespoon parsley
- A pinch of sweet paprika
- 2 tablespoons melted ghee

Directions:

Divide ghee, parsley, paprika and garlic in each oyster. Add the water to your instant pot, add steamer basket, add oysters, cover pot and cook on High for 6 minutes. Arrange oysters on a platter and serve with lemon wedges on the side. Enjoy!

Nutrition: calories 90, fat 1, fiber 1, carbs 2, protein 4

Tuna Patties

Preparation time: 10 minutes
Cooking time: 8 minutes
Servings: 12

Ingredients:
- 15 ounces canned tuna, drained and flaked
- 3 eggs
- ½ teaspoon dill, chopped
- 1 teaspoon parsley, dried
- ½ cup red onion, chopped
- 1 and ½ cups water
- 1 teaspoon garlic powder
- Salt and black pepper to the taste
- A drizzle of olive oil

Directions:
In a bowl, mix tuna with salt, pepper, dill, parsley, onion, garlic powder and eggs, stir and shape medium patties out of this mix. Set your instant pot on sauté mode, add a drizzle of oil, heat it up, add tuna patties, cook them for 2 minutes on each side and transfer to a plate. Clean the pot, add the water, add steamer basket, add tuna cakes, cover pot and cook on High for 4 minutes. Arrange patties on a platter and serve. Enjoy!

Nutrition: calories 140, fat 2, fiber 1, carbs 0.6, protein 6

Worcestershire Shrimp

Preparation time: 10 minutes
Cooking time: 8 minutes
Servings: 2

Ingredients:
- ½ pound big shrimp, peeled and deveined
- 2 teaspoons Worcestershire sauce
- 2 teaspoons olive oil
- Juice of 1 lemon
- Salt and black pepper to the taste
- 1 teaspoon Creole seasoning

Directions:
In your instant pot, mix shrimp with Worcestershire sauce, oil, lemon juice, salt, pepper and seasoning, stir, cover and cook on High for 4 minutes. Arrange shrimp on a lined baking sheet, introduce in preheated broiler and broil for 4 minutes more. Arrange on a platter and serve. Enjoy!

Nutrition: calories 120, fat 3, fiber 1, carbs 6, protein 5

Side Dish Recipes

Napa Cabbage Side Salad

Preparation time: 40 minutes
Cooking time: 5 minutes
Servings: 6

Ingredients:
- Salt and black pepper to the taste
- 1 pound napa cabbage, chopped
- 1 carrot, julienned
- 2 tablespoons veggie stock
- ½ cup daikon radish
- 3 garlic cloves, minced
- 3 green onion stalks, chopped
- 1 tablespoon coconut aminos
- 3 tablespoons chili flakes
- 1 tablespoon olive oil
- ½ inch ginger, grated

Directions:
In a bowl, mix cabbage with salt and black pepper, massage well for 10 minutes, cover and leave aside for 30 minutes. In another bowl, mix chili flakes with aminos, garlic, oil and ginger and stir whisk well. Drain cabbage well, transfer to your instant pot, add stock, carrots, green onions, radish and the chili paste you made, stir, cover and cook on High for 5 minutes. Divide between plates and serve as a side dish. Enjoy!

Nutrition: calories 100, fat 3, fiber 4, carbs 5, protein 2

Asian Brussels Sprouts

Preparation time: 10 minutes
Cooking time: 4 minutes
Servings: 4

Ingredients:
- 1 pound Brussels sprouts, halved
- 3 tablespoons chicken stock
- Salt and black pepper to the taste
- 1 teaspoon sesame seeds, toasted
- 1 tablespoon green onions, chopped
- 1 and ½ tablespoons stevia
- 1 tablespoon coconut aminos
- 2 tablespoons olive oil
- 1 tablespoon keto sriracha sauce

Directions:
In a bowl, mix oil with coconut aminos, sriracha, stevia, salt and black pepper and whisk well. Put Brussels sprouts in your instant pot; add sriracha mix, stock, green onions and sesame seeds, stir, cover and cook on High for 4 minutes. Divide between plates and serve as a side dish. Enjoy!

Nutrition: calories 110, fat 4, fiber 2, carbs 4, protein 2

Cauliflower and Parmesan

Preparation time: 10 minutes
Cooking time: 4 minutes
Servings: 6

Ingredients:
- 1 cauliflower head, florets separated
- ½ cup veggie stock
- 2 garlic cloves, minced
- Salt and black pepper to the taste
- 1/3 cup parmesan, grated
- 1 tablespoon parsley, chopped
- 3 tablespoons olive oil

Directions:
In a bowl, mix oil with garlic, salt, pepper and cauliflower florets, toss and transfer to your instant pot. Add stock, cover pot and cook on High for 4 minutes. Add parsley and parmesan, toss, divide between plates and serve as a side dish. Enjoy!

Nutrition: calories 120, fat 2, fiber 3, carbs 5, protein 3

Swiss Chard and Garlic

Preparation time: 10 minutes
Cooking time: 6 minutes
Servings: 2

Ingredients:
- 2 tablespoons ghee
- 3 tablespoons lemon juice
- ½ cup chicken stock
- 4 bacon slices, chopped
- 1 bunch Swiss chard, roughly chopped
- ½ teaspoon garlic paste
- Salt and black pepper to the taste

Directions:
Set your instant pot on sauté mode, add bacon, stir and cook for a couple of minutes. Add ghee, lemon juice and garlic paste and stir. Add Swiss chard, salt, pepper and stock, cover pot and cook on High for 3 minutes. Divide between plates and serve as a side dish. Enjoy!

Nutrition: calories 160, fat 7, fiber 3, carbs 6, protein 4

Mushroom and Arugula Side Dish

Preparation time: 10 minutes
Cooking time: 5 minutes
Servings: 4

Ingredients:
- 2 tablespoons ghee
- Salt and black pepper to the taste
- 1 pound cremini mushrooms, chopped
- 4 tablespoons veggie stock
- 4 bunches arugula
- 8 slices prosciutto, chopped
- 2 tablespoons balsamic vinegar
- 8 sun-dried tomatoes in oil, chopped
- 1 tablespoon parsley, chopped

Directions:
Set your instant pot on sauté mode, add prosciutto, stir and cook for 2 minutes. Add ghee, melt it, add mushrooms, salt and pepper, stir and cook for 2 minutes. Add vinegar, stock and tomatoes, stir, cover and cook on High for 3 minutes. Add parsley, stir and transfer this mix to a bowl. Add arugula, toss, divide between plates and serve as a side dish. Enjoy!

Nutrition: calories 200, fat 3, fiber 2, carbs 5, protein 6

Red Chard and Olives

Preparation time: 10 minutes
Cooking time: 5 minutes
Servings: 4

Ingredients:
- 2 tablespoons olive oil
- 1 bunch red chard, roughly chopped
- 3 tablespoons veggie stock
- 2 tablespoons capers
- 1 yellow onion, chopped
- Juice of 1 lemon
- Salt and black pepper to the taste
- 1 teaspoon stevia
- ¼ cup kalamata olives, pitted and chopped

Directions:
Set your instant pot on sauté mode, add oil, heat it up, add onion, stir and cook for 2 minutes. Add stevia, olives, chard, salt, pepper and stock, stir, cover and cook on High for 3 minutes. Add capers and lemon juice, stir, divide between plates and serve as a side dish. Enjoy!

Nutrition: calories 123, fat 4, fiber 3, carbs 4, protein 5

Kale and Almonds

Preparation time: 10 minutes
Cooking time: 7 minutes
Servings: 4

Ingredients:
- 1 cup water
- 1 big kale bunch, roughly chopped
- 1 tablespoon balsamic vinegar
- 1/3 cup almonds, toasted
- 3 garlic cloves, minced
- 1 small yellow onion, chopped
- 2 tablespoons olive oil

Directions:

Set your instant pot on sauté mode, add oil, heat it up, add onion, stir and cook for 3 minutes. Add garlic, water and kale, stir, cover and cook on High for 4 minutes. Add salt, pepper, vinegar and almonds, toss well, divide between plates and serve as a side dish. Enjoy!

Nutrition: calories 140, fat 6, fiber 3, carbs 5, protein 3

Green Cabbage and Paprika

Preparation time: 10 minutes
Cooking time: 7 minutes
Servings: 4

Ingredients:
- 1 and ½ pound green cabbage, shredded
- Salt and black pepper to the taste
- 3 tablespoons ghee
- 1 cup veggie stock
- ¼ teaspoon sweet paprika

Directions:

Set your instant pot on sauté mode, add ghee, melt it, add cabbage, salt, pepper and stock, stir, cover and cook on High for 7 minutes. Add paprika, toss a bit, divide between plates and serve as a side dish. Enjoy!

Nutrition: calories 170, fat 4, fiber 2, carbs 5, protein 5

Coconut Cream and Sausage Gravy

Preparation time: 10 minutes
Cooking time: 7 minutes
Servings: 4

Ingredients:
- 4 ounces sausages, minced
- Salt and black pepper to the taste
- 1 cup coconut cream
- 2 tablespoons ghee
- ½ teaspoon stevia

Directions:

Set your instant pot on sauté mode, add minced sausage, stir and cook for a couple of minutes. Add ghee, cream, stevia, salt and pepper, stir, cover and cook on High for 5 minutes. Serve this with a steak. Enjoy!

Nutrition: calories 125, fat 7, fiber 1, carbs 5, protein 4

Vietnamese Eggplant Side Dish

Preparation time: 10 minutes
Cooking time: 10 minutes
Servings: 4

Ingredients:
- 1 big eggplant, roughly chopped
- 1 yellow onion, chopped
- 2 tablespoons olive oil
- 2 teaspoons chili paste

For the sauce:
- 1 teaspoon stevia
- ½ cup chicken stock
- 2 teaspoons garlic, minced
- ½ cup water
- 3 tablespoons coconut milk
- 4 green onions, chopped
- 2 tablespoons coconut aminos

Directions:

Set your instant pot on sauté mode, add oil, heat it up, add eggplant and brown for a couple of minutes. Add yellow onion, garlic, water, chili paste and coconut milk and stir. Heat up a pan with the chicken stock over medium heat, add stevia and aminos, stir, cook for a couple of minutes and transfer to the instant pot as well. Cover your instant pot and cook on High for 4 minutes. Add green onions as well, stir, divide between plates and serve as a side dish. Enjoy!

Nutrition: calories 182, fat 3, fiber 4, carbs 7, protein 4

Baby Mushrooms Sauté

Preparation time: 10 minutes
Cooking time: 10 minutes
Servings: 4

Ingredients:

- 4 tablespoons ghee
- 3 tablespoons veggie stock
- 1 teaspoon garlic powder
- 16 ounces baby mushrooms
- Salt and black pepper to the taste
- 3 tablespoons onion, dried
- 3 tablespoons parsley flakes

Directions:

In a bowl, mix parsley flakes with onion, salt, pepper, garlic powder and mushrooms and toss well. Set your instant pot on sauté mode, add ghee, melt it, add mushrooms mix, stir and cook for 3-4 minutes. Add stock, cover pot and cook on High for 6 minutes. Divide between plates and serve as a side dish. Enjoy!

Nutrition: calories 172, fat 6, fiber 5, carbs 6, protein 2

Cauliflower and Eggs Salad

Preparation time: 10 minutes
Cooking time: 5 minutes
Servings: 10

Ingredients:

- 21 ounces cauliflower, florets separated
- 1 cup red onion, chopped
- 1 cup celery, chopped
- ½ cup water
- Salt and black pepper to the taste
- 2 tablespoons balsamic vinegar
- 1 teaspoon stevia
- 4 eggs, hard-boiled, peeled and chopped
- 1 cup mayonnaise

Directions:

Put the water in your instant pot, add steamer basket, add cauliflower, cover pot and cook on High for 5 minutes. Transfer cauliflower to a bowl, add eggs, celery and onion and toss. In a separate bowl, mix mayo with salt, pepper, vinegar and stevia and whisk well. Add this to your salad, toss, divide between plates and serve as a side dish. Enjoy!

Nutrition: calories 171, fat 6, fiber 2, carbs 6, protein 3

Asparagus and Cheese Side Dish

Preparation time: 10 minutes
Cooking time: 6 minutes
Servings: 4

Ingredients:

- 10 ounces asparagus, cut into medium pieces
- Salt and black pepper to the taste
- 2 tablespoons parmesan, grated
- 1/3 cup Monterey jack cheese, shredded
- 2 tablespoons mustard
- 2 ounces cream cheese
- 1/3 cup coconut cream
- 3 tablespoons bacon, cooked and crumbled

Directions

In your instant pot, mix asparagus with salt, pepper, parmesan, Monterey jack cheese, mustard, cream cheese, coconut cream and bacon, stir, cover and cook on High for 6 minutes. Divide between plates and serve as a side dish. Enjoy!

Nutrition: calories 156, fat 3, fiber 2, carbs 5, protein 7

Sprouts and Apple Side Dish

Preparation time: 10 minutes
Cooking time: 7 minutes
Servings: 4

Ingredients:

- 1 green apple, cored and julienned
- 1 and ½ teaspoons olive oil
- 4 cups alfalfa sprouts
- Salt and black pepper to the taste
- ¼ cup coconut milk

Directions:

Set your instant pot on sauté mode, add oil, heat it up, add apple and sprouts, stir, cover pot and cook on High for 5 minutes. Add salt, pepper and coconut milk, stir, cover pot again and cook on High for 2 minutes more. Divide between plates and serve as a side dish. Enjoy!

Nutrition: calories 120, fat 3, fiber 1, carbs 3, protein 3

Radishes and Chives

Preparation time: 10 minutes
Cooking time: 7 minutes
Servings: 2

Ingredients:

- 2 cups radishes, cut into quarters
- ½ cup chicken stock
- Salt and black pepper to the taste
- 2 tablespoons ghee, melted
- 1 tablespoon chives, chopped
- 1 tablespoon lemon zest, grated

Directions:

In your instant pot, mix radishes with stock, salt, pepper and lemon zest, stir, cover pot and cook on High for 7 minutes. Add melted ghee, toss a bit, divide between plates, sprinkle chives on top and serve as a side dish. Enjoy!

Nutrition: calories 102, fat 4, fiber 1, carbs 6, protein 5

Hot Radishes with Bacon and Cheese

Preparation time: 10 minutes
Cooking time: 10 minutes
Servings: 1

Ingredients:

- 7 ounces red radishes, halved
- ½ cup veggie stock
- 2 tablespoons coconut cream
- 2 bacon slices, chopped
- 1 tablespoon green onion, chopped
- 1 tablespoon cheddar cheese, grated
- Hot sauce to the taste
- Salt and black pepper to the taste

Directions:

Set your instant pot on sauté mode, add bacon, stir and cook for a couple of minutes. Add radishes, salt, pepper and stock, stir, cover and cook on High for 4 minutes. Add green onion, cream, cheese and hot sauce, stir, cover the pot again and cook on High for 2 minutes more. Divide between plates and serve as a side dish. Enjoy!

Nutrition: calories 170, fat 16, fiber 3, carbs 6, protein 12

Avocado Side Salad

Preparation time: 10 minutes
Cooking time: 7 minutes
Servings: 4

Ingredients:

- 4 cups mixed lettuce leaves, torn
- 4 eggs
- 2 cups water
- 2 teaspoons mustard
- 1 avocado, pitted and sliced
- ¼ cup mayonnaise
- 2 garlic cloves, minced
- 1 tablespoon chives, chopped
- Salt and black pepper to the taste

Directions:

Put the water in your instant pot, add steamer basket, add eggs inside, cover pot, cook on High for 7 minutes, cool them down, chop and transfer to a bowl. Add lettuce, avocado, garlic, chives, salt and pepper and toss. In a small bowl, mix mustard with mayo, salt and pepper, whisk well, add to salad, toss to coat and serve as a side salad. Enjoy!

Nutrition: calories 134, fat 7, fiber 4, carbs 7, protein 10

Swiss Chard and Pine Nuts

Preparation time: 10 minutes
Cooking time: 5 minutes
Servings: 4

Ingredients:

- 1 bunch Swiss chard, cut into strips
- 2 tablespoons olive oil
- 1 tablespoon balsamic vinegar
- 1 small yellow onion, chopped
- ¼ teaspoon red pepper flakes
- ¼ cup pine nuts, toasted
- ¼ cup raisins
- 1 tablespoon balsamic vinegar
- Salt and black pepper to the taste

Directions:

Set your instant pot on sauté mode, add oil, heat it up, add onion and chard, stir and cook for 2 minutes. Add pepper flakes, salt, pepper and vinegar, stir, cover and cook on High for 3 minutes. Add raisins and pine nuts, toss, divide between plates and serve as a side dish. Enjoy!

Nutrition: calories 120, fat 2, fiber 1, carbs 2, protein 4

Spinach and Chard Mix

Preparation time: 10 minutes
Cooking time: 6 minutes
Servings: 4

Ingredients:

- 1 apple, cored and chopped
- 1 yellow onion, sliced
- 4 tablespoons pine nuts, toasted
- 3 tablespoons olive oil
- ¼ cup raisins
- 6 garlic cloves, chopped
- ¼ cup balsamic vinegar
- 2 and ½ cups baby spinach
- 2 and ½ cups Swiss chard, roughly torn
- Salt and black pepper to the taste
- A pinch of nutmeg

Directions:

Set your instant pot on sauté mode, add oil, heat it up, add onion and apple, stir and cook for 3 minutes. Add garlic, raisins, spinach, chard and vinegar, stir, cover and cook on High for 3 minutes. Add salt, pepper, nutmeg and pine nuts, stir, divide between plates and serve as a side dish. Enjoy!

Nutrition: calories 140, fat 1, fiber 2, carbs 3, protein 3

Cherry Tomatoes and Parmesan Mix

Preparation time: 10 minutes
Cooking time: 7 minutes
Servings: 8

Ingredients:

- 1 jalapeno pepper, chopped
- 4 garlic cloves, minced
- Salt and black pepper to the taste
- 2 pounds cherry tomatoes, cut into halves
- 1 yellow onion, cut into wedges
- ¼ cup olive oil
- ½ teaspoon oregano, dried
- 1 and ½ cups chicken stock
- ¼ cup basil, chopped
- ½ cup parmesan, grated

Directions:

Set your instant pot on sauté mode, add oil, heat it up, add onion and garlic, stir and cook for 2-3 minutes. Add jalapeno, tomatoes, oregano, salt, pepper and stock, stir, cover and cook on High for 4 minutes. Add basil and parmesan, toss a bit, divide between plates and serve as a side dish. Enjoy!

Nutrition: calories 120, fat 2, fiber 3, carbs 5, protein 4

Almond Cauliflower Rice

Preparation time: 10 minutes
Cooking time: 7 minutes
Servings: 4

Ingredients:

- ½ cup yellow onion, finely chopped
- 1 tablespoon ghee
- 1 celery stalk, chopped
- 1 and ½ cups cauliflower rice
- 4 ounces chicken stock
- Salt and black pepper to the taste
- ½ cup almonds, toasted and chopped
- 2 tablespoons parsley, chopped

Directions:

Set your instant pot on Sauté mode, add ghee, melt it, add celery and onion, stir and sauté for 3 minutes. Add cauliflower, salt, pepper and stock, stir, cover and cook on High for 4 minutes. Add parsley and almonds, toss, divide between plates and serve as a side dish. Enjoy!

Nutrition: calories 172, fat 3, fiber 5, carbs 7, protein 12

Saffron Cauliflower Rice

Preparation time: 10 minutes
Cooking time: 7 minutes
Servings: 6

Ingredients:

- 2 tablespoons olive oil
- ½ teaspoon saffron threads, crushed
- ½ cup onion, chopped
- 2 tablespoons coconut milk
- 1 and ½ cups cauliflower rice
- 2 cups veggie stock
- Salt and black pepper to the taste
- 1 tablespoon stevia
- 1 cinnamon stick
- 1/3 cup almonds, chopped

Directions:

In a bowl, mix milk with saffron and stir. Set your instant pot on sauté mode, add oil, heat it up, add onion, stir and cook for 2 minutes. Add cauliflower rice, stock, saffron mix, stevia, almonds, salt, pepper and cinnamon, stir, cover and cook on High for 5 minutes. Stir your rice one more time, discard cinnamon, divide between plates and serve as a side dish. Enjoy!

Nutrition: calories 162, fat 4, fiber 3, carbs 7, protein 4

Hot Cauliflower Rice and Avocado

Preparation time: 10 minutes
Cooking time: 4 minutes
Servings: 8

Ingredients:
- 1 cup cauliflower rice
- 1 and ¼ cups veggie stock
- ¼ cup green hot sauce
- ½ cup cilantro, chopped
- ½ avocado, pitted, peeled and chopped
- Salt and black pepper to the taste

Directions:
In your instant pot, mix cauliflower rice with stock, salt and pepper, stir, cover and cook on High for 4 minutes. In your blender, mix avocado with hot sauce and cilantro, pulse well and add to cauliflower rice. Stir everything, divide between plates and serve as a side dish. Enjoy!

Nutrition: calories 154, fat 1, fiber 2, carbs 5, protein 7

Celery and Rosemary Side Dish

Preparation time: 10 minutes
Cooking time: 6 minutes
Servings: 4

Ingredients:
- 1 pound celery, peeled and cubed
- 1 cup water
- 2 garlic cloves, minced
- Salt and black pepper to the taste
- ¼ teaspoon rosemary, dried
- 1 tablespoon olive oil

Directions:
Put the water in your instant pot, add steamer basket, add celery cubes inside, cover pot and cook on High for 4 minutes. In a bowl, mix oil with garlic and rosemary and whisk well. Add steamed celery, toss well, spread on a lined baking sheet and introduce in a preheated broiler for 3 minutes. Divide between plates and serve as a side dish. Enjoy!

Nutrition: calories 100, fat 3, fiber 3, carbs 8, protein 3

Lemon Cauliflower Rice

Preparation time: 10 minutes
Cooking time: 10 minutes
Servings: 6

Ingredients:
- 1 and ½ cup cauliflower rice
- 2 tablespoons ghee
- 1 tablespoon olive oil
- 1 yellow onion, chopped
- 2 tablespoons lemon juice
- 1 teaspoon lemon zest, grated
- 2 cups chicken stock
- 2 tablespoons parsley, chopped
- Salt and black pepper to the taste
- 2 tablespoons parmesan, grated

Directions:
Set your instant pot on sauté mode, add ghee and oil, heat them up, add onion, stir and sauté them for 3 minutes. Add cauliflower rice, stock, lemon juice, salt and pepper, stir, cover and cook on High for 4 minutes. Add parmesan, lemon zest and parsley, stir well, cover pot and leave aside for 3 minutes more. Divide between plates and serve as a side dish. Enjoy!

Nutrition: calories 172, fat 3, fiber 3, carbs 4, protein 3

Spinach Cauliflower Rice

Preparation time: 10 minutes
Cooking time: 8 minutes
Servings: 6

Ingredients:
- 2 garlic cloves, minced
- 2 tablespoons olive oil
- ¾ cup yellow onion, chopped
- 1 and ½ cups cauliflower rice
- 12 ounces spinach, chopped
- 2 and ½ cups hot veggie stock
- Salt and black pepper to the taste
- 4 ounces goat cheese, crumbled
- 2 tablespoons lemon juice

Directions:
Set your instant pot on sauté mode, add oil, heat it up, add onion and garlic, stir and cook for 2 minutes. Add cauliflower rice, stock, salt and pepper, cover and cook on High for 4 minutes. Add lemon juice and spinach, stir, cover and cook on High for 2 minutes more. Add goat cheese, stir your rice, divide between plates and serve as a side dish. Enjoy!

Nutrition: calories 210, fat 4, fiber 4, carbs 6, protein 8

Squash Puree

Preparation time: 10 minutes
Cooking time: 20 minutes
Servings: 4

Ingredients:
- ½ cup water
- 2 acorn squash, cut into halves and seeded
- Salt and black pepper to the taste
- ¼ teaspoon baking soda
- 2 tablespoons ghee, melted
- ½ teaspoon nutmeg, grated
- 2 tablespoons stevia

Directions:

Add the water to your instant pot, add the steamer basket, add squash halves, season them with salt, pepper and baking soda, cover pot and cook on High for 20 minutes. Scrape squash flesh, transfer to a bowl, Add salt, pepper, ghee, nutmeg and stevia, mash well, divide between plates and serve as a side dish. Enjoy!

Nutrition: calories 152, fat 3, fiber 2, carbs 4, protein 3

Celeriac Fries

Preparation time: 10 minutes
Cooking time: 10 minutes
Servings: 4

Ingredients:
- 2 big celeriac, peeled and cut into medium wedges
- 1 cup water
- Salt to the taste
- ¼ teaspoon baking soda
- Olive oil for frying

Directions:

Put the water in your instant pot, add salt and the baking soda, and the steamer basket, add celeriac fries inside, cover, cook on High for 4 minutes, drain and transfer them to a bowl. Heat up a pan with some olive oil over medium high heat, add celeriac fries, cook until they are gold on all sides, drain grease, transfer them to plates and serve as a side dish. Enjoy!

Nutrition: calories 182, fat 5, fiber 5, carbs 7, protein 10

Green Beans Side Dish

Preparation time: 10 minutes
Cooking time: 10 minutes
Servings: 4

Ingredients:

- 1 pound fresh green beans, trimmed
- 1 small yellow onion, chopped
- 6 ounces bacon, chopped
- 1 garlic clove, minced
- 8 ounces mushrooms, sliced
- Salt and black pepper to the taste
- A splash of balsamic vinegar

Directions:

Put green beans in your instant pot, add water to cover them, cover the pot, cook at High for 3 minutes, drain and transfer them to a bowl. Clean your instant pot, set on sauté mode, add bacon, stir and cook for 2 minutes. Add onion, mushroom and garlic, stir and cook for 3 minutes more. Return green beans to the pot, add salt, pepper and vinegar, toss well, divide between plates and serve as a side dish. Enjoy!

Nutrition: calories 152, fat 6, fiber 3, carbs 6, protein 6

Cauliflower and Pineapple Risotto

Preparation time: 10 minutes
Cooking time: 6 minutes
Servings: 6

Ingredients:

- 2 cups cauliflower rice
- 3 cups water
- ¼ teaspoon sweet paprika
- ½ pineapple, peeled and chopped
- Salt and black pepper to the taste
- 2 teaspoons olive oil

Directions:

In your instant pot, mix cauliflower rice with pineapple, water, oil, salt and pepper, stir, cover and cook on High for 6 minutes. Add paprika and more salt and pepper if needed, toss a bit, divide between plates and serve as a side dish. Enjoy!

Nutrition: calories 162, fat 4, fiber 3, carbs 6, protein 6

Parsnips Mash

Preparation time: 10 minutes
Cooking time: 10 minutes
Servings: 4

Ingredients:

- 2 and ½ pounds parsnips, chopped
- 4 tablespoons ghee, melted
- Salt and black pepper to the taste
- 1 and ½ cups beef stock
- 1 thyme sprigs, chopped
- 1 yellow onion, roughly chopped

Directions:

Set your instant pot on Sauté mode, add 3 tablespoons ghee, melt it, add onion, stir and cook for 3 minutes. Add parsnips, stir and cook for 3 minutes more. Add thyme and stock, cover pot and cook on High for 4 minutes. Transfer this to your blender, add the rest of the ghee, pulse well, divide between plates and serve as a side dish. Enjoy!

Nutrition: calories 152, fat 3, fiber 3, carbs 6, protein 8

Cauliflower Mash

Preparation time: 10 minutes
Cooking time: 6 minutes
Servings: 4

Ingredients:

- 1 cauliflower, florets separated
- Salt and black pepper to the taste
- 1 and ½ cups water
- ½ teaspoon turmeric, ground
- 1 tablespoon ghee, melted
- 3 chives, chopped

Directions:

Put the water in your instant pot, add the steamer basket, add cauliflower inside, cover and cook on High for 6 minutes. Transfer cauliflower to a bowl, mash using a potato masher, add melted ghee, turmeric, salt and pepper and whisk really well. Divide between plates and serve as a side dish with chives sprinkled on top. Enjoy!

Nutrition: calories 100, fat 3, fiber 2, carbs 5, protein 5

Turnips Puree

Preparation time: 10 minutes
Cooking time: 5 minutes
Servings: 4

Ingredients:
- 4 turnips, peeled and chopped
- ½ cup chicken stock
- Salt and black pepper to the taste
- 1 yellow onion, chopped
- ¼ cup coconut cream

Directions:

In your instant pot, mix turnips with stock and onion, stir, cover, cook on High for 5 minutes, blend using an immersion blender and transfer to a bowl. Add salt, pepper and cream blend again with your immersion blender, divide between plates and serve as a side dish. Enjoy!

Nutrition: calories 100, fat 3, fiber 3, carbs 7, protein 3

Carrot Mash

Preparation time: 5 minutes
Cooking time: 4 minutes
Servings: 4

Ingredients:
- 1 and ½ pounds carrots, peeled and chopped
- 1 tablespoon ghee, melted
- Salt and white pepper to the taste
- 1 cup water
- 1 tablespoon stevia

Directions:

Put carrots in your instant pot, add water, cover, cook at High for 4 minutes, drain, transfer to a bowl and mash using an immersion blender. Add ghee, salt, pepper and stevia, blend again, divide between plates and serve as a side dish. Enjoy!

Nutrition: calories 100, fat 3, fiber 2, carbs 5, protein 2

Carrots with Thyme and Dill

Preparation time: 10 minutes
Cooking time; 5 minutes
Servings: 4

Ingredients:
- ½ cup water
- 1 pound baby carrots
- 3 tablespoons stevia
- 1 tablespoon thyme, chopped
- 1 tablespoon dill, chopped
- Salt to the taste
- 2 tablespoons ghee

Directions:
Put the water in your instant pot, add the steamer basket, add carrots inside, cover, cook on High for 3 minutes, drain and transfer to a bowl. Set your instant pot on Sauté mode, add ghee, melt it, add stevia, thyme, dill and return carrots as well. Stir, cook for a couple of minutes, divide between plates and serve as a side dish. Enjoy!

Nutrition: calories 162, fat 4, fiber 4, carbs 8, protein 3

Lemon Broccoli

Preparation time: 5 minutes
Cooking time: 15 minutes
Servings: 6

Ingredients:
- 31 oz broccoli, florets separated
- 1 cup water
- 5 lemon slices
- Salt and black pepper to the taste

Directions:
Pour the water in your instant pot, add broccoli, salt, pepper and lemon slices, cover and cook on High for 15 minutes. Drain broccoli, divide between plates, season with more salt and pepper and serve as a side dish. Enjoy!

Nutrition: calories 82, fat 1, fiber 2, carbs 6, protein 3

Poached Fennel

Preparation time: 5 minutes
Cooking time: 6 minutes
Servings: 3

Ingredients:
- 2 big fennel bulbs, sliced
- 2 tablespoons ghee
- 1 tablespoon coconut flour
- 2 cups coconut milk
- ¼ teaspoon nutmeg, ground
- Salt and black pepper to the taste.

Directions:
Set your instant pot on Sauté mode, add ghee, melt it, add fennel, stir and cook for 2 minutes. Add coconut flour, salt, pepper, milk and nutmeg, stir, cover and cook on High for 4 minutes. Divide poached fennel between plates and serve as a side dish. Enjoy!

Nutrition: calories 121, fat 2, fiber 3, carbs 6, protein 3

Mixed Bell Peppers Side Dish

Preparation time: 10 minutes
Cooking time: 8 minutes
Servings: 4

Ingredients:
- 2 yellow bell peppers, thinly sliced
- 1 green bell pepper, thinly sliced
- 2 red bell peppers, thinly sliced
- 2 tomatoes, chopped
- 2 garlic cloves, minced
- 1 red onion, thinly sliced
- Salt and black pepper to the taste
- 1 bunch parsley, finely chopped
- A drizzle of olive oil

Directions:
Set your instant pot on Sauté mode, add oil, heat it up, add onion, stir and cook for 2 minutes, Add red, yellow and green peppers, tomatoes, salt and pepper, stir, cover and cook at High for 6 minutes. Add garlic and parsley, stir, divide between plates and serve as a side dish. Enjoy!

Nutrition: calories 152, fat 3, fiber 3, carbs 5, protein 4

Beet and Garlic

Preparation time: 10 minutes
Cooking time: 18 minutes
Servings: 4

Ingredients:

- 3 beets, washed
- 2 cups water
- 1 tablespoon olive oil
- Salt and black pepper to the taste
- 2 garlic cloves, minced
- 1 teaspoon lemon juice

Directions:

Put the water in your instant pot, add steamer basket, add beets inside, cover, cook on High for 15 minutes, drain, transfer them to a cutting board, cool them down, peel and cut them into medium cubes. Clean your instant pot, set on sauté mode, add oil heat it up, add beets, stir and cook for 3 minutes. Add garlic, lemon juice, salt and pepper, toss well, divide between plates and serve as a side dish, Enjoy!

Nutrition: calories 100, fat 1, fiber 2, carbs 6, protein 3

Green Beans and Tomatoes

Preparation time: 10 minutes
Cooking time: 6 minutes
Servings: 4

Ingredients:

- 2 cups tomatoes, chopped
- 1 tablespoon olive oil
- 1 garlic clove, minced
- 1 pound green beans, trimmed
- Salt to the taste
- ½ tablespoon basil, chopped

Directions:

Set your instant pot on Sauté mode, add oil, heat it up, add garlic, stir and cook for 1 minute. Add tomatoes and green beans, stir, cover and cook on High for 5 minutes. Add salt, pepper and basil, toss well, divide between plates and serve as a side dish. Enjoy!

Nutrition: calories 100, fat 4, fiber 3, carbs 3, protein 2

Bok Choy and Garlic

Preparation time: 10 minutes
Cooking time: 10 minutes
Servings: 4

Ingredients:
- 5 bunches bok choy
- 5 cups water
- 2 garlic cloves, minced
- 1 teaspoon ginger, grated
- 1 tablespoon olive oil
- Salt and black pepper to the taste

Directions:
Put bok choy in your instant pot, add water, cover the pot, cook on High for 7 minutes, drain, chop and transfer to a bowl. Clean your instant pot, set on sauté mode, add oil, heat it up, add bok choy, salt, pepper, garlic and ginger, stir, cook for 2 minutes, divide between plates and serve as a side dish. Enjoy!

Nutrition: calories 100, fat 1, fiber 2, carbs 3, protein 2

Red Cabbage and Applesauce

Preparation time: 10 minutes
Cooking time: 13 minutes
Servings: 4

Ingredients:
- 4 garlic cloves, minced
- ½ cup yellow onion, chopped
- 1 tablespoon olive oil
- 6 cups red cabbage, chopped
- 1 cup water
- 1 tablespoon balsamic vinegar
- 1 cup natural applesauce
- Salt and black pepper to the taste

Directions:
Set your instant pot on Sauté mode, add the oil, heat it up, add onion and garlic, stir and cook for 3 minutes. Add cabbage, water, applesauce, vinegar, salt and pepper, stir, cover, cook on High for 10 minutes, divide between plates and serve as a side dish. Enjoy!

Nutrition: calories 152, fat 4, fiber 6, carbs 10, protein 4

Beets and Capers

Preparation time: 10 minutes
Cooking time: 30 minutes
Servings: 4

Ingredients:

- 4 beets
- 1 cup water
- 2 tablespoons balsamic vinegar
- 2 tablespoons capers
- A bunch of parsley, chopped
- Salt and black pepper to the taste
- 1 tablespoon olive oil
- 1 garlic clove, minced

Directions:

Put the water in your instant pot, add the steamer basket, add beets inside, cover and cook on High for 20 minutes. In a bowl, mix parsley with garlic, salt, pepper, olive oil and capers and whisk. Transfer beets to a cutting board, cool them down, peel and slice them and divide them between plates. Add vinegar and capers mix, toss a bit and serve as a side dish. Enjoy!

Nutrition: calories 63, fat 2, fiber 1, carbs 2, protein 4

Beet and Arugula Side Salad

Preparation time: 10 minutes
Cooking time: 7 minutes
Servings: 4

Ingredients:

- 1 and ½ pounds beets, washed and halved
- 2 teaspoons lemon zest, grated
- 2 tablespoons balsamic vinegar
- 2 tablespoons lemon juice
- 2 tablespoons stevia
- 2 scallions, chopped
- 2 teaspoons mustard
- 2 cups arugula

Directions:

In your instant pot, mix vinegar and lemon juice and beets, stir, cover and cook on High for 7 minutes. Peel beets, roughly chop them and transfer them to a bowl, Add mustard, stevia, scallions and lemon zest and toss. Add arugula, toss well, divide between plates and serve as a side salad. Enjoy!

Nutrition: calories 142, fat 3, fiber 2, carbs 6, protein 4

Tomato and Beet Side Salad

Preparation time: 10 minutes
Cooking time: 30 minutes
Servings: 8

Ingredients:

- 2 and ½ cups water
- 8 small beets, trimmed
- 1 red onion, sliced
- 4 ounces goat cheese
- 1 cup balsamic vinegar
- Salt and black pepper to the taste
- 2 tablespoons stevia
- 1 pint mixed cherry tomatoes, halved
- 2 tablespoons olive oil

Directions:

Put 1 and ½ cups water in your instant pot, add the steamer basket, add beets, cover, cook on High for 20 minutes, transfer them to a cutting board, cool them down, peel, chop and put them into a bowl. Clean your instant pot, add the rest of the water, vinegar, stevia, salt and pepper, stir, set the pot on simmer mode and cook for a couple of minutes. Strain this into a bowl, add onion, leave aside for 10 minutes, drain them well and add to the bowl with the beets. Also add tomatoes, oil, salt, pepper, 2 tablespoons liquid from the onions and goat cheese, toss everything, divide between plates and serve as a side salad. Enjoy!

Nutrition: calories 152, fat 4, fiber 3, carbs 4, protein 3

Broccoli and Garlic

Preparation time: 10 minutes
Cooking time: 12 minutes
Servings: 4

Ingredients:

- 1 broccoli head, cut into 4
- ½ cup water
- 1 tablespoon olive oil
- 6 garlic cloves, minced
- 1 tablespoon balsamic vinegar
- Salt and black pepper to the taste

Directions:

Put the water in your instant pot, add the steamer basket, add broccoli inside, cover, cook on Low for 12 minutes, transfer to a bowl filled with ice water, cool it down and drain it. Clean your instant pot, set it on sauté mode, add oil, heat it up, add garlic, stir and cook for 2 minutes. Add broccoli, vinegar, salt and pepper, stir, cook for 1 minute more, divide among plates and serve as a side dish. Enjoy!

Nutrition: calories 100, fat 2, fiber 1, carbs 2, protein 7

Brussels Sprouts and Dill

Preparation time: 4 minutes
Cooking time: 8 minutes
Servings: 4

Ingredients:
- 1 pound Brussels sprouts, trimmed and halved
- ½ cup bacon, chopped
- Salt and black pepper to the taste
- 1 tablespoon mustard
- 1 cup chicken stock
- 1 tablespoon ghee
- 2 tablespoons dill, chopped

Directions:
Set your instant pot on Sauté mode, add bacon, stir and cook for 2 minutes. Add sprouts, mustard, stock, salt and pepper, stir, cover and cook on High for 4 minutes. Add ghee and dill, stir, set the pot on sauté mode, cook everything for a couple more minutes, divide between plates and serve as a side dish. Enjoy!

Nutrition: calories 162, fat 4, fiber 3, carbs 6, protein 6

Savoy Cabbage and Bacon

Preparation time: 10 minutes
Cooking time: 9 minutes
Servings: 4

Ingredients:
- 1 cup bacon, chopped
- 1 Savoy cabbage head, shredded
- ¼ teaspoon nutmeg, ground
- 1 yellow onion, chopped
- 2 cups beef stock
- Salt and black pepper to the taste
- 1 bay leaf
- 1 cup coconut milk
- 2 tablespoons parsley flakes

Directions:
Set your instant pot on Sauté mode, add bacon and onion, stir and cook for 2 minutes. Add stock, cabbage, bay leaf, salt, pepper and nutmeg, stir, cover, cook on High for 5 minutes, mix with milk and parsley, stir and cook on sauté mode for 4 minutes more. Divide between plates and serve as a side dish. Enjoy!

Nutrition: calories 157, fat 3, fiber 3, carbs 6, protein 6

Sweet Cabbage

Preparation time: 10 minutes
Cooking time: 8 minutes
Servings: 4

Ingredients:
- 1 cabbage, cut into 8 wedges
- 1 tablespoon olive oil
- 1 carrot, grated
- ¼ cup balsamic vinegar
- 1 and ¼ cups water
- 1 teaspoon stevia
- A pinch of cayenne pepper
- ½ teaspoon red pepper flakes

Directions:
Set your instant pot on Sauté mode, add oil, heat it up, add cabbage, stir and cook for 3 minutes. Add carrots, water, stevia, vinegar, cayenne and pepper flakes, stir, cover and cook at High for 5 minutes. Divide between plates and serve right away. Enjoy!

Nutrition: calories 100, fat 3, fiber 3, carbs 4, protein 4

Collard Greens and Tomato Sauce

Preparation time: 10 minutes
Cooking time: 20 minutes
Servings: 4

Ingredients:
- 1 bunch collard greens, trimmed
- 2 tablespoons olive oil
- ½ cup chicken stock
- 2 tablespoons tomato puree
- 1 yellow onion, chopped
- 3 garlic cloves, minced
- Salt and black pepper to the taste
- 1 tablespoon balsamic vinegar
- 1 teaspoon stevia

Directions:
In your instant pot, mix stock with oil, garlic, vinegar, onion, tomato puree, collard greens, salt, pepper and stevia, stir a bit, cover and cook on High for 20 minutes. Divide between plates and serve right away. Enjoy!

Nutrition: calories 132, fat 2, fiber 2, carbs 5, protein 3

Dessert Recipes

Raspberry Dessert

Preparation time: 10 minutes
Cooking time: 2 minutes
Servings: 12

Ingredients:
- ½ cup coconut butter
- ½ cup coconut oil
- ½ cup coconut, unsweetened and shredded
- ½ cup raspberries, dried
- 3 tablespoons stevia

Directions:
Set your instant pot on sauté mode, add coconut butter, melt it, add stevia, oil, coconut and raspberries, stir, cover and cook on High for 2 minutes. Spread this on a lined baking sheet, spread well, introduce in the fridge for a couple of hours, slice and serve. Enjoy!

Nutrition: calories 174, fat 5, fiber 2, carbs 4, protein 7

Blueberries and Strawberries Cream

Preparation time: 10 minutes
Cooking time: 2 minutes
Servings: 12

Ingredients:
- 8 ounces mascarpone cheese
- ¾ teaspoon vanilla stevia
- 1 cup coconut cream
- ½ pint blueberries
- ½ pint strawberries

Directions:
In your instant pot, mix cream with stevia, mascarpone, blueberries and strawberries, stir, cover and cook on High for 2 minutes. Divide into small dessert bowls and serve cold. Enjoy!

Nutrition: calories 183, fat 4, fiber 1, carbs 3, protein 1

Lemon Cream

Preparation time: 10 minutes
Cooking time: 2 minutes
Servings: 5

Ingredients:

- 1 cup coconut cream
- A pinch of salt
- 1 teaspoon lemon stevia
- ¼ cup lemon juice
- 8 ounces mascarpone cheese

Directions:

In your instant pot, mix cream with mascarpone, lemon juice, stevia and a pinch of salt, stir, cover and cook on High for 2 minutes. Divide into small dessert bowls and keep in the fridge until you serve it. Enjoy!

Nutrition: calories 165, fat 7, fiber 0, carbs 2, protein 3

Cream Cheese Bars

Preparation time: 10 minutes
Cooking time: 16 minutes
Servings: 8

Ingredients:

- 5 ounces coconut oil, melted
- ½ teaspoon baking powder
- 4 tablespoons stevia
- 1 teaspoon vanilla extract
- 4 ounces cream cheese
- 6 eggs
- ½ cup blueberries
- 1 and ½ cups water

Directions:

In a bowl, mix oil with eggs, cream cheese, vanilla, stevia, blueberries and baking powder, blend using an immersion blender and pour into a baking dish. Add the water to your instant pot, add steamer basket, add baking dish inside, cover and cook on High for 16 minutes. Leave aside to cool down, cut into medium bars and serve them cold. Enjoy!

Nutrition: calories 162, fat 4, fiber 2, carbs 6, protein 8

Cocoa Pudding

Preparation time: 50 minutes
Cooking time: 3 minutes
Servings: 2

Ingredients:
- 1 and ½ cups water+ 2 tablespoons water
- 1 tablespoon gelatin
- 2 tablespoons stevia
- 2 tablespoons cocoa powder
- 1 cup coconut milk, hot

Directions:

In a bowl, mix milk with stevia and cocoa powder and stir well. In a bowl, mix gelatin with 2 tablespoons water, stir well, add to the cocoa mix, stir and divide into 2 ramekins. Add the water to your instant pot, add the steamer basket, add ramekins inside, cover and cook on High for 3 minutes. Keep puddings in the fridge until you serve. Enjoy!

Nutrition: calories 120, fat 2, fiber 1, carbs 4, protein 3

Avocado Pudding

Preparation time: 10 minutes
Cooking time: 2 minutes
Servings: 4

Ingredients:
- 2 avocados, pitted, peeled and chopped
- 2 teaspoons vanilla extract
- 80 drops stevia
- 1 tablespoon lime juice
- 14 ounces coconut milk
- 1 and ½ cups water

Directions:

In your instant pot, mix avocado with coconut milk, vanilla extract, stevia and lime juice, blend well and divide into 4 ramekins. Add the water to your instant pot, add the steamer basket, add ramekins inside, cover and cook on High for 2 minutes. Keep puddings in the fridge until you serve them. Enjoy!

Nutrition: calories 150, fat 3, fiber 1, carbs 3, protein 4

Peppermint Pudding

Preparation time: 2 hours
Cooking time: 2 minutes
Servings: 3

Ingredients:

- ½ cup coconut oil, melted
- 13 stevia drops
- 1 tablespoon cocoa powder
- 1 teaspoon peppermint oil
- 14 ounces canned coconut milk
- 1 avocado, pitted, peeled and chopped
- 10 drops stevia

Directions:

In a bowl, mix coconut oil with cocoa powder and 3 drops stevia, stir well, transfer to a lined container, keep in the fridge for 1 hour and chop into small pieces. In your instant pot, mix coconut milk with avocado, 10 drops stevia and peppermint oil, blend using an immersion blender, cover pot and cook on High for 2 minutes. Add chocolate chips, stir, divide pudding into bowls and keep in the fridge for 1 hour before serving. Enjoy!

Nutrition: calories 140, fat 3, fiber 2, carbs 3, protein 4

Coconut Pudding

Preparation time: 10 minutes
Cooking time: 3 minutes
Servings: 4

Ingredients:

- 1 and 2/3 cups coconut milk
- 1 tablespoon gelatin
- 6 tablespoons swerve
- 3 egg yolks
- ½ teaspoon vanilla extract

Directions:

In a bowl, mix gelatin with 1 tablespoon coconut milk, stir well and leave aside for now. Set your instant pot on simmer mode, add milk, heat it up, add swerve, egg yolks, vanilla extract and gelatin, stir well, cover pot and cook on High for 2 minutes. Divide everything into 4 ramekins and serve them cold. Enjoy!

Nutrition: calories 140, fat 2, fiber 1, carbs 3, protein 2

Orange Cake

Preparation time: 10 minutes
Cooking time: 25 minutes
Servings: 12

Ingredients:
- 6 eggs
- 1 orange, cut into quarters
- 1 and ½ cups water
- 1 teaspoon vanilla extract
- 1 teaspoon baking powder
- 9 ounces almond meal
- 4 tablespoons swerve
- 2 tablespoons orange zest, grated
- 2 ounces stevia
- 4 ounces cream cheese
- 4 ounces coconut yogurt

Directions:
In your food processor, mix orange with almond meal, swerve, eggs, baking powder and vanilla extract, pulse well and transfer to a cake pan. Add the water to your instant pot, add steamer basket, add cake pan inside, cover and cook on High for 25 minutes. In a bowl, mix cream cheese with orange zest, coconut yogurt and stevia and stir well. Spread this well over cake, slice and serve it. Enjoy!

Nutrition: calories 170, fat 13, fiber 2, carbs 4, protein 4

Walnuts Cream

Preparation time: 10 minutes
Cooking time: 1 minute
Servings: 6

Ingredients:
- 2 ounces coconut oil
- 4 tablespoons cocoa powder
- 1 teaspoon vanilla extract
- 1 cup walnuts, chopped
- 4 tablespoons stevia

Directions:
In your instant pot, mix cocoa powder with oil, vanilla, walnuts and stevia, blend using an immersion blender, cover pot and cook on High for 1 minute. Transfer to a bowl, leave in the fridge for a couple of hours and serve. Enjoy!

Nutrition: calories 100, fat 5, fiber 1, carbs 3, protein 4

Lemon Cream

Preparation time: 10 minutes
Cooking time: 30 minutes
Servings: 6

Ingredients:
- 1 and 1/3 pint coconut milk
- 1 and ½ cups water
- 4 tablespoons lemon zest
- 4 eggs
- 5 tablespoons swerve
- 2 tablespoons lemon juice

Directions:

In a bowl, mix eggs with milk, swerve, lemon zest and lemon juice, whisk well and pour into 6 ramekins. Add the water to your instant pot, add steamer basket, add ramekins, cover pot and cook on High for 20 minutes. Leave cream to cool down before servings. Enjoy!

Nutrition: calories 120, fat 2, fiber 2, carbs 5, protein 3

Chocolate Cream

Preparation time: 1 minute
Cooking time: 3 minutes
Servings: 6

Ingredients:
- ½ cup coconut cream
- 4 ounces dark chocolate, unsweetened and chopped

Directions:

In your instant pot, mix cream with dark chocolate, cover pot and cook on High for 3 minutes. Stir your cream really well, divide into dessert cups and serve cold. Enjoy!

Nutrition: calories 78, fat 2, fiber 1, carbs 3, protein 1

Berry Cream

Preparation time: 10 minutes
Cooking time: 2 minutes
Servings: 4

Ingredients:
- 3 tablespoons cocoa powder
- 14 ounces coconut cream
- 1 cup blackberries
- 1 cup raspberries
- 2 tablespoons stevia

Directions:
In your instant pot, mix cream with cocoa, stevia, blackberries and raspberries, stir, cover and cook on High for 2 minutes. Divide into dessert cups and serve cold. Enjoy!

Nutrition: calories 145, fat 4, fiber 2, carbs 6, protein 2

Strawberry Cream

Preparation time: 10 minutes
Cooking time: 2 minutes
Servings: 4

Ingredients:
- 1 and ¾ cups coconut cream
- 2 teaspoons stevia
- 1 cup strawberries

Directions:
In your instant pot, mix cream with stevia and strawberries, stir, cover and cook on High for 2 minutes. Divide into bowls and serve cold. Enjoy!

Nutrition: calories 155, fat 2, fiber 1, carbs 5, protein 4

Caramel Pudding

Preparation time: 10 minutes
Cooking time: 25 minutes
Servings: 2

Ingredients:
- 1 and ½ teaspoons caramel extract
- 1 cup water
- 2 ounces cream cheese
- 2 eggs
- 1 and ½ tablespoons swerve

For the sauce:
- 2 tablespoons swerve
- 2 tablespoons ghee
- ¼ teaspoon caramel extract

Directions:

In your blender, mix cream cheese with water, 1 and ½ tablespoons swerve, 1 and ½ teaspoons caramel extract and eggs, pulse well and divide into 2 greased ramekins. Add the water to your instant pot, add steamer basket, add ramekins inside, cover and cook on High for 20 minutes. Meanwhile, put the ghee in a pot, heat up over medium heat, add ¼ teaspoon caramel extract and 2 tablespoons swerve, stir well, cook for a few minutes and pour over caramel pudding. Enjoy!

Nutrition: calories 174, fat 7, fiber 1, carbs 2, protein 4

Peanut and Chia Pudding

Preparation time: 10 minutes
Cooking time: 2 minutes
Servings: 4

Ingredients:
- ½ cup chia seeds
- 2 cups almond milk, unsweetened
- 1 teaspoon vanilla extract
- ¼ cup peanut butter, unsweetened
- 1 teaspoon vanilla stevia

Directions:

In your instant pot, mix milk with chia seeds, peanut butter, vanilla extract and stevia, stir, cover and cook on High for 2 minutes. Divide into dessert glasses and leave in the fridge for 10 minutes before serving, Enjoy!

Nutrition: calories 120, fat 1, fiber 2, carbs 4, protein 2

Pumpkin Cream

Preparation time: 10 minutes
Cooking time: 5 minutes
Servings: 6

Ingredients:

- 1 tablespoon gelatin
- ¼ cup warm water
- 14 ounces coconut milk
- 14 ounces pumpkin puree
- A pinch of salt
- 2 teaspoons vanilla extract
- 1 teaspoon cinnamon powder
- 1 teaspoon pumpkin pie spice
- 8 scoops stevia
- 3 tablespoons erythritol

Directions:

In your instant pot, mix pumpkin puree with coconut milk, a pinch of salt, vanilla extract, cinnamon powder, stevia, erythritol and pumpkin pie spice, stir well, cover and cook on High for 4 minutes. In a bowl, mix gelatin and water and stir. Add this over pumpkin cream, stir, divide custard into ramekins and serve them cold. Enjoy!

Nutrition: calories 160, fat 2, fiber 1, carbs 3, protein 4

Chia Jam

Preparation time: 15 minutes
Cooking time: 5 minutes
Servings: 22

Ingredients:

- 3 tablespoons chia seeds
- 2 and ½ cups cherries, pitted
- ½ teaspoon vanilla powder
- Zest from ½ lemon, grated
- ¼ cup erythritol
- 10 drops stevia
- 1 cup water

Directions:

In your instant pot, mix cherries with water, stevia, erythritol, vanilla powder, chia seeds and lemon peel, stir, cover and cook on High for 5 minutes. Divide into dessert cups and serve cold. Enjoy!

Nutrition: calories 160, fat 1, fiber 1, carbs 2, protein 0.5

Melon Cream

Preparation time: 5 minutes
Cooking time: 10 minutes
Servings: 6

Ingredients:
- Flesh from 1 melon
- 1 ounce stevia
- 1 cup natural apple juice
- 1 tablespoon ghee
- Juice of 1 lemon

Directions:
Put melon and apple juice in your instant pot, cover, cook on High for 7 minutes, transfer to a blender, add lemon juice, ghee and stevia, pulse well and return to your instant pot. Set on simmer mode, cook for a couple more minutes, divide into dessert cups and serve. Enjoy!

Nutrition: calories 73, fat 1, fiber 1, carbs 2, protein 2

Peach Cream

Preparation time: 5 minutes
Cooking time: 3 minutes
Servings: 6

Ingredients:
- 10 ounces peaches, stoned and chopped
- A pinch of nutmeg, ground
- 2 tablespoons coconut flakes
- 3 tablespoons stevia
- ½ cup water
- 1/8 teaspoon cinnamon powder
- 1/8 teaspoon almond extract

Directions:
In your instant pot, mix peaches with nutmeg, coconut, stevia, almond extract and cinnamon, stir, cover and cook at High for 3 minutes. Divide into small cups and serve. Enjoy!

Nutrition: calories 90, fat 2, fiber 1, carbs 3, protein 5

Peaches and Sweet Sauce

Preparation time: 10 minutes
Cooking time: 10 minutes
Servings: 6

Ingredients:
- 4 tablespoons stevia
- 3 cups peaches, cored and roughly chopped
- 6 tablespoons natural apple juice
- 2 teaspoons lemon zest, grated

Directions:
In your instant pot mix peaches with stevia, apple juice and lemon zest, stir, cover and cook at High for 10 minutes. Divide into small cups and serve cold. Enjoy!

Nutrition: calories 80, fat 2, fiber 2, carbs 5, protein 5

Chestnut Cream

Preparation time: 10 minutes
Cooking time: 20 minutes
Servings: 6

Ingredients:
- 11 ounces stevia
- 11 ounces water
- 1 and ½ pounds chestnuts, halved and peeled

Directions:
In your instant pot, mix stevia with water and chestnuts, stir, cover and cook on High for 20 minutes. Blend using your immersion blender, divide into small cups and serve. Enjoy!

Nutrition: calories 82, fat 1, fiber 0, carbs 5, protein 3

Cheesecake

Preparation time: 60 minutes
Cooking time: 50 minutes
Servings: 12

Ingredients:
For the crust:
- 4 tablespoons melted ghee
- 1 and ½ cups chocolate cookie crumbs

For the filling:
- 24 ounces cream cheese, soft
- 2 tablespoons coconut flakes
- 3 tablespoons stevia
- 3 eggs
- 1 tablespoon vanilla extract
- Cooking spray
- 1 cup water
- ½ cup Greek yogurt
- 5 ounces white chocolate, unsweetened and melted
- 5 ounces bittersweet chocolate, melted

Directions:
In a bowl mix cookie crumbs with ghee, stir well, press on the bottom of a cake pan that you've greased with cooking spray, and lined with parchment paper. In a bowl, mix cream cheese with coconut, stevia, eggs, vanilla and yogurt, whisk well and leave aside for a few minutes. Put milk chocolate in a heatproof bowl and heat up in the microwave for 30 seconds. Add white and bittersweet chocolate, stir well again and pour over cookie crust. Add the water to your instant pot, add steamer basket, and cake, cover and cook on High for 45 minutes. Slice and serve cold. Enjoy!

Nutrition: calories 267, fat 4, fiber 7, carbs 10, protein 7

Banana Cake

Preparation time: 10 minutes
Cooking time: 30 minutes
Servings: 6

Ingredients:
- 4 tablespoons stevia
- 1/3 cup ghee, soft
- 1 teaspoon vanilla extract
- 1 egg
- 2 bananas, peeled and mashed
- 1 teaspoon baking powder
- 1 and ½ cups coconut flour
- ½ teaspoons baking soda
- 1/3 cup coconut milk
- 1 and ½ teaspoons keto cream of tartar
- 2 cups water
- Olive oil cooking spray

Directions:
In a bowl, mix milk with cream of tartar, stevia, ghee, egg, vanilla and bananas and stir everything. Add flour, baking powder and baking soda, stir well and pour into a cake pan that you've greased with cooking spray. Add the water to your instant pot, add steamer basket, and cake pan, cover and cook on High for 30 minutes. Slice and serve cold. Enjoy!

Nutrition: calories 214, fat 2, fiber 2, carbs 6, protein 8

Pumpkin Cake

Preparation time: 10 minutes
Cooking time: 35 minutes
Servings: 12

Ingredients:
- 2 cups coconut flour
- 1 teaspoon baking soda
- ¾ teaspoon pumpkin pie spice
- ¾ cup stevia
- 1 banana, mashed
- ½ teaspoon baking powder
- 2 tablespoons coconut oil
- ½ cup Greek yogurt
- 8 ounces canned pumpkin puree
- Cooking spray
- 1-quart water
- 1 egg
- ½ teaspoon vanilla extract
- 2/3 cup chocolate chips

Directions:

In a bowl, mix flour with baking soda, baking powder, pumpkin spice, stevia, oil, banana, yogurt, pumpkin puree, vanilla and egg and stir using a mixer. Add chocolate chips, stir, pour into a cake pan greased with cooking spray and cover with some tin foil. Add the water to your instant pot, add steamer basket, add cake pan inside, cover and cook on High for 35 minutes. Slice cake and serve cold. Enjoy!

Nutrition: calories 200, fat 3, fiber 3, carbs 6, protein 8

Apple Cake

Preparation time: 10 minutes
Cooking time: 1 hour and 10 minutes
Servings: 6

Ingredients:
- 3 cups apples, cored and cubed
- 4 tablespoons stevia
- 1 tablespoon vanilla extract
- 2 eggs
- 1 tablespoon apple pie spice
- 2 cups coconut flour
- 2 tablespoons ghee, melted
- 1 tablespoon baking powder
- 1 cup water

Directions:

In a bowl mix egg with ghee, apple pie spice, stevia, apples, flour and baking powder, stir and pour into a cake pan. Add the water to your instant pot, add steamer basket, add cake pan inside, cover and cook on High for 1 hour. Leave the cake to cool down, slice and serve. Enjoy!

Nutrition: calories 89, fat 1, fiber 2, carbs 5, protein 4

Upside Down Cake

Preparation time: 10 minutes
Cooking time: 25 minutes
Servings: 8

Ingredients:
- 1 apple, sliced
- 1 apple, chopped
- 1 cup ricotta cheese
- 3 tablespoons stevia
- 1 tablespoon lemon juice
- 1 egg
- 1 teaspoon vanilla extract
- 3 tablespoons olive oil
- 1 cup coconut flour
- 2 teaspoons baking powder
- 1/8 teaspoon cinnamon powder
- 1 teaspoon baking soda
- 2 cups water

Directions:
In a bowl, mix all apples with lemon juice and half of the stevia, toss and leave aside. Line a cake pan with some parchment paper, grease with some oil, dust with some flour and spread half of the apples. In a bowl, mix the egg with cheese, the rest of the stevia, vanilla extract, oil, flour, baking powder and soda, the rest of the apples and cinnamon and stir. Pour everything into the cake pan and cover with tin foil. Add the water to your instant pot, add steamer basket, and cake pan, cover and cook on High for 25 minutes. Turn cake upside down, slice and serve. Enjoy!

Nutrition: calories 210, fat 4, fiber 5, carbs 12, protein 5

Almond Cake

Preparation time: 10 minutes
Cooking time: 20 minutes
Servings: 4

Ingredients:
- 1/8 teaspoon almond extract
- 2 cups water
- 1 cup coconut flour
- ½ cup cocoa powder
- 4 tablespoons stevia
- 3 tablespoons olive oil
- 3 eggs
- 2 teaspoons baking powder
- ½ cup almonds, sliced

Directions:
In a bowl, mix cocoa powder, almond extract, flour, eggs, stevia, oil, baking powder and almonds, whisk well and pour everything into a greased cake pan. Add the water to your instant pot, add steamer basket, and cake pan, cover and cook on High for 20 minutes. Slice and serve cold. Enjoy!

Nutrition: calories 162, fat 4, fiber 2, carbs 18, protein 3

French Coconut Cream

Preparation time: 1 hour
Cooking time: 15 minutes
Servings: 6

Ingredients:
- 2 cups coconut cream
- 1 teaspoon cinnamon powder
- 6 egg yolks
- 5 tablespoons stevia
- Zest from 1 lemon, grated
- A pinch of nutmeg
- 2 cups water

Directions:

Heat up a pan with the coconut cream over medium heat, add cinnamon and orange zest, stir, bring to a simmer, take off heat and leave aside to cool down. Add egg yolks and stevia, stir well, strain and divide this into small ramekins. Add the water to your instant pot, add steamer basket, add ramekins, cover pot and cook on Low for 10 minutes. Sprinkle nutmeg on top and serve cold. Enjoy!

Nutrition: calories 200, fat 5, fiber 2, carbs 10, protein 13

Flavored Pears

Preparation time: 10 minutes
Cooking time: 10 minutes
Servings: 4

Ingredients:
- 4 pears
- Juice of 1 lemon
- Zest from 1 lemon, grated
- 26 ounces grape juice
- ½ vanilla bean
- 4 peppercorns
- 2 rosemary sprigs

Directions:

In your instant pot, mix grape juice with lemon juice, lemon zest, vanilla, rosemary, peppercorns and pears, cover pot and cook on High for 10 minutes. Divide into bowls and serve. Enjoy!

Nutrition: calories 152, fat 3, fiber 6, carbs 8, protein 12

Pumpkin Pudding

Preparation time: 30 minutes
Cooking time: 18 minutes
Servings: 6

Ingredients:
- 1 cup cauliflower rice
- ½ cup water
- 3 cups coconut milk
- ½ cup dates, chopped
- 1 cinnamon stick
- 1 cup pumpkin puree
- 4 tablespoons stevia
- 1 teaspoon vanilla extract

Directions:
Put cauliflower rice in your instant pot, add water, milk, dates and cinnamon, stir, cover and cook on High for 13 minutes. Add pumpkin puree, stevia and vanilla, stir, set the pot on Simmer mode and cook for 5 minutes. Discard cinnamon, divide pudding into bowls and serve. Enjoy!

Nutrition: calories 120, fat 3, fiber 3, carbs 8, protein 5

Strawberries and Cranberries Marmalade

Preparation time: 10 minutes
Cooking time: 15 minutes
Servings: 8

Ingredients:
- 1 pound cranberries
- 1 pound strawberries
- ½ pound blueberries
- 3.5 ounces blackcurrant
- Stevia to the taste
- Zest from 1 lemon, grated
- ½ cup water

Directions:
In your instant pot, mix strawberries with cranberries, blueberries, currants, lemon zest, stevia and water, stir, set the pot on simmer mode, cook for 5 minutes, then cover and cook on High for 10 minutes. Divide into dessert cups and serve. Enjoy!

Nutrition: calories 100, fat 0, fiber 1, carbs 7, protein 3

Pear Marmalade

Preparation time: 10 minutes
Cooking time: 4 minutes
Servings: 12

Ingredients:
- 8 pears, cored and roughly chopped
- 2 apples, peeled, cored and roughly chopped
- ¼ cup natural apple juice
- 1 teaspoon cinnamon powder

Directions:
In your instant pot, mix pears with apples, cinnamon and apple juice, stir, cover, cook on High for 4 minutes, blend with your immersion blender, leave aside to cool down, divide into small dessert cups and serve. Enjoy!

Nutrition: calories 90, fat 0, fiber 2, carbs 19, protein 2

Peach Marmalade

Preparation time: 10 minutes
Cooking time: 10 minutes
Servings: 6

Ingredients:
- 4 and ½ cups peaches, peeled and cubed
- Stevia to the taste
- 1 teaspoon ginger, grated
- 2 cups water

Directions:
In your instant pot, mix peaches with stevia, ginger and water, stir, cover and cook on High for 10 minutes. Divide into small cups, cool down and serve. Enjoy!

Nutrition: calories 82, fat 1, fiber 2, carbs 3, protein 2

Strawberries Compote

Preparation time: 10 minutes
Cooking time: 7 minutes
Servings: 8

Ingredients:
- 1 cup blueberries
- 2 cups strawberries, chopped
- 2 tablespoons lemon juice
- Stevia to the taste
- 1 tablespoon water

Directions:

In your instant pot, mix blueberries with strawberries, lemon juice, stevia and water, stir, cover and cook on High for 7 minutes. Divide into cups and serve cold. Enjoy!

Nutrition: calories 200, fat 1, fiber 3, carbs 12, protein 3

Sweet Peaches

Preparation time: 10 minutes
Cooking time: 6 minutes
Servings: 3

Ingredients:
- 6 peaches, insides discarded
- ¼ cup coconut flour
- 2 tablespoons stevia
- 2 tablespoons coconut butter
- ½ teaspoon cinnamon powder
- 1 teaspoon almond extract
- 1 cup water

Directions:

In a bowl, mix flour with stevia, butter, cinnamon and almond, stir well and stuff peaches with this mix. Add the water to your instant pot, add steamer basket, add peaches, cover and cook on High for 6 minutes. Divide into cups and serve them cold. Enjoy!

Nutrition: calories 152, fat 2, fiber 2, carbs 9, protein 3

Simple Peach Compote

Preparation time: 10 minutes
Cooking time: 4 minutes
Servings: 4

Ingredients:
- 8 peaches, chopped
- Stevia to the taste
- 1 teaspoon cinnamon powder
- 1 teaspoon vanilla extract
- 1 cup water

Directions:
In your instant pot, mix peaches with stevia, water, cinnamon and vanilla, stir, cover and cook on High for 4 minutes. Divide into bowls and serve cold. Enjoy!

Nutrition: calories 120, fat 2, fiber 2, carbs 8, protein 2

Apple Cobbler

Preparation time: 10 minutes
Cooking time: 12 minutes
Servings: 4

Ingredients:
- 3 apples, cored and roughly chopped
- 2 pears, cored and roughly chopped
- 1 and ½ cup hot water
- 2 tablespoons coconut flakes
- 3 tablespoon stevia
- 1 teaspoon cinnamon powder

Directions:
In your instant pot, mix apples with pears, water, coconut, stevia and cinnamon, stir, cover and cook on High for 12 minutes. Divide into bowls and serve cold. Enjoy!

Nutrition: calories 162, fat 2, fiber 2, carbs 6, protein 2

Zucchini Cake

Preparation time: 10 minutes
Cooking time: 25 minutes
Servings: 6

Ingredients:
- 1 cup natural applesauce
- 3 eggs, whisked
- 1 tablespoon vanilla extract
- 4 tablespoons stevia
- 2 cups zucchini, grated
- 2 and ½ cups coconut flour
- ½ cup baking cocoa powder
- 1 teaspoon baking soda
- ¼ teaspoon baking powder
- 1 teaspoon cinnamon powder
- ½ cup walnuts, chopped
- 2 cups water

Directions:
In a bowl, mix zucchini with stevia, vanilla, eggs, applesauce, flour, cocoa powder, baking soda, baking powder, cinnamon and walnuts, stir and pour into a cake pan. Add the water to your instant pot, add steamer basket, and cake pan, cover and cook on High for 20 minutes. Slice and serve cold. Enjoy!

Nutrition: calories 192, fat 3, fiber 6, carbs 8, protein 3

Pineapple and Cauliflower Pudding

Preparation time: 10 minutes
Cooking time: 5 minutes
Servings: 8

Ingredients:
- 1 tablespoon coconut oil
- 1 and ½ cups water
- 1 cup cauliflower rice
- 14 ounces coconut milk
- 8 ounces pineapple, chopped
- 2 eggs, whisked
- 4 tablespoons stevia
- ½ teaspoon vanilla extract

Directions:
In your instant pot, mix oil, water and cauliflower rice, stir, cover, cook on High for 3 minutes and mix with coconut milk and stevia. Add eggs, vanilla and pineapple, stir, cover again and cook on High for 2 minutes more. Divide into bowls and serve cold. Enjoy!

Nutrition: calories 100, fat 4, fiber 1, carbs 6, protein 4

Chocolate Pudding

Preparation time: 10 minutes
Cooking time: 20 minutes
Servings: 4

Ingredients:
- 6 ounces dark chocolate, chopped and melted
- ½ cup hot coconut milk
- 1 cup coconut cream
- 5 egg yolks
- 4 tablespoons stevia
- 2 teaspoons vanilla extract
- 2 cups water
- ¼ teaspoon cardamom powder

Directions:
In a bowl, mix egg yolks with vanilla, stevia, cardamom, melted chocolate, coconut milk and coconut cream, whisk really well and strain into 4 ramekins. Add the water to your instant pot, add steamer basket, add ramekins inside, cover and cook on High for 12 minutes. Serve cold. Enjoy!

Nutrition: calories 162, fat 4, fiber 1, carbs 12, protein 7

Strawberries Compote

Preparation time: 10 minutes
Cooking time: 30 minutes
Servings: 4

Ingredients:
- 1/3 cup water
- 1 pound strawberries, chopped
- 1 pound rhubarb, chopped
- 3 tablespoon stevia
- 1 tablespoon mint, chopped
- 1 pound strawberries, chopped

Directions:
In your instant pot, mix water with strawberries, rhubarb and stevia, stir, cover and cook on High for 20 minutes. Add mint, stir, divide into cups and serve cold. Enjoy!

Nutrition: calories 91, fat 1, fiber 1, carbs 8, protein 1

Carrot, Pecans and Raisins Cake

Preparation time: 10 minutes
Cooking time: 1 hour
Servings: 6

Ingredients:

- 1 and ½ cups water
- A drizzle of coconut oil, melted
- 4 tablespoons stevia
- 2 eggs
- ½ cup coconut flour
- ½ teaspoon allspice
- ½ teaspoon cinnamon powder
- A pinch of nutmeg
- ½ teaspoon baking soda
- ½ cup pecans, chopped
- ½ cup carrots, grated
- ½ cup raisins
- 1 cup coconut flakes

For the sauce:

- 4 tablespoons ghee
- Stevia to the taste
- ¼ cup coconut cream
- ¼ teaspoon cinnamon powder

Directions:

In a bowl, mix eggs with 4 tablespoons stevia, flour, allspice, cinnamon powder, nutmeg, baking soda, carrots, pecans, raisins and coconut flakes, whisk well and pour into a cake pan greased with some coconut oil. Add the water to your instant pot, add the steamer basket, add cake pan inside, cover and cook on High for 50 minutes. Meanwhile, heat up a pan with the ghee over medium heat, add stevia to the taste, coconut cream and cinnamon powder, stir and cook for 2 minutes. Drizzle this over cake, slice and serve. Enjoy!

Nutrition: calories 271, fat 4, fiber 4, carbs 17, protein 6

Fresh Figs

Preparation time: 10 minutes
Cooking time: 3 minutes
Servings: 4

Ingredients:

- 1 cup natural grape juice
- 1 pound figs
- ½ cup pine nuts, toasted
- 4 tablespoons stevia

Directions:

In your instant pot, mix grape juice with figs and stevia, cover pot and cook on High for 3 minutes. Divide this into bowls, sprinkle pine nuts on top and serve. Enjoy!

Nutrition: calories 100, fat 0, fiber 1, carbs 9, protein 1

Sweet Carrots

Preparation time: 10 minutes
Cooking time: 10 minutes
Servings: 4

Ingredients:
- 1 tablespoon stevia
- 2 cups baby carrots
- 1 tablespoon ghee
- ½ cup water

Directions:
In your instant pot, mix carrots with stevia, ghee and water, stir, cover and cook on High for 10 minutes. Divide into dessert cups and serve. Enjoy!

Nutrition: calories 100, fat 1, fiber 1, carbs 2, protein 2

Pear Pudding

Preparation time: 5 minutes
Cooking time: 7 minutes
Servings: 4

Ingredients:
- 1 cup water
- 2 cups pears, chopped
- 2 cups coconut milk
- 1 tablespoon ghee
- 3 tablespoons stevia
- ½ teaspoon cinnamon powder
- 1 cup coconut flakes
- ½ cup walnuts, chopped

Directions:
In a pudding pan, mix milk with stevia, ghee, coconut, cinnamon, pears and walnuts and stir. Add the water to your instant pot, add steamer basket, add pudding pan, cover and cook on High for 7 minutes. Divide into bowls and serve. Enjoy!

Nutrition: calories 172, fat 3, fiber 4, carbs 8, protein 7

Winter Fruit Cobbler

Preparation time: 10 minutes
Cooking time: 10 minutes
Servings: 4

Ingredients:
- 1 plum, chopped
- 1 and ½ cups water
- 1 pear, chopped
- 1 apple, chopped
- 2 tablespoons stevia
- 3 tablespoons coconut oil
- ½ teaspoon cinnamon powder
- ¼ cup pecans, toasted and chopped
- ¼ cup coconut, shredded

Directions:
In a bowl, mix plum with pear, apple, stevia, oil, cinnamon, coconut and pecans, stir and transfer to a round pan. Add water to your instant pot, add steamer basket, add pan inside, cover and cook on High for 10 minutes. Divide into bowls and serve. Enjoy!

Nutrition: calories 152, fat 2, fiber 2, carbs 8, protein 7

Pumpkin Granola

Preparation time: 10 minutes
Cooking time: 13 minutes
Servings: 6

Ingredients:
- 2 cups water
- 1 tablespoon melted ghee
- 1 cup pumpkin puree
- 1 cup coconut flakes
- 3 tablespoons stevia
- 2 teaspoons cinnamon powder
- 1 teaspoon pumpkin pie spice

Directions:
Set your instant pot on sauté mode, add ghee, heat it up, add coconut flakes, pumpkin, water, cinnamon, stevia and spice, stir, cover and cook on High for 13 minutes. Divide into bowls and serve. Enjoy!

Nutrition: calories 182, fat 2, fiber 1, carbs 8, protein 4

Carrot and Chia Seed Pudding

Preparation time: 10 minutes
Cooking time: 10 minutes
Servings: 4

Ingredients:
- 1 cup coconut flakes
- 2 cups water
- 1 tablespoon ghee
- 3 tablespoons stevia
- 2 teaspoons cinnamon powder
- 1 cup carrots, grated
- ¼ cup chia seeds

Directions:
Select the Sauté mode on your instant pot, add ghee, heat it up, add coconut, water, stevia, cinnamon, carrots and chia seeds, stir, cover and cook on High for 10 minutes. Divide into bowls and serve cold. Enjoy!

Nutrition: calories 132, fat 2, fiber 2, carbs 9, protein 4

Cinnamon Rice Pudding

Preparation time: 10 minutes
Cooking time: 10 minutes
Servings: 4

Ingredients:
- 1 and ½ cups cauliflower rice
- 1 and ½ teaspoon cinnamon powder
- 4 tablespoons stevia
- 2 tablespoons ghee
- 2 apples, cored and sliced
- 1 cup natural apple juice
- 3 cups coconut milk

Directions:
Set your instant pot on Sauté mode, add ghee, heat it up, add cauliflower rice, stevia, apples, apple juice, milk and cinnamon, stir, cover and cook on High for 10 minutes. Divide into bowls and serve warm. Enjoy!

Nutrition: calories 110, fat 2, fiber 3, carbs 12, protein 4

Breakfast Recipes

Colored Cauliflower and Eggs Breakfast

Preparation time: 10 minutes
Cooking time: 15 minutes
Servings: 2

Ingredients:

- 1 cauliflower head, florets separated and chopped
- 1 tablespoon olive oil
- 1 small yellow onion, chopped
- ¼ red bell pepper, sliced
- ¼ yellow bell pepper, sliced
- ¼ green bell pepper, sliced
- ¼ teaspoon poultry seasoning
- ¼ teaspoon dill, dried
- A pinch of salt and black pepper
- 2 eggs
- 1 cup water+ 2 tablespoons

Directions:

Put the cauliflower in a heatproof bowl, add some water, introduce in your microwave for a couple of minutes, drain and leave aside for now. Set your instant pot on sauté mode, add the oil, heat it up, add onion, red, green and yellow bell pepper, stir and cook for 2-3 minutes. Add cauliflower and 2 tablespoons water, stir and cook for 2 minutes more. Add dill, salt, pepper, and poultry seasoning, stir cook for 2 minutes more, transfer to a heatproof dish and crack eggs on top. Clean your instant pot, add 1 cup water and the trivet, add dish inside, cover and cook on High for 6 minutes. Divide between 2 plates and serve for breakfast. Enjoy!

Nutrition: calories 200, fat 3, fiber 4, carbs 7, protein 4

Simple Breakfast Hash Browns

Preparation time: 10 minutes
Cooking time: 10 minutes
Servings: 2

Ingredients:

- 1 egg, whisked
- A pinch of salt and black pepper
- 2 cups cauliflower, riced
- 1 teaspoon red bell pepper, chopped
- 1tablespoon onion, chopped
- 1 teaspoon green bell pepper, chopped
- ½ tablespoon olive oil
- 1 cup water
- 1 small block onion and chives cheese, grated

Directions:

Set your instant pot on sauté mode, add the oil heat it up, add onion, stir and cook for 2 minutes. Add cauliflower rice, red and green bell pepper, stir, cook for 1 minute more and transfer everything to a bowl. Cool this down, add salt, pepper and egg and whisk everything. Pour this into a greased baking dish and sprinkle onion and chives cheese all over. Clean your instant pot, add the water, and the trivet, and the dish with the cauliflower mix inside, cover pot and cook on High for 6 minutes. Divide between 2 plates and serve for breakfast. Enjoy!

Nutrition: calories 100, fat 4, fiber 2, carbs 8, protein 5

Delicious Breakfast Meatloaf

Preparation time: 10 minutes
Cooking time: 20 minutes
Servings: 4

Ingredients:
- 1 pound Italian sausage
- 4 ounces cream cheese
- 6 eggs
- 1 tablespoon ghee
- 2 cups water
- 1 small yellow onion, chopped
- 2 tablespoons scallions, chopped
- 1 cup cheddar cheese, shredded

Directions:

In a bowl, mix sausage with half of the cheese, eggs, onion and scallions and stir really well. Grease a loaf pan with the ghee, add sausage mixture and spread evenly. Add the rest of the cream cheese and sprinkle cheddar cheese on top. Add the water to your instant pot, add the steamer basket, add loaf pan inside, cover pot and cook on High for 15 minutes. Take loaf pan out of the instant pot, introduce in preheated broiler and broil for 5 minutes. Slice, divide between plates and serve for breakfast. Enjoy!

Nutrition: calories 200, fat 4, fiber 2, carbs 8, protein 7

Cajun Breakfast Hash Browns

Preparation time: 10 minutes
Cooking time: 10 minutes
Servings: 2

Ingredients:
- 2 tablespoons olive oil
- 1 small onion, chopped
- 2 tablespoons garlic, minced
- 1 pound cauliflower, riced
- 1 teaspoon Cajun seasoning
- 8 ounces pastrami, shaved
- 2 tablespoons veggie stock
- 1 small green bell pepper, chopped

Directions:

Set your instant pot on sauté mode, add the oil and heat it up. Add onion, stir and cook for 2 minutes. Add garlic and cauliflower, stir and cook for 2 minutes more. Add pastrami, green bell pepper and Cajun seasoning, stir and cook for 2 minutes. Add stock, cover and cook on High for 4 minutes. Divide between plates and serve for breakfast. Enjoy!

Nutrition: calories 182, fat 4, fiber 2, carbs 4, protein 7

Eggs and Chives

Preparation time: 10 minutes
Cooking time: 2 minutes
Servings: 3

Ingredients:

- 3 tablespoons ghee
- 3 tablespoons cream cheese
- 3 eggs
- 1 tablespoon chives, chopped
- A pinch of salt and black pepper
- 1 cup water

Directions:

Divide grease 3 ramekins with the ghee and divide cream cheese in each. Crack an egg into each ramekin, season with a pinch of salt and black pepper and sprinkle chives on top. Add the water to your instant pot, add the steamer basket, add ramekins inside, cover and cook on High for 2 minutes. Serve hot. Enjoy!

Nutrition: calories 163, fat 4, fiber 2, carbs 7, protein 6

Eggs and Cheese Breakfast

Preparation time: 10 minutes
Cooking time: 16 minutes
Servings: 4

Ingredients:

- 2 cup cauliflower, riced
- 6 bacon slices, chopped
- 6 eggs
- ¼ cup coconut milk
- ½ cup cheddar cheese, shredded
- A pinch of salt and black pepper
- 1 small yellow onion, chopped
- 1 and ½ cups water

Directions:

Set your instant pot on sauté mode, add bacon, stir and cook for 2 minutes. Add onion, stir and cook for 2 minutes more. Add cauliflower rice, stir and cook for 2 minutes. In a bowl, mix eggs with cheese, salt, pepper, coconut milk and the veggie mix, stir everything and pour into a heatproof dish. Clean your instant pot, add the water and the trivet, add the baking dish inside, cover and cook on High for 10 minutes. Divide between plates and serve. Enjoy!

Nutrition: calories 182, fat 3, fiber 6, carbs 7, protein 7

Breakfast Blueberry Cake

Preparation time: 10 minutes
Cooking time: 30 minutes
Servings: 4

Ingredients:

- 2 cups coconut flour
- Zest from 1 lemon, grated
- 2 teaspoons baking powder
- ½ cup ghee
- ¾ cup stevia
- 1 teaspoon vanilla extract
- 1 egg
- ½ cup coconut milk
- 2/3 cup water
- 2 cups blueberries

Directions:

In a bowl, mix ghee with flour, baking powder, lemon zest and stevia and stir well. Add egg, vanilla and coconut milk and stir really well. Add blueberries, stir gently and pour into a cake pan. Add the water to your instant pot, add the steamer basket, add cake pan inside, cover pot and cook on Manual for 30 minutes. Divide between plates and serve for breakfast. Enjoy!

Nutrition: calories 172, fat 4, fiber 3, carbs 7, protein 7

Egg Casserole

Preparation time: 10 minutes
Cooking time: 25 minutes
Servings: 4

Ingredients:

- 2 cups water
- 1 yellow onion, chopped
- 1 and ½ cups ham, chopped
- 2 cups cheddar cheese, shredded
- 10 eggs
- 1 cup coconut milk
- A pinch of salt and black pepper
- A drizzle of olive oil

Directions:

Spray a baking dish with olive oil. In a bowl, mix onion with ham, cheese, eggs, coconut milk, salt and pepper and stir well. Pour this into the baking dish and spread evenly. Add the water to your instant pot, add the steamer basket, add the baking dish inside, cover and cook on Manual for 25 minutes. Slice, divide between plates and serve for breakfast. Enjoy!

Nutrition: calories 192, fat 4, fiber 2, carbs 6, protein 8

Breakfast Pancake

Preparation time: 10 minutes
Cooking time: 45 minutes
Servings: 4

Ingredients:
- 2 cups coconut flour
- 2 tablespoons stevia
- 2 eggs
- 2 teaspoons baking powder
- 1 and ½ cups coconut milk
- A drizzle of olive oil

Directions:

In a bowl, mix eggs with stevia and milk and whisk well. Add flour and baking powder and stir everything well again. Grease your instant pot with the oil, add the batter, spread into the pot, cover and cook on Low for 45 minutes. Slice pancake, divide between plates and serve for breakfast. Enjoy!

Nutrition: calories 182, fat 3, fiber 2, carbs 6, protein 8

Tomato and Spinach Eggs

Preparation time: 10 minutes
Cooking time: 20 minutes
Servings: 6

Ingredients:
- ½ cup coconut milk
- A pinch of salt and black pepper
- 12 eggs
- 3 cups spinach, chopped
- 1 cup tomato, chopped
- 3 green onions, chopped
- ¼ cup parmesan, grated
- 1 and ½ cups water
- A drizzle of olive oil

Directions:

In a bowl, mix eggs with salt, pepper, milk, green onion, spinach and tomato and stir well. Grease a baking dish with the olive oil, pour eggs mix, spread and sprinkle parmesan on top. Add the water to your instant pot, add the steamer basket, add baking dish inside, cover and cook on High for 20 minutes. Divide between plates and serve for breakfast. Enjoy!

Nutrition: calories 183, fat 4, fiber 4, carbs 7, protein 8

Breakfast Frittata

Preparation time: 10 minutes
Cooking time: 30 minutes
Servings: 4

Ingredients:
- 1 cup coconut cream
- 4 eggs
- 10 ounces canned green chilies
- A pinch of salt and black pepper
- ½ teaspoon cumin, ground
- 1 cup Mexican cheese, shredded
- ¼ cup cilantro, chopped
- 2 cups water

Directions:
In a bowl, mix eggs with coconut cream, salt, pepper, chilies, cumin and half of the cheese, stir well and pour this into a round pan. Add the water to your instant pot, add the trivet, place pan inside, cover and cook on High for 20 minutes. Spread the rest of the cheese and the cilantro over frittata, introduce in a preheated broiler for 5 minutes, slice and serve. Enjoy!

Nutrition: calories 254, fat 6, fiber 1, carbs 6, protein 14

Mexican Breakfast Casserole

Preparation time: 10 minutes
Cooking time: 25 minutes
Servings: 8

Ingredients:
- 1 pound sausage, ground
- 8 eggs, whisked
- 1 red bell pepper, chopped
- 1 red onion, chopped
- ½ cup green onions, chopped
- ½ cup coconut flour
- 1 cup cotija cheese, shredded
- 1 cup mozzarella cheese, shredded
- 1 tablespoon cilantro, chopped

Directions:
Set your instant pot on sauté mode, add sausage, stir and cook for 3 minutes. Add eggs, bell pepper, onion, green onions, coconut flour, cotija and mozzarella cheese, stir, cover and cook on High for 20 minutes. Add cilantro, stir your mix gently, divide between plates and serve for breakfast. Enjoy!

Nutrition: calories 265, fat 3, fiber 6, carbs 8, protein 8

Burrito Casserole

Preparation time: 10 minutes
Cooking time: 13 minutes
Servings: 6

Ingredients:

- 2 pound celeriac, peeled and cubed
- 4 eggs
- ¼ cup yellow onion, chopped
- 1 jalapeno, chopped
- 6 ounces ham, chopped
- A pinch of salt and black pepper
- ¼ teaspoon chili powder
- ¾ teaspoon taco seasoning
- Keto salsa for serving
- 1 cup water+ 1 tablespoon

Directions:

In a bowl, mix eggs with onion, jalapeno, celeriac, ham, salt, pepper, chili powder and taco seasoning and stir. Add 1 tablespoon water, stir again and pour everything into a casserole. Add the water to your instant pot, add the trivet, and casserole, cover pot and cook on Manual for 13 minutes. Divide between plates and serve for breakfast with some keto salsa on top. Enjoy!

Nutrition: calories 213, fat 4, fiber 6, carbs 7, protein 7

Breakfast Oatmeal

Preparation time: 10 minutes
Cooking time: 10 minutes
Servings: 2

Ingredients:

- ¼ cup chia seeds
- ¼ cup coconut, unsweetened and shredded
- 1/3 coconut, flaked
- 1/3 cup almonds, flaked
- ½ cup coconut milk
- 1 teaspoon vanilla extract
- 1 cup water
- 2 tablespoons swerve

Directions:

In your instant pot, mix coconut with almonds, coconut milk, vanilla, water and swerve, stir, cover and cook on High for 6 minutes. Add chia seeds, stir, cover the pot and leave it aside for 4 minutes more. Divide into bowls and serve for breakfast. Enjoy!

Nutrition: calories 173, fat 3, fiber 4, carbs 5, protein 6

Chocolate Oatmeal

Preparation time: 10 minutes
Cooking time: 10 minutes
Servings: 4

Ingredients:

- 1 cup coconut milk
- 2 and ½ tablespoon cocoa powder
- 4 cups water
- 2 cups coconut, shredded
- 1 teaspoon vanilla extract
- 1 teaspoon cinnamon powder
- 10 ounces cherries, pitted

Directions:

In your instant pot, mix coconut milk with water, cocoa powder, coconut, vanilla extract, cinnamon and cherries, stir, cover and cook on High for 10 minutes. Stir your chocolate oatmeal once again, divide into bowls and serve for breakfast. Enjoy!

Nutrition: calories 183, fat 4, fiber 2, carbs 5, protein 7

Blueberry and Yogurt Bowl

Preparation time: 10 minutes
Cooking time: 6 minutes
Servings: 1

Ingredients:

- 1/3 cup coconut milk
- 1/3 cup coconut, unsweetened and flaked
- 1/3 cup yogurt
- 1/3 cup blueberries
- 1 tablespoon chia seeds
- ½ teaspoon stevia
- ¼ teaspoon vanilla extract
- A sprinkle of cinnamon powder
- 1 and ½ cups water

Directions:

In a heatproof jar, mix coconut milk with coconut, yogurt, blueberries, chia, stevia, vanilla and cinnamon, stir well and cover with tin foil. Put the water in your instant pot, add the jar, cover and cook on High for 6 minutes. Transfer blueberry mix to a bowl and serve. Enjoy!

Nutrition: calories 152, fat 3, fiber 3, carbs 4, protein 6

Breakfast Cauliflower Pudding

Preparation time: 10 minutes
Cooking time: 10 minutes
Servings: 6

Ingredients:
- 2 cups coconut milk
- 1 and ¼ cups water
- 1 cup cauliflower rice
- ¾ cup coconut cream
- 2 tablespoons swerve
- 1 teaspoon vanilla extract

Directions:

In your instant pot, mix coconut milk with water, swerve and cauliflower rice, stir, cover and cook on High for 10 minutes. Add cream and vanilla extract, stir, divide into bowls and serve for breakfast. Enjoy!

Nutrition: calories 153, fat 3, fiber 2, carbs 6, protein 7

Scotch Eggs

Preparation time: 10 minutes
Cooking time: 12 minutes
Servings: 4

Ingredients:
- 1 pound sausage, ground
- 4 eggs
- 1 tablespoon olive oil
- 2 cups water

Directions:

Put 1 cup water in your instant pot, add the steamer basket, add eggs inside, cover, cook on High for 6 minutes, transfer eggs to a bowl filled with ice water, cool them down and peel. Divide sausage mix into 4 pieces, place them on a cutting board and flatten them. Divide eggs on sausage mix, wrap well and shape 4 balls. Add the oil to your instant pot, set on sauté mode, heat it up, add scotch eggs and brown them on all sides. Clean the pot, add 1 cup water, and the steamer basket, and scotch eggs inside, cover the pot and cook on High for 6 minutes. Serve them for breakfast. Enjoy!

Nutrition: calories 192, fat 4, fiber 2, carbs 4, protein 7

Celeriac and Bacon Breakfast

Preparation time: 10 minutes
Cooking time: 9 minutes
Servings: 6

Ingredients:

- 2 teaspoons parsley, dried
- 3 bacon strips
- 2 pounds celeriac, peeled and cubed
- 4 ounces cheddar cheese, shredded
- 1 teaspoon garlic powder
- A pinch of salt and black pepper
- 2 tablespoons water

Directions:

Set your instant pot on sauté mode, add bacon, stir and cook for a couple of minutes. Add garlic powder, salt, pepper, water and parsley and stir. Add celeriac, stir, cover and cook on Manual for 7 minutes. Divide between plates and serve for breakfast. Enjoy!

Nutrition: calories 164, fat 3, fiber 2, carbs 6, protein 7

Meat Quiche

Preparation time: 10 minutes
Cooking time: 30 minutes
Servings: 4

Ingredients:

- ½ cup coconut milk
- A pinch of salt and black pepper
- 6 eggs, whisked
- 4 bacon slices, cooked and crumbled
- 1 cup sausage, ground and cooked
- ½ cup ham, chopped
- 2 green onions, chopped
- 1 cup cheddar cheese, shredded
- 1 cup water

Directions:

In a bowl, mix eggs with salt, pepper, milk, sausage, bacon, ham, green onions and cheese and stir well. Pour this into a soufflé dish and spread. Add the water to your instant pot, add the trivet, add soufflé dish inside, cover pot and cook on High for 30 minutes. Serve hot for breakfast. Enjoy!

Nutrition: calories 200, fat 3, fiber 3, carbs 6, protein 6

Cinnamon Oatmeal

Preparation time: 10 minutes
Cooking time: 5 minutes
Servings: 2

Ingredients:
- 1 and ½ cups water
- ½ cup coconut, unsweetened and flaked
- ½ teaspoon cinnamon powder
- 2 apples, cored, peeled and chopped
- ¼ teaspoon ginger powder
- Stevia to the taste

Directions:

In your instant pot, mix water with coconut, cinnamon, apples, ginger and stevia to the taste, stir, cover and cook on High for 5 minutes. Stir again, divide into bowls and serve for breakfast. Enjoy!

Nutrition: calories 172, fat 4, fiber 2, carbs 6, protein 6

Cauliflower Congee

Preparation time: 10 minutes
Cooking time: 20 minutes
Servings: 4

Ingredients:
- 1 cup cauliflower rice
- 3 cups veggie stock
- 2 cups bok choy, chopped
- 2 tablespoons ginger, grated
- 2 cups shitake mushrooms, chopped
- 2 garlic cloves, minced
- 1 cup water
- 1 tablespoon coconut aminos

Directions:

In your instant pot, mix cauliflower rice with veggie stock, bok choy, mushrooms, garlic, water and aminos, stir, cover and cook on Manual for 20 minutes. Divide into bowls and serve for breakfast. Enjoy!

Nutrition: calories 183, fat 3, fiber 2, carbs 6, protein 3

Breakfast Avocado Cups

Preparation time: 10 minutes
Cooking time: 5 minutes
Servings: 4

Ingredients:
- 2 avocados, cut into halves and pitted
- 1 cup water
- A drizzle of olive oil
- 1 tablespoon chives, chopped
- A pinch of salt and black pepper
- 4 eggs

Directions:
Arrange all avocado cups on a cutting board and drizzle some olive oil over them. Crack an egg into each avocado cup, season with salt and pepper and sprinkle chives all over. Add the water to your instant pot, add the trivet, add avocado cups inside, cover and cook on High for 5 minutes. Divide avocado cups between plates and serve for breakfast. Enjoy!

Nutrition: calories 200, fat 3, fiber 3, carbs 7, protein 5

Smoked Salmon and Shrimp Breakfast

Preparation time: 10 minutes
Cooking time: 10 minutes
Servings: 4

Ingredients:
- 1 cup mushrooms, sliced
- 4 ounces salmon, smoked and chopped
- 4 ounces shrimp, deveined
- A pinch of salt and black pepper
- 4 bacon slices, chopped
- ½ cup coconut cream

Directions:
Set your instant pot on sauté mode, add bacon, stir and cook for 2 minutes, Add mushrooms, stir and cook for 1 minute more. Add salmon, shrimp, salt, pepper and coconut cream, stir, cover and cook on High for 5 minutes. Divide into bowls and serve for breakfast. Enjoy!

Nutrition: calories 180, fat 3, fiber 1, carbs 5, protein 8

Beef Breakfast Pie

Preparation time: 10 minutes
Cooking time: 30 minutes
Servings: 8

Ingredients:

- ½ onion, chopped
- 1 keto pie crust
- 1 small red bell pepper, chopped
- 1 pound beef, ground
- 8 eggs
- 1 and ½ cups water
- A pinch of salt and black pepper
- 1 tablespoon Italian seasoning
- A handful cilantro, chopped
- 1 teaspoon olive oil
- 1 teaspoon baking soda

Directions:

Set your instant pot on sauté mode, add the oil, heat it up, add beef, salt, pepper and Italian seasoning, stir and brown for 2 minutes. Add bell pepper and onion, stir and cook for 2 minutes more. Add baking soda and eggs, stir, cook for 3 minutes more and transfer to a bowl. Fill your piecrust with this mix and spread it well. Add the water to your instant pot, add the steamer basket, add pie inside, cover and cook on High for 20 minutes. Leave the pie to cool down, sprinkle cilantro on top, slice and serve for breakfast. Enjoy!

Nutrition: calories 258, fat 4, fiber 5, carbs 6, protein 5

Delicious Breakfast Skillet
It's going to be so tasty!

Preparation time: 10 minutes
Cooking time: 20 minutes
Servings: 4

Ingredients:

- 8 ounces mushrooms, chopped
- 2 tablespoons veggie stock
- A pinch of salt and black pepper
- 1 pound pork, minced
- 1 tablespoon olive oil
- ½ teaspoon garlic powder
- ½ teaspoon basil, dried
- 2 tablespoons Dijon mustard
- 2 zucchinis, chopped

Directions:

Set your instant pot on sauté mode, add oil, heat it up, add mushrooms, stir and sauté for 2 minutes. Add zucchini, salt, pepper, pork meat, garlic powder and basil, stir and cook for 3 minutes more. Add mustard and stock, stir, cover and cook on High for 15 minutes. Divide between plates and serve for breakfast. Enjoy!

Nutrition: calories 180, fat 5, fiber 2, carbs 5, protein 6

Pork Sausage Quiche

Preparation time: 10 minutes
Cooking time: 20 minutes
Servings: 5

Ingredients:
- 12 ounces pork sausage, chopped
- Salt and black pepper to the taste
- 2 teaspoons coconut cream
- 2 tablespoons parsley, chopped
- 10 mixed cherry tomatoes, halved
- 6 eggs
- 2 tablespoons parmesan, grated
- 2 cups water
- 5 eggplant slices

Directions:
Spread sausage pieces on the bottom of a baking dish and add eggplant and cherries over them. In a bowl, mix eggs with salt, pepper, parmesan, parsley and cream, whisk well and pour over sausage mixture. Add the water to your instant pot, add the steamer basket, add the baking dish inside, cover and cook on High for 20 minutes. Leave quiche to cool down a bit, slice and serve. Enjoy!

Nutrition: calories 240, fat 6, fiber 3, carbs 6, protein 7

Sausage, Leeks and Eggs Casserole

Preparation time: 10 minutes
Cooking time: 25 minutes
Servings: 4

Ingredients:
- 1 pound sausage, chopped
- ¼ cup coconut milk
- 4 asparagus stalks, chopped
- 1 leek, chopped
- 8 eggs, whisked
- 1 tablespoon dill, chopped
- A pinch of salt and black pepper
- ¼ teaspoon garlic powder
- 1 tablespoon olive oil
- 1 and ½ cups water

Directions:
Set your instant pot on sauté mode, add sausage, stir and brown for 3 minutes. Add asparagus and leek, stir and cook for 2 minutes more. In a bowl, mix eggs with garlic powder, salt, pepper, milk and dill and whisk well. Add sausage and veggie mix and stir. Drizzle the oil in a baking dish and add eggs and sausage mix. Add the water to your instant pot, add the trivet, add baking dish inside, cover and cook on High for 20 minutes. Slice, divide between plates and serve for breakfast. Enjoy!

Nutrition: calories 240, fat 5, fiber 3, carbs 5, protein 14

Almond Porridge

Preparation time: 5 minutes
Cooking time: 7 minutes
Servings: 2

Ingredients:

- 1 teaspoon cinnamon powder
- A pinch of nutmeg, ground
- A pinch of cloves, ground
- A pinch of cardamom, ground
- ½ cup almonds, ground
- 1 teaspoon stevia
- ¾ cup coconut cream

Directions:

In your instant pot, mix almonds with cream, stevia, cardamom, cloves, nutmeg and cinnamon, stir, cover and cook on High for 7 minutes. Divide into 2 bowls and serve for breakfast. Enjoy!

Nutrition: calories 163, fat 5, fiber 2, carbs 4, protein 8

Almond and Chia Breakfast

Preparation time: 5 minutes
Cooking time: 5 minutes
Servings: 2

Ingredients:

- 2 tablespoons almonds, chopped
- 1 tablespoon chia seeds
- 2 tablespoon pepitas, roasted
- 1/3 cup coconut milk
- 1/3 cup water
- A handful blueberries

Directions:

In your food processor, mix pepitas with almonds and pulse them well. In your instant pot, mix chia seeds with water and coconut milk and stir. Add pepitas mix, stir, cover pot and cook on High for 5 minutes. Add blueberries, toss a bit, divide into 2 bowls and serve for breakfast. Enjoy!

Nutrition: calories 150, fat 1, fiber 2, carbs 4, protein 2

Nuts Bowl

Preparation time: 5 minutes
Cooking time: 5 minutes
Servings: 1

Ingredients:
- 1 teaspoon pecans, chopped
- 1 teaspoon walnuts, chopped
- 1 teaspoon almonds, chopped
- 1 teaspoon pistachios, chopped
- 1 teaspoon pine nuts, chopped
- 1 teaspoon sunflower seeds
- 1 teaspoon stevia
- 1 teaspoon pepitas, raw
- 2 teaspoons raspberries
- 1 cup coconut milk

Directions:
In your instant pot, mix pecans with walnuts, almonds, pistachios, pine nuts, sunflower seeds, pepitas and stevia and stir. Add milk, stir, cover pot and cook on High for 5 minutes. Add raspberries, toss a bit, transfer to a bowl and serve for breakfast. Enjoy!

Nutrition: calories 100, fat 1, fiber 2, carbs 2, protein 4

Kale and Prosciutto Muffins

Preparation time: 10 minutes
Cooking time: 15 minutes
Servings: 4

Ingredients:
- ½ cup coconut milk
- 6 eggs
- 1 tablespoon olive oil
- Salt and black pepper to the taste
- ¼ cup kale, chopped
- 8 prosciutto slices
- ¼ cup chives, chopped
- 1 and ½ cups water

Directions:
In a bowl, mix eggs with milk, chives, salt, pepper and kale and whisk well. Grease a muffin tray with the oil, line with prosciutto slices and pour eggs and kale mix over them. Add the water to your instant pot, add the trivet, add muffin tray inside, cover pot and cook on High for 15 minutes. Leave muffins to cool down a bit, divide between plates and serve for breakfast. Enjoy!

Nutrition: calories 130, fat 1, fiber 1, carbs 2, protein 7

Bacon Muffins

Preparation time: 10 minutes
Cooking time: 20 minutes
Servings: 12

Ingredients:
- 1 cup bacon, chopped
- A pinch of salt and black pepper
- 1 and ½ cups water
- ½ cup ghee, melted
- 3 cups coconut flour
- 1 teaspoon baking soda
- 4 eggs
- 2 teaspoons lemon zest, grated

Directions:

In a bowl, mix flour with baking soda, eggs, lemon zest, ghee, salt, pepper and bacon, stir well and pour into a greased muffin tray. Add the water to your instant pot, add the trivet, add muffin tray inside, cover and cook on High for 20 minutes. Leave muffins to cool down a bit, divide between plates and serve them for breakfast. Enjoy!

Nutrition: calories 173, fat 3, fiber 2, carbs 5, protein 6

Cheddar and Parmesan Muffins

Preparation time: 10 minutes
Cooking time: 20 minutes
Servings: 6

Ingredients:
- 2 tablespoons olive oil
- 2 cups water
- 2 tablespoon parmesan, grated
- 1 cup cheddar cheese, grated
- 1 egg
- ½ teaspoon oregano, dried
- ¼ teaspoon baking soda
- 1 cup coconut flour
- A pinch of salt and black pepper
- ½ cup coconut milk

Directions:

In a bowl, mix flour with oregano, salt, pepper, parmesan, baking soda, milk, oil, egg and cheddar cheese, stir really well and pour into a greased muffin tray. Add the water to your instant pot, add the trivet, and the muffin tray inside, cover and cook on High for 15 minutes. Sprinkle parmesan over muffins, introduce them in a preheated broiler, broil for 5 minutes, divide them between plates and serve for breakfast. Enjoy!

Nutrition: calories 160, fat 1, fiber 2, carbs 3, protein 6

Eggs and Turkey

Preparation time: 10 minutes
Cooking time: 10 minutes
Servings: 4

Ingredients:
- 4 avocado slices
- A pinch of salt and black pepper
- 4 bacon slices, cooked
- 4 turkey breast slices, already cooked
- 2 tablespoons olive oil
- 4 eggs, whisked
- 2 tablespoons veggie stock

Directions:
Set your instant pot on sauté mode, add bacon, brown on both sides and transfer to a plate. Add the oil to your instant pot, heat it up, add eggs, salt, pepper and veggie stock, stir, cover and cook on High for 5 minutes. Divide turkey and bacon slices among 4 plates. Divide eggs and avocado slices as well and serve for breakfast. Enjoy!

Nutrition: calories 155, fat 2, fiber 2, carbs 4, protein 6

Chia Pudding

Preparation time: 2 minutes
Cooking time: 3 minutes
Servings: 4

Ingredients:
- ½ cup chia seeds
- 2 cups coconut milk
- ¼ cup almonds, chopped
- ¼ cup coconut, unsweetened and shredded
- 4 teaspoons stevia

Directions:
Put chia seeds in your instant pot, add milk, almonds, coconut and stevia, stir, cover and cook on High for 3 minutes. Divide into bowls and serve for breakfast. Enjoy!

Nutrition: calories 140, fat 1, fiber 1, carbs 2, protein 3

Pumpkin Spread

Preparation time: 10 minutes
Cooking time: 10 minutes
Servings: 4

Ingredients:

- 2 apples, peeled, cored and chopped
- 20 ounces pumpkin puree
- 1 tablespoon pumpkin pie spice
- 1 tablespoon stevia
- 10 ounces apple cider

Directions:

In your instant pot, mix apples with pumpkin puree, spice, stevia and cider, stir, cover, cook on High for 10 minutes, divide into jars and serve cold for breakfast. Enjoy!

Nutrition: calories 140, fat 3, fiber 1, carbs 3, protein 4

Mushroom, Tomatoes and Zucchini Mix

Preparation time: 10 minutes
Cooking time: 5 minutes
Servings: 5

Ingredients:

- 1 and ½ cups yellow onion, chopped
- 12 ounces mushrooms, chopped
- 15 ounces tomatoes, chopped
- 8 cups zucchini, sliced
- 1 tablespoon olive oil
- 2 garlic cloves, minced
- 1 basil sprigs, chopped
- A pinch of sea salt and black pepper

Directions:

Set your instant pot on sauté mode add the oil, heat it up, add garlic and onion, stir and cook for 2 minutes. Add salt, pepper, basil and mushrooms, stir and sauté for 30 seconds more. Add tomatoes and zucchini, stir, cover pot, cook on High for 3 minutes, divide between plates and serve for breakfast. Enjoy!

Nutrition: calories 136, fat 2, fiber 3, carbs 3, protein 4

Okra and Zucchinis Breakfast

Preparation time: 10 minutes
Cooking time: 10 minutes
Servings: 4

Ingredients:

- 1 and ½ cups red onion, roughly chopped
- 3 tablespoons olive oil
- 2 cups okra, sliced
- 1 cup mushrooms, sliced
- 1 cup cherry tomatoes, halved
- 1 cup water
- 2 cups zucchini, roughly chopped
- 2 cups yellow bell pepper, chopped
- Black pepper to the taste
- 2 tablespoons basil, chopped
- 1 tablespoon thyme, chopped
- ½ cup balsamic vinegar

Directions:

Put onion, tomatoes, okra, mushrooms, zucchini, bell pepper, basil, thyme, vinegar and oil in your instant pot and toss. Add black pepper, toss again well, also add the water, cover pot and cook on High for 10 minutes. Divide between plates and serve for breakfast. Enjoy!

Nutrition: calories 120, fat 2, fiber 2, carbs 3, protein 6

Squash and Cranberry Sauce

Preparation time: 10 minutes
Cooking time: 7 minutes
Servings: 4

Ingredients:

- ¼ cup raisins
- 2 acorn squash, peeled and roughly chopped
- 14 ounces cranberry sauce, unsweetened
- ¼ teaspoon cinnamon powder
- A pinch of sea salt and black pepper

Directions:

In your instant pot, mix squash with cranberry sauce, raisins, cinnamon, salt and pepper, stir, cover, cook on High for 7 minutes, divide into bowls and serve. Enjoy!

Nutrition: calories 140, fat 3, fiber 2, carbs 3, protein 4

Beef and Radish Hash

Preparation time: 10 minutes
Cooking time: 16 minutes
Servings: 2

Ingredients:

- 1 tablespoon olive oil
- 1 yellow onion, chopped
- 2 cups corned beef, cubed
- 2 garlic cloves, minced
- ½ cup beef stock
- A pinch of salt and black pepper
- 1 pound radishes, cut into quarters

Directions:

Set your instant pot on sauté mode, add oil, heat it up, add onion, stir and cook for 2 minutes. Add garlic and radishes, stir and sauté them for 4 minutes more. Add beef, stock, salt and pepper, stir, cover and cook on High for 10 minutes. Divide into bowls and serve for breakfast. Enjoy!

Nutrition: calories 160, fat 3, fiber 3, carbs 5, protein 4

Sweet Carrots Breakfast

Preparation time: 10 minutes
Cooking time: 4 minutes
Servings: 4

Ingredients:

- 1 and ½ cups coconut milk
- A pinch of cloves, ground
- A pinch of nutmeg, ground
- 1 small zucchini, grated
- 1 carrot, grated
- 2 tablespoons swerve
- ½ teaspoon cinnamon powder
- ¼ cup pecans, chopped

Directions:

In your instant pot, mix milk with cloves, nutmeg, zucchini, carrot, swerve, cinnamon and pecans, stir, cover and cook on High for 4 minutes. Divide into bowls and serve hot. Enjoy!

Nutrition: calories 100, fat 1, fiber 2, carbs 3, protein 4

Breakfast Omelet

Preparation time: 10 minutes
Cooking time: 10 minutes
Servings: 1

Ingredients:

- 1 ounces rotisserie chicken, shredded
- 1 teaspoon mustard
- 1 tablespoon homemade mayonnaise
- 1 tomato, chopped
- 2 bacon slices, cooked and crumbled
- 3 eggs, whisked
- 1 small avocado, pitted, peeled and chopped
- Salt and black pepper to the taste
- A drizzle of olive oil

Directions:

In a bowl, mix eggs with chicken, mustard, mayo, tomato, bacon, avocado, salt and pepper and whisk well. Set your instant pot on sauté mode, add the oil, heat it up, add eggs mix, spread and cook for 2 minutes. Cover your instant pot, cook your omelet on High for 2 minutes, divide it between plates and serve for breakfast. Enjoy!

Nutrition: calories 150, fat 2, fiber 6, carbs 8, protein 10

Nuts, Squash and Apples Breakfast

Preparation time: 10 minutes
Cooking time: 10 minutes
Servings: 4

Ingredients:

- ½ cup almonds, soaked for 12 hours and drained
- ½ cup walnuts, soaked for 12 hours and drained
- 2 apples, peeled, cored and cubed
- 1 butternut squash, peeled and cubed
- 1 teaspoon cinnamon powder
- 1 tablespoon stevia
- ½ teaspoon nutmeg, ground
- 1 cup coconut milk

Directions:

Put the almonds in your blender, pulse them well and transfer them to your instant pot. Add walnuts, apples, squash, cinnamon, stevia, milk and nutmeg, stir, cover and cook on High for 10 minutes. Divide into bowls and serve for breakfast. Enjoy!

Nutrition: calories 140, fat 1, fiber 2, carbs 6, protein 3

Leek and Beef Breakfast Mix

Preparation time: 10 minutes
Cooking time: 10 minutes
Servings: 4

Ingredients:

- 1 and 1/3 cups leek, chopped
- 1 cup kale, chopped
- ½ cup water
- 2 tablespoons olive oil
- 2 teaspoons garlic, minced
- 8 eggs
- 2/3 cup celeriac, peeled and grated
- 1 and ½ cups beef sausage, casings removed and chopped

Directions:

Set your instant pot on Sauté mode, add the oil, heat it up, add leeks, stir and sauté for 1 minutes. Add celeriac, kale, water and garlic, stir and sauté for 1 minute more. Add beef sausage and eggs, stir, cover and cook on High for 6 minutes. Divide this mix on plates and serve for breakfast. Enjoy!

Nutrition: calories 150, fat 2, fiber 2, carbs 5, protein 6

Strawberries and Coconut Breakfast

Preparation time: 10 minutes
Cooking time: 10 minutes
Servings: 2

Ingredients:

- 3 tablespoons coconut flakes, unsweetened
- 2 tablespoon strawberries, chopped
- 1 cup water
- 2/3 cup coconut milk
- ½ teaspoon stevia

Directions:

In your instant pot, mix strawberries with coconut flakes, water, milk and stevia, stir, cover and cook on High for 10 minutes. Divide into 2 bowls and serve for breakfast. Enjoy!

Nutrition: calories 110, fat 5, fiber 3, carbs 3, protein 3

Chorizo and Veggies Mix

Preparation time: 10 minutes
Cooking time: 15 minutes
Servings: 2

Ingredients:

- 1 pound chorizo, chopped
- 1 small yellow onion, chopped
- 2 garlic cloves, minced
- 4 bacon slices, chopped
- ½ cup beef stock
- 2 poblano peppers, chopped
- 1 cup kale, chopped
- 8 mushrooms, chopped
- ½ cup cilantro, chopped
- 1 avocado, peeled, pitted and chopped
- 4 eggs

Directions:

Set your instant pot on sauté mode, add chorizo and bacon, stir and cook for 2 minutes. Add garlic, onion and poblano peppers, stir and cook for 2 minutes more. Add kale, mushrooms and stock, stir, make 4 holes in this mix, crack an egg in each, cover pot and cook on High for 4 minutes. Divide this between plates, add avocado and cilantro on top and serve for breakfast. Enjoy!

Nutrition: calories 160, fat 5, fiber 3, carbs 5, protein 7

Delicious Vanilla and Espresso Oatmeal

Preparation time: 10 minutes
Cooking time: 10 minutes
Servings: 4

Ingredients:

- 1 cup coconut milk
- 1 cup coconut flakes
- 2 cups water
- 2 tablespoons stevia
- 1 teaspoon espresso powder
- 2 teaspoons vanilla extract
- Grated dark and bitter chocolate for serving

Directions:

In your instant pot, mix coconut flakes with water, stevia, milk and espresso powder, stir, cover and cook on High for 10 minutes. Add vanilla extract, stir, divide into bowls and serve with grated chocolate on top. Enjoy!

Nutrition: calories 172, fat 2, fiber 4, carbs 7, protein 8

Coconut and Pomegranate Oatmeal

Preparation time: 5 minutes
Cooking time: 2 minutes
Servings: 2

Ingredients:
- 1 cup coconut, shredded
- 1 cup water
- ¾ cup pomegranate juice
- Seeds from 1 pomegranate

Directions:
In your instant pot, mix coconut with water and pomegranate juice, stir, cover and cook on High for 2 minutes. Add pomegranate seeds, stir oatmeal, divide into bowls and serve for breakfast. Enjoy!

Nutrition: calories 183, fat 3, fiber 6, carbs 9, protein 6

Cauliflower Rice Bowl

Preparation time: 5 minutes
Cooking time: 7 minutes
Servings: 4

Ingredients:
- 1 cup cauliflower, riced
- ½ cup coconut chips
- 1 cup coconut milk
- 3 tablespoons stevia
- ¼ cup raisins
- ¼ cup almonds, chopped
- A pinch of cinnamon powder

Directions:
In your instant pot, mix cauliflower rice with coconut, coconut milk, stevia, raisins, almonds and cinnamon, stir, cover and cook on High for 7 minutes. Divide into bowls and serve for breakfast. Enjoy!

Nutrition: calories 172, fat 2, fiber 3, carbs 7, protein 10

Conclusion

The Ketogenic diet can really change your life! It will transform you into a healthy and happy person! It's one of the best diets ever! The best thing about this amazing lifestyle is that you don't have to make drastic changes. You only have to respect some simple rules and everything will be ok.

The purpose of this amazing cookbook you've discovered is to help you make the most delicious Ketogenic recipes ever using one of the most popular kitchen appliances: instant pots.

All the recipes are so easy to make at home and professionals in the field have tested them all.
So, what are you waiting for?
Get your instant pot and start your Ketogenic diet today!

. Copyright 2017 by Vincent Brian All rights reserved.

All rights Reserved. No part of this publication or the information in it may be quoted from or reproduced in any form by means such as printing, scanning, photocopying or otherwise without prior written permission of the copyright holder.

Disclaimer and Terms of Use: Effort has been made to ensure that the information in this book is accurate and complete, however, the author and the publisher do not warrant the accuracy of the information, text and graphics contained within the book due to the rapidly changing nature of science, research, known and unknown facts and internet. The Author and the publisher do not hold any responsibility for errors, omissions or contrary interpretation of the subject matter herein. This book is presented solely for motivational and informational purposes only.

Introduction

You can start a new life today! You can forget about everything you lived before and you can transform into a new person!
Don't worry! You don't need to make significant changes in your life! You don't need to try some magical pills or treatments! You just need to start living healthier!
You only need to adopt a new lifestyle!
We are here to help you make this transformation! We are here to help you become a happier person!

You might be asking yourself how can we help you in this case.
Well, the answer is so simple: you just have to start a Paleo diet!
This wonderful and special diet will soon show you all its benefits: your overall health will improve, your skin will glow and you will be able to lose those extra pounds that bother you so much!
This might sound too good to be true but we can assure you that everything is so simple and real!

A Paleo diet is easy to follow as long as you follow some simple rules.
First of all, you have to forget about processed foods or artificial ingredients.
You have to stop eating products that contain added sugars and salt.
Also, you are not allowed to eat any dairy foods, vegetable oils, beans, legumes and alcohol.

Instead, you can consume a lot of veggies, fruits, organic meats, seafood and fish, nuts and healthy oils.

Now that you know what you are allowed to eat during a Paleo diet, it's time to discover some wonderful Paleo recipes!
This is when things get even better!
We prepared something really special and unique for you! It's not your average Paleo cookbook!
It's a unique one that presents to you the best Paleo dishes made in your instant pot!
All these recipes you are about to discover are easy to make at home and they are full of great tastes and flavors!

So, what do you think?
Are you interested in a Paleo diet?
If you are determined to start a Paleo lifestyle, then you must really get your hands on this great cookbook as well!
We guarantee it's the best choice you'll ever make!

Main Dish Recipes

Butternut And Chard Soup

Preparation time: 10 minutes
Cooking time: 20 minutes
Servings: 6

Ingredients:
- 1 tablespoon olive oil
- 1 yellow onion, chopped
- 3 big carrots, chopped
- 3 celery stalks, chopped
- 4 thyme sprigs
- 8 cups chicken stock
- A pinch of salt and pepper
- 1 teaspoon rosemary, chopped
- 4 cups Swiss chard leaves, chopped
- 2 cups butternut squash, peeled and cubed
- 4 garlic cloves, minced
- 1 cup coconut cream

Directions:
Set your instant pot on sauté mode, add the oil, heat it up, add carrots, onion and celery, stir and sauté for a couple of minutes. Add thyme spring, chicken stock, salt, pepper, butternut squash, garlic and rosemary, stir, cover and cook on High for 18 minutes. Discard thyme, add Swiss chard and coconut cream, stir, set on sauté mode for a couple more minutes, ladle into bowls and serve. Enjoy!

Nutrition: calories 210, fat 3, fiber 1, carbs 5, protein 8

Tender Pork Chops

Preparation time: 10 minutes
Cooking time: 20 minutes
Servings: 4

Ingredients:
- 4 pork chops, boneless
- 1 cup water
- 2 tablespoons olive oil
- 10 ounces Paleo cream of mushroom soup
- 1 cup coconut cream
- A pinch of sea salt and black pepper
- A handful parsley, chopped

Directions:
Set your instant pot on Sauté mode, add oil, heat it up, add pork chops, salt and pepper and brown them for a few minutes. Add water, stir, cover and cook on High for 10 minutes. Transfer pork chops to a platter and leave aside. Set the pot on Simmer mode, heat up the cooking liquid, add mushroom soup, stir, cook for 2 minutes and take off heat. Add parsley and coconut cream and stir. Divide pork chops on plates, drizzle the sauce all over and serve. Enjoy!

Nutrition: calories 244, fat 8, fiber 1, carbs 7, protein 22

Asian Style Salmon

Preparation time: 10 minutes
Cooking time: 4 minutes
Servings: 2

Ingredients:

- 2 salmon fillets, boneless
- 1 cup water
- A pinch of sea salt and black pepper
- 2 tablespoons coconut aminos
- 2 tablespoons maple syrup
- 16 ounces broccoli and cauliflower florets
- 2 tablespoons lemon juice
- 1 teaspoon sesame seeds

Directions:

Put the cauliflower, broccoli florets and salmon in a heat proof dish. In a bowl, mix maple syrup with aminos and lemon juice and whisk well. Pour this over salmon and veggies, season with black pepper to the taste and sprinkle sesame seeds on top. Put the water in your instant pot, add the steamer basket, add the dish with the salmon and veggies, cover and cook on High for 4 minutes. Divide everything between plates and serve. Enjoy!

Nutrition: calories 180, fat 4, fiber 2, carbs 6, protein 5

Creamy Soup

Preparation time: 6 minutes
Cooking time: 15 minutes
Servings: 8

Ingredients:

- 6 bacon slices, cooked and chopped
- 1 pound chicken sausage, ground and cooked
- 1 tablespoon ghee, melted
- 1 cup yellow onion, chopped
- 2 garlic cloves, minced
- 14 ounces chicken stock
- A pinch of sea salt and black pepper
- A pinch of red pepper flakes
- 3 sweet potatoes, chopped
- 2 tablespoons arrowroot powder
- 12 ounces coconut milk
- 2 cups spinach, chopped

Directions:

Put the ghee, onion, garlic, stock, salt, pepper, red pepper flakes and sausage in your instant pot, stir, cover and cook on High for 10 minutes. In a bowl, mix arrowroot powder with coconut milk, whisk and add to the soup. Add spinach, stir, cover and cook on High for 3 minutes more. Add bacon, stir, ladle into bowls and serve. Enjoy!

Nutrition: calories 184, fat 3, fiber 3, carbs 6, protein 8

Easy Tomato Soup

Preparation time: 10 minutes
Cooking time: 15 minutes
Servings: 4

Ingredients:

- 35 oz tomatoes, chopped
- 1 yellow onion, chopped
- 2 garlic cloves, minced
- 1 tablespoon olive oil
- 2 teaspoons thyme, chopped
- 1 tablespoon ghee, melted
- 1 cup veggie stock
- ½ cup coconut cream
- A pinch of sea salt and black pepper

Directions:

Set your instant pot on Sauté mode, add the oil and the ghee and heat up. Add onion and garlic, stir and sauté for 3 minutes. Add tomatoes, thyme, stock, salt and pepper, stir, cover and cook on High for 12 minutes. Add cream, stir, ladle into bowls and serve. Enjoy!

Nutrition: calories 200, fat 1, fiber 3, carbs 5, protein 7

Carrot And Ginger Soup

Preparation time: 10 minutes
Cooking time: 20 minutes
Servings: 4

Ingredients:

- 2 and ½ pounds carrots, chopped
- 2 tablespoons ginger, grated
- 2 tablespoons olive oil
- 2 garlic cloves, minced
- 1 cup yellow onion, chopped
- 4 cups veggie stock
- 4 ounces coconut milk
- 1 cup water
- 3 tablespoons ghee, melted
- Salt and pepper to the taste

Directions:

Put carrots, ginger, olive oil, onion, garlic, veggie stock, water, milk, ghee, salt and pepper in your instant pot, stir, cover and cook on High for 20 minutes. Blend soup using an immersion blender, stir, ladle into bowls and serve. Enjoy!

Nutrition: calories 178, fat 4, fiber 2, carbs 3, protein 5

Red Peppers Soup

Preparation time: 5 minutes
Cooking time: 15 minutes
Servings: 4

Ingredients:

- 6 red bell peppers, sliced
- 2 red onions, chopped
- 2 garlic cloves, minced
- 4 plum tomatoes, sliced
- 1 sweet potato, chopped
- 6 cups chicken stock
- 2 tablespoons olive oil
- A pinch of sea salt and black pepper

Directions:

Set your instant pot on Sauté mode, add the oil and heat it up. Add red peppers, garlic and onion, stir and sauté for 3 minutes Add tomatoes, chicken stock and sweet potato, stir, cover and cook on High for 13 minutes more. Add a pinch of salt and black pepper, stir, ladle into bowls and serve. Enjoy!

Nutrition: calories 193, fat 3, fiber 1, carbs 5, protein 7

Delicious Fish Stew

Preparation time: 10 minutes
Cooking time: 10 minutes
Servings: 8

Ingredients:

- 14 ounces chicken stock
- 4 sweet potatoes, cubed
- 3 carrots, chopped
- 1 yellow onion, chopped
- 2 garlic cloves, minced
- ¼ cup parsley, chopped
- 1 bay leaf
- ¼ teaspoon saffron powder
- 1 pound halibut, boneless and cubed
- 1 red bell pepper, chopped

Directions:

Put the chicken stock in your instant pot, add sweet potatoes, carrots, onion, garlic, saffron, parsley and bay leaf, stir, cover and cook on High for 4 minutes Add fish and red bell pepper, cover and cook on High for 6 minutes more. Discard bay leaf, divide fish stew between plates and serve. Enjoy!

Nutrition: calories 200, fat 3, fiber 1, carbs 5, protein 6

Chicken Stew

Preparation time: 10 minutes
Cooking time: 20 minutes
Servings: 4

Ingredients:

- 3 sweet potatoes, cubed
- 1 yellow onion, cut into medium chunks
- 1 whole chicken, cut into 8 pieces
- 2 bay leaves
- 1 cup water
- 4 tomatoes, cut into medium chunks
- A pinch of sea salt and pepper

Directions:

Put chicken pieces in your instant pot, add sweet potatoes, onions, tomatoes, bay leaves, water, salt and pepper, stir, cover and cook on High for 20 minutes. Divide among plates and serve hot. Enjoy!

Nutrition: calories 200, fat 2, fiber 1, carbs 5, protein 8

Veggie Stew

Preparation time: 10 minutes
Cooking time: 12 minutes
Servings: 4

Ingredients:

- 1 eggplant, chopped
- 1 zucchini, chopped
- 1 yellow squash, peeled and cubed
- 1 red bell pepper, chopped
- 1 and ½ cups tomatoes, chopped
- 1 yellow onion, chopped
- 1 bay leaf
- 1 cup water
- 3 garlic cloves, minced
- 3 tablespoons olive oil
- 2 tablespoons thyme, chopped
- 2 tablespoons parsley, chopped
- ½ cup basil, chopped
- A pinch of salt and black pepper

Directions:

Set your instant pot on Sauté mode, add oil and heat it up. Add onion, garlic, eggplant, zucchini, yellow squash, bell pepper, tomatoes and bay leaf, stir and sauté for a couple of minutes. Add thyme, basil, parsley, salt, pepper and the water, stir, cover and cook on High for 10 minutes. Divide among plates and serve hot. Enjoy!

Nutrition: calories 219, fat 2, fiber 2, carbs 6, protein 10

Special Pork And Sauce

Preparation time: 10 minutes
Cooking time: 1 hour
Servings: 4

Ingredients:

- 1 and ½ pounds pork shoulder, cubed
- 3 garlic cloves, minced
- 1 yellow onion, chopped
- 1 cinnamon stick
- Juice from 1 orange
- ½ cup water
- A pinch of sea salt and black pepper
- 1 tablespoon ginger, grated
- 2 whole cloves
- 1 teaspoon rosemary, dried
- 1 tablespoon maple syrup
- 2 tablespoons coconut aminos
- 1 tablespoon olive oil
- 1 tablespoon honey
- 1 and ½ tablespoons arrowroot powder

Directions:

Set your instant pot on Sauté mode, add the oil, heat it up, add pork, salt and pepper, brown for 5 minutes on each side and transfer to a plate. Add onions, ginger, salt and pepper to the pot, stir and sauté them for 1 minute. Add garlic and sauté for 1 minute more. Add orange juice, water, aminos, honey, maple syrup, cinnamon, cloves, rosemary and return pork, stir, cover and cook on High for 50 minutes. Discard cinnamon and cloves, add arrowroot powder, stir well, set pot on Sauté mode and cook until it thickens. Divide everything between plates and serve.
Enjoy!

Nutrition: calories 240, fat 6, fiber 1, carbs 6, protein 16

Beef Stew

Preparation time: 10 minutes
Cooking time: 25 minutes
Servings: 6

Ingredients:

- 1 tablespoon olive oil
- 2 pound beef chuck, cubed
- 1 teaspoon rosemary, chopped
- 1 yellow onion, chopped
- 2 carrots, chopped
- 1 ounce porcini mushrooms, chopped
- 1 celery stalk, chopped
- 1 and ½ cups beef stock
- A pinch of salt and black pepper
- 2 tablespoons coconut flour
- 2 tablespoons ghee, melted

Directions:

Set your instant pot on Sauté mode, add oil and beef, stir, brown for 5 minutes and mix with onion, celery, rosemary, salt, pepper, carrots, mushrooms and stock. Cover pot, cook on High for 15 minutes and then transfer to Simmer mode. Heat up a pan with the ghee over medium high heat, add flour and 6 tablespoons cooking liquid from the stew, stir and pour over beef stew. Simmer for 5 minutes, divide into bowls and serve. Enjoy!

Nutrition: calories 261, fat 4, fiber 3, carbs 8, protein 18

Cold Veggie Delight

Preparation time: 10 minutes
Cooking time: 10 minutes
Servings: 4

Ingredients:

- ½ cup olive oil
- 1 yellow onion, finely chopped
- 3 tomatoes, chopped
- 1 garlic clove, minced
- ¼ cup parsley, chopped
- ¼ cup dill, chopped
- 1 teaspoon basil, chopped
- 1 cup veggie stock
- 3 sweet potatoes, chopped
- 2 zucchinis, chopped
- 2 carrots, chopped
- 3 celery stalks, chopped
- 1 green bell pepper, thinly sliced
- Salt and black pepper to the taste

Directions:

Set your instant pot on sauté mode, add the oil, heat it up, add onion, stir and cook for 2 minutes. Add parsley, garlic and dill, stir and sauté for 1 minute more. Add stock, basil, tomatoes, zucchinis, sweet potatoes, carrots, green bell pepper, celery, salt and pepper, stir, cover and cook on High for 6 minutes. Divide among plates and serve cold Enjoy!

Nutrition: calories 140, fat 5, fiber 2, carbs 3, protein 8

Mushroom Stew

Preparation time: 10 minutes
Cooking time: 15 minutes
Servings: 4

Ingredients:

- 8 ounces shiitake mushrooms, roughly chopped
- 4 ounces white mushrooms, roughly chopped
- 1 tablespoon ginger, grated
- 1 and ¼ cups veggie stock
- ½ cup red onion, finely chopped
- ½ cup celery, chopped
- ½ cup carrot, chopped
- 5 garlic cloves, minced
- Salt and black pepper to the taste
- ¼ teaspoon oregano, dry
- 28 ounces canned tomatoes, chopped
- 1 and ½ teaspoons turmeric powder
- ¼ cup basil leaves, chopped

Directions:

Set your instant pot on sauté mode, add ¼ cup stock and heat it up. Add mushrooms, onion, celery, carrot, ginger and garlic, stir and sauté for 5 minutes. Add the rest of the stock, tomatoes, salt, pepper, turmeric and oregano, stir, cover and cook on High for 10 minutes. Add basil, divide among plates and serve right away. Enjoy!

Nutrition: calories 70, fat 3, fiber 1, carbs 5, protein 3

Different And Special Stew

Preparation time: 10 minutes
Cooking time: 25 minutes
Servings: 4

Ingredients:
- 1 pound beef, cubed
- 2 bacon slices, cooked and crumbled
- 2 tablespoons olive oil
- ½ cup coconut flour
- 2 cups beef stock
- A pinch of sea salt and black pepper
- 1 cup pearl onions, peeled
- 4 carrots, chopped
- 4 garlic cloves, minced
- 1 tablespoon tomato paste
- ½ cup water
- A small bunch thyme, chopped
- A small bunch rosemary, chopped
- 2 bay leaves

Directions:
In a bowl, mix coconut flour with a pinch of salt and pepper, dredge beef cubes in this mix and place them on a plate Set your instant pot on Sauté mode, add oil, heat up, add meat, brown on all sides and transfer to a clean plate. Add garlic, water, stock, thyme, carrots, tomato paste, rosemary and onions, stir and sauté for a couple of minutes. Return beef to pot, add bay leaves and bacon, cover and cook at High for 20 minutes Discard bay leaves, divide into bowls and serve right away. Enjoy!

Nutrition: calories 298, fat 4, fiber 6, carbs 9, protein 18

Mexican Chicken Soup

Preparation time: 10 minutes
Cooking time: 17 minutes
Servings: 4

Ingredients:
- 4 chicken breasts, skinless and boneless
- 2 tablespoons olive oil
- 16 ounces Paleo salsa
- 1 yellow onion, chopped
- 3 garlic cloves, minced
- 29 ounces canned tomatoes, peeled and chopped
- 29 ounces chicken stock
- A pinch of sea salt and black pepper
- 2 tablespoons parsley, chopped
- 1 teaspoon garlic powder
- 1 tablespoon onion powder
- 1 tablespoon chili powder

Directions:
Set your instant pot on Sauté mode, add oil, heat it up, add onion and garlic, stir and sauté for 5 minutes. Add chicken breasts, salsa, tomatoes, stock, salt, pepper, parsley, garlic powder, onion and chili powder, stir, cover and cook at High for 8 minutes. Transfer chicken breasts to a cutting board, shred, return to pot, stir, and set the pot on Simmer mode, cook soup for 3 minutes more, ladle into bowls and serve. Enjoy!

Nutrition: calories 210, fat 3, fiber 4, carbs 7, protein 14

Creamy Carrot Soup

Preparation time: 10 minutes
Cooking time: 15 minutes
Servings: 4

Ingredients:
- 1 tablespoon olive oil
- 1 yellow onion, chopped
- 1 tablespoon ghee
- 1 garlic clove, minced
- 1 pound carrots, chopped
- 1 inch ginger piece, grated
- A pinch of sea salt and black pepper
- ¼ teaspoon stevia
- 2 cups chicken stock
- 14 ounces canned coconut milk
- A handful cilantro, chopped

Directions:
Set your instant pot on Sauté mode, add ghee and oil, heat up, add onion, garlic and ginger, stir and sauté for 4 minutes. Add carrots, stevia, salt and pepper, stir and cook 2 minutes more. Add coconut milk and stock, stir, cover and cook at High for 6 minutes. Blend soup using an immersion blender, add cilantro, stir gently, ladle into bowls and serve. Enjoy!

Nutrition: calories 84, fat 2, fiber 3, carbs 8, protein 9

Cauliflower Soup

Preparation time: 10 minutes
Cooking time: 30 minutes
Servings: 8

Ingredients:
- ½ teaspoon cumin seeds
- 1 tablespoon ginger, grated
- 3 garlic cloves, minced
- 1 yellow onion, chopped
- 1 chili pepper, minced
- A pinch of cinnamon powder
- 4 cups veggie stock
- 3 cups water
- 1 pound sweet potatoes, peeled and cubed
- 1 tablespoon curry powder
- 1 cauliflower head, florets separated
- 15 ounces canned tomatoes, chopped
- A pinch of sea salt and cayenne pepper
- 1 tablespoon cashew butter

Directions:
Set your instant pot on sauté mode, add onions, stir and brown for a couple of minutes. Add ginger, cumin seeds, chili and garlic, stir and cook 1 minute more. Add potatoes, stock, curry powder and cinnamon, stir, cover and cook on High for 16 minutes. Add tomatoes, cauliflower, the water, salt and cayenne, stir, cover and cook on High for 10 more minutes. Add cashews butter, stir, ladle into bowls and serve hot. Enjoy!

Nutrition: calories 113, fat 1, fiber 3, carbs 6, protein 6

Cod Fillets And Orange Sauce

Preparation time: 10 minutes
Cooking time: 10 minutes
Servings: 4

Ingredients:

- 4 spring onions, chopped
- 1 inch ginger piece, grated
- 1 tablespoon olive oil
- 4 cod fillets, boneless and skinless
- Juice from 1 orange
- Zest from 1 orange, grated
- A pinch of salt and black pepper
- 1 cup veggie stock

Directions:

Season cod with salt and pepper, rub them with oil and leave aside for now. Put ginger, orange juice, orange zest, onions and stock in your instant pot, add the steamer basket, place the fish inside, cover the pot and cook on High for 10 minutes. Divide fish on plates, top with the orange sauce from the pot and serve right away. Enjoy!

Nutrition: calories 187, fat 3, fiber 2, carbs 4, protein 6

Special Cod Dish

Preparation time: 5 minutes
Cooking time: 10 minutes
Servings: 4

Ingredients:

- 1 garlic clove, minced
- 1 tablespoon olive oil
- 1 cup water
- 17 ounces cherry tomatoes, halved
- 4 cod fillets, boneless and skinless
- 2 tablespoons capers, chopped
- 1 cup black olives, pitted and chopped
- A pinch of sea salt and black pepper
- 1 tablespoon parsley, finely chopped

Directions:

In a heat proof dish, mix tomatoes with salt, pepper, parsley, oil, fish, olives, capers and garlic and toss to coat. Put the water in your instant pot, add the steamer basket, place the dish inside, cover and cook on High for 8 minutes. Divide fish mix between plates and serve. Enjoy!

Nutrition: calories 187, fat 3, fiber 3, carbs 6, protein 7

Light Salmon

Preparation time: 5 minutes
Cooking time: 5 minutes
Servings: 4

Ingredients:

- 4 medium salmon fillets, boneless and skin on
- 1 bay leaf
- 1 teaspoon fennel seeds
- 4 scallions, chopped
- Zest from 1 lemon, grated
- 1 teaspoon balsamic vinegar
- 3 peppercorns
- ¼ cup dill, chopped
- 2 cups chicken stock
- A pinch of sea salt and black pepper

Directions:

In your instant pot, mix scallions with stock, peppercorns, lemon zest, vinegar, fennel, wine, dill and bay leaf, stir, add the steamer basket and place salmon fillets inside. Season with a pinch of salt and pepper, cover and cook on High for 5 minutes. Divide fish fillets between plates and leave them aside. Set the pot on Simmer more, cook the sauce for a couple more minutes, drizzle over salmon and serve right away. Enjoy!

Nutrition: calories 187, fat 3, fiber 3, carbs 6, protein 7

Wonderful Salmon And Veggies

Preparation time: 10 minutes
Cooking time: 10 minutes
Servings: 2

Ingredients:

- 1 cinnamon stick
- 1 tablespoon olive oil
- 1 cup water
- 2 salmon fillets, boneless and skin on
- 1 bay leaf
- 3 cloves
- 2 cups broccoli florets
- 1 cup baby carrots
- A pinch of sea salt and black pepper
- Some lime wedges for serving

Directions:

Put the water in your instant pot and add cinnamon, cloves and bay leaf. Add the steamer basket, place salmon inside, season with salt and pepper, brush it with the oil and mix with carrots and broccoli. Cover instant pot and cook on High for 6 minutes. Divide salmon and veggies on plates, discard bay leaf, cloves and cinnamon, drizzle the sauce from the pot and serve with lime wedges on the side. Enjoy!

Nutrition: calories 172, fat 3, fiber 1, carbs 2, protein 3

White Fish Delight

Preparation time: 5 minutes
Cooking time: 25 minutes
Servings: 6

Ingredients:

- 1 yellow onion, chopped
- 6 white fish fillets, cut into medium cubes
- A pinch of salt and black pepper
- 13 ounces sweet potatoes, peeled and cubed
- 13 ounces coconut milk
- 14 ounces chicken stock
- 14 ounces coconut cream
- 14 ounces water

Directions:

Put potatoes, fish, onion, milk, stock and water in your instant pot, stir, cover and cook on High for 10 minutes Set your instant pot on Simmer more, add coconut cream, salt and pepper, stir and cook for 10 minutes more. Divide this into serving bowls and serve. Enjoy!

Nutrition: calories 254, fat 3, fiber 2, carbs 5, protein 12

Healthy Mackerel

Preparation time: 10 minutes
Cooking time: 6 minutes
Servings: 4

Ingredients:

- 8 shallots, chopped
- 1 teaspoon shrimp powder
- 3 garlic cloves, minced
- 18 ounces mackerel, boneless and chopped
- 1 teaspoon turmeric powder
- 2 lemongrass sticks, halved
- 1 tablespoon chili paste
- 1 inch ginger, grated
- 4 ounces water
- 5 tablespoons olive oil
- 6 laska leaves stalks
- 1 tablespoon stevia
- A pinch of salt

Directions:

In a food processor, mix chili paste with shrimp powder, shallots and turmeric and blend well. Set your instant pot on Sauté mode, add the oil, heat it up, add the paste you've made, mackerel,, lemon grass, laska leaves, ginger, salt and stevia, stir and sauté for 1 minute. Add water, stir, cover and cook on High for 5 minutes Divide fish mix between plates and serve. Enjoy!

Nutrition: calories 212, fat 2, fiber 1, carbs 3, protein 7

Fast Mussels

Preparation time: 5 minutes
Cooking time: 5 minutes
Servings: 4

Ingredients:
- 1 yellow onion, chopped
- 1 radicchio, chopped
- 2 pounds mussels, scrubbed and debearded
- 1 pound baby spinach
- 1 garlic clove, minced
- 1 cup water
- A drizzle of olive oil
- A pinch of sea salt and black pepper

Directions:

Set your instant pot on Sauté mode, add the oil, heat it up, add onion and garlic, stir and sauté them for 2 minutes. Add water, salt and pepper, stir, add the steamer basket, place mussels inside, cover and cook on High for 3 minutes Arrange spinach and radicchio on a platter, add mussels, drizzle the juices from the pot and serve. Enjoy!

Nutrition: calories 192, fat 2, fiber 1, carbs 2, protein 3

Simple Octopus

Preparation time: 5 minutes
Cooking time: 35 minutes
Servings: 6

Ingredients:
- 4 sweet potatoes
- 2 pound octopus, head discarded, tentacles separated
- 1 bay leaf
- ½ teaspoon peppercorns
- 3 garlic cloves
- 4 cups water
- 2 tablespoons parsley, chopped
- 2 tablespoons olive oil
- A pinch of sea salt and black pepper
- 5 tablespoons vinegar

Directions:

Put 2 cups water in your instant pot, add sweet potatoes, stir, cover and cook on High for 15 minutes. Transfer potatoes to a bowl, cool them down, peeled and chop them. Clean your instant pot, add octopus, 2 cups water, 1 garlic clove, bay leaf, a pinch of salt and peppercorns, stir, cover and cook on High for 20 minutes. Drain octopus, chop and add this to the bowl with the potatoes. In a separate bowl, mix the rest of the garlic with oil, vinegar, a pinch of salt and pepper and whisk well. Add this to your salad, sprinkle parsley, toss to coat and serve. Enjoy!

Nutrition: calories 200, fat 2, fiber 2, carbs 3, protein 3

Easy Artichoke Soup

Preparation time: 10 minutes
Cooking time: 20 minutes
Servings: 4

Ingredients:
- 5 artichoke hearts, washed and trimmed
- 1 leek, sliced
- 5 garlic cloves, minced
- 4 tablespoons ghee, melted
- ½ cup shallots, chopped
- 8 ounces sweet potatoes, peeled and cubed
- 12 cups chicken stock
- 1 bay leaf
- A pinch of sea salt
- 4 parsley sprigs
- 2 thyme sprigs
- ¼ teaspoon black peppercorns, crushed
- ¼ cup coconut cream

Directions:
Set your instant pot on Sauté mode, add ghee, melt it, add artichoke hearts, shallots, leek and garlic, stir and sauté for 3-4 minutes. Add potatoes, stock, bay leaf, thyme, parsley, peppercorns and salt, stir, cover and cook at High for 15 minutes. Discard herbs, blend using an immersion blender, add cream, stir well, ladle into bowls and serve. Enjoy!

Nutrition: calories 97, fat 2, fiber 3, carbs 7, protein 4

Incredible Beet Soup

Preparation time: 10 minutes
Cooking time: 10 minutes
Servings: 4

Ingredients:
- 1 tablespoon olive oil
- 1 red onion, chopped
- 2 carrots, chopped
- 3 beets, chopped
- 3 bay leaves
- 6 cups veggie stock
- ½ teaspoon thyme leaves, chopped
- 1 and ½ tablespoons parsley, chopped
- Salt and black pepper to the taste

Directions:
Set your instant pot on Sauté mode, add oil, heat it up, add onion, stir and cook for 5 minutes. Add carrots, beets, thyme, bay leaves, stock, salt and pepper, stir, cover and cook at High for 5 minutes. Discard bay leaves, blend using an immersion blender, add parsley, stir, divide into soup bowls and serve. Enjoy!

Nutrition: calories 100, fat 2, fiber 1, carbs 3, protein 3

Refreshing Fennel Soup

Preparation time: 10 minutes
Cooking time: 15 minutes
Servings: 3

Ingredients:
- 1 fennel bulb, chopped
- 1 leek, chopped
- 1 tablespoon olive oil
- 1 bay leaf
- 2 cups water
- ½ cube Italian seasoning
- A pinch of sea salt and black pepper
- 2 teaspoons cashew cheese, grated

Directions:
In your instant pot, mix fennel with leek, bay leaf, seasoning and water, stir, cover and cook on High for 15 minutes Add cheese, oil, salt and pepper, stir, divide into bowls and serve. Enjoy!

Nutrition: calories 100, fat 2, fiber 2, carbs 5, protein 6

Unbelievable Chicken

Preparation time: 10 minutes
Cooking time: 10 minutes
Servings: 2

Ingredients:
- 2 tomatoes, chopped
- 2 red onions, chopped
- 2 chicken breasts, boneless and skinless
- 1 tablespoon maple syrup
- 2 garlic cloves, minced
- 1 teaspoon chili powder
- 1 teaspoon basil, dried
- 1 cup water
- 1 teaspoon cloves

Directions:
In your instant pot, mix onion with tomatoes, chicken, garlic, maple syrup, chili powder, basil, water and cloves, toss well, cover and cook on High for 10 minutes Shred chicken and divide among plates and serve with a side salad Enjoy!

Nutrition: calories 200, fat 3, fiber 3, carbs 5, protein 5

Flavored And Delicious Chicken

Preparation time: 10 minutes
Cooking time: 12 minutes
Servings: 4

Ingredients:

- 4 chicken breasts, skinless and boneless
- ½ cup water
- 16 ounces Paleo salsa
- 1 and ½ tablespoons parsley, chopped
- ½ tablespoon cilantro, chopped
- ½ tablespoon oregano, dried
- 1 teaspoon garlic powder
- 1 teaspoon onion powder
- ½ teaspoon smoked paprika
- 1 teaspoon chili powder
- ½ teaspoon cumin, ground
- Black pepper to the taste

Directions:

Put the water in your instant pot, add chicken breasts, salsa, parsley, garlic powder, cilantro, onion powder, oregano, paprika, chili powder, cumin and black pepper, stir, cover and cook on High for 12 minutes Divide chicken on plates, drizzle the sauces on top and serve. Enjoy!

Nutrition: calories 200, fat 4, fiber 2, carbs 5, protein 12

Superb Stuffed Tomatoes

Preparation time: 10 minutes
Cooking time: 10 minutes
Servings: 4

Ingredients:

- 4 tomatoes, tops cut off, pulp scooped out and chopped
- 1 tablespoon ghee
- A pinch of salt and black pepper
- 1 yellow onion, chopped
- 2 tablespoons celery, chopped
- ½ cup mushrooms, chopped
- 1 tablespoon flax meal
- 1 cup almond cream cheese
- ¼ teaspoon caraway seeds
- 1 tablespoon parsley, chopped
- ½ cup water

Directions:

Set your instant pot on sauté mode, add the ghee, heat it up, add onion and celery, stir and cook for 3 minutes. Add tomato pulp and mushrooms, stir and cook for 1 minute more. Add salt, pepper, flax meal, almond cheese, caraway seeds and parsley, stir, cook for 4 minutes more and stuff tomatoes with this mix. Clean your instant pot, add the water, also add the steamer basket, place tomatoes inside, cover and cook at High for 2 minutes. Divide stuffed tomatoes on plates and serve. Enjoy!

Nutrition: calories 142, fat 2, fiber 1, carbs 3, protein 7

Sweet Potato Salad

Preparation time: 10 minutes
Cooking time: 10 minutes
Servings: 6

Ingredients:
- 1 yellow onion, chopped
- 6 sweet potatoes
- 1 celery stalk, chopped
- 1 cup water
- A pinch of salt and black pepper
- 3 teaspoons dill, chopped
- 1 teaspoon mustard
- 1 teaspoon cider vinegar
- 3 ounces Paleo mayonnaise

Directions:
Put potatoes in your instant pot, add the water, cover and cook on High for 3 minutes. Leave potatoes to cool down, peel, chop and put them in a salad bowl. Add onion, celery, salt, pepper and dill and toss. In a small bowl, mix mayo with vinegar and mustard and whisk well. Add this to the salad, toss to coat and serve. Enjoy!

Nutrition: calories 140, fat 2, fiber 1 carbs 2, protein 4

Beef Soup

Preparation time: 10 minutes
Cooking time: 15 minutes
Servings: 6

Ingredients:
- 1 pound beef, ground
- 3 garlic cloves, minced
- 1 yellow onion, chopped
- 1 tablespoon olive oil
- 1 celery rib, chopped
- 28 ounces beef stock
- 14 ounces canned tomatoes, crushed
- 12 ounces tomato juice
- 1 sweet potato, peeled and cubed
- Salt and black pepper to the taste
- 2 carrots, sliced

Directions:
Set your instant pot on Sauté mode, add beef, stir, brown and transfer to a plate. Add the oil to your pot, heat it up, add celery, garlic and onion, stir and sauté for 6 minutes. Add tomato juice, stock, tomatoes, carrots, potatoes, beef, salt and pepper, stir, cover, cook on High for 5 minutes, ladle into bowls and serve. Enjoy!

Nutrition: calories 212, fat 2, fiber 3, carbs 6, protein 3

Rich Beef Stew

Preparation time: 10 minutes
Cooking time: 30 minutes
Servings: 8

Ingredients:
- 1 tablespoon olive oil
- 2 pounds beef, cubed
- 1 yellow onion, chopped
- 5 carrots, chopped
- 4 sweet potatoes, peeled cubed
- 2 teaspoons arrowroot powder
- A pinch of sea salt and black pepper
- 2 cups water

Directions:
Set your instant pot on Sauté mode, add oil, heat it up, add beef and onion, stir and sauté for a couple of minutes Add carrots, water, potatoes, salt and pepper, stir, cover and cook on Medium for 20 minutes. Add arrowroot powder, set the pot on Simmer mode, cook for a few minutes more, divide into bowls and serve. яяEnjoy!

Nutrition: calories 273, fat 4, fiber 2, carbs 6, protein 17

Perfect Chicken Stew

Preparation time: 10 minutes
Cooking time: 35 minutes
Servings: 6

Ingredients:
- 6 chicken thighs
- 1 teaspoon olive oil
- A pinch of sea salt and black pepper
- 1 yellow onion, chopped
- ¼ pound baby carrots, sliced
- 1 celery stalk, chopped
- ½ teaspoon thyme, dried
- 2 tablespoons tomato paste
- 2 cups chicken stock
- 15 ounces canned tomatoes, chopped
- 1 pound sweet potatoes, peeled and cubed

Directions:
Set your instant pot on Sauté mode, add oil, heat it up, add chicken, salt and pepper, brown for 4 minutes on each side and transfer to a plate. Add celery, onion, tomato paste, carrots, thyme, salt and pepper to your instant pot, stir and sauté for 5 minutes. Add stock, return chicken, add tomatoes and potatoes, stir, cover and cook on High for 15 minutes. Transfer chicken pieces to a cutting board, leave aside to cool down for a few minutes, discard bones, shred meat and return it to the stew. Stir, divide into bowls and serve hot. Enjoy!

Nutrition: calories 251, fat 2, fiber 3, carbs 7, protein 13

Turkey Stew

Preparation time: 10 minutes
Cooking time: 10 minutes
Servings: 4

Ingredients:

- 1 pound turkey meat, ground
- 5 ounces water
- A pinch of salt and cayenne pepper
- 1 yellow onion, chopped
- 1 yellow bell pepper, chopped
- 3 garlic cloves, minced
- 2 and ½ tablespoons chili powder
- 1 and ½ teaspoons cumin, ground
- 12 ounces veggies stock

Directions:

Put turkey meat in your instant pot, add water, stir, cover and cook on High for 5 minutes. Add bell pepper, onion, garlic, chili powder, cumin, salt, cayenne and veggie stock, stir, cover again and cook on High for 5 minutes more. Divide it between plates and serve right away. Enjoy!

Nutrition: calories 212, fat 3, fiber 4, carbs 6, protein 14

Special Turkey Wings

Preparation time: 10 minutes
Cooking time: 20 minutes
Servings: 4

Ingredients:

- 4 turkey wings
- 2 tablespoons ghee, melted
- 2 tablespoons olive oil
- 1 and ½ cups cranberries, dried
- 1 cup walnuts
- A pinch of sea salt and black pepper
- 1 yellow onion, roughly chopped
- 1 cup orange juice
- 1 bunch thyme, chopped

Directions:

Set your instant pot on Sauté mode, add ghee and oil, heat up, add turkey wings, salt and pepper, brown on all sides and transfer to a plate. Add onion, walnuts, cranberries and thyme to the pot, stir and cook for 2 minutes. Add orange juice, return turkey wings to pot, stir, cover and cook on High for 20 minutes. Divide turkey wings between plates and keep warm. Set instant pot on Simmer mode, cook cranberry mix for 5 minutes more, drizzle over turkey wings and serve. Enjoy!

Nutrition: calories 232, fat 4, fiber 2, carbs 6, protein 15

Flavored Chicken And Veggies

Preparation time: 10 minutes
Cooking time: 25 minutes
Servings: 4

Ingredients:

- 3 garlic cloves, minced
- 2 tablespoons olive oil
- 3 bird's eye chilies, chopped
- 1 inch piece ginger, grated
- 2 tablespoons green curry paste
- A pinch of cumin, ground
- ¼ teaspoon coriander, ground
- 14 ounces coconut milk
- 6 cups squash, peeled and cubed
- 1 eggplant, cubed
- 8 chicken pieces
- A pinch of sea salt and black pepper
- 1 tablespoon coconut aminos
- 4 cups spinach, chopped
- ½ cup cilantro, chopped
- ½ cup basil, chopped

Directions:

Set your instant pot on Sauté mode, add oil, heat it up, add garlic, ginger, chilies, cumin and coriander, stir and cook for 1 minute. Add curry paste and coconut milk, stir and cook 4 minutes. Add chicken, squash, eggplant, salt and pepper, stir, cover and cook at High for 20 minutes. Add spinach, aminos, basil and cilantro, stir, divide among plates and serve. Enjoy!

Nutrition: calories 152, fat 3, fiber 3, carbs 6, protein 8

Crazy Carrots Casserole

Preparation time: 10 minutes
Cooking time: 10 minutes
Servings: 4

Ingredients:

- 3 tablespoons olive oil
- 3 tablespoons flax meal
- 1 teaspoon lemon juice
- 1 and ¾ cup water
- 1 tablespoon parsley, chopped
- 1 pound carrots, cut into thin matchsticks
- 1 pound broccoli florets
- A pinch of salt and black pepper

Directions:

In a bowl mix, parsley, flax meal and lemon juice, stir well and leave aside for now. Put carrots, broccoli, salt, pepper and the water in your instant pot, cover and cook on High for 10 minutes. Drain veggies, transfer them to plates, sprinkle flax meal mix all over and serve. Enjoy!

Nutrition: calories 170, fat 2, fiber 2, carbs 7, protein 13

Rich Cabbage Salad

Preparation time: 5 minutes
Cooking time: 5 minutes
Servings: 4

Ingredients:
- 2 cups red cabbage, shredded
- ½ cup water
- A pinch of sea salt and black pepper
- 1 tablespoon olive oil
- ¼ cup white onion, chopped
- 2 teaspoons balsamic vinegar
- ½ teaspoon maple syrup

Directions:
Put shredded cabbage and the water in your instant pot, cover and cook on High for 5 minutes. Drain cabbage, transfer it to a salad bowl, add salt, pepper, onion, oil, maple syrup and vinegar, toss to coat and serve right away.
Enjoy!

Nutrition: calories 110, fat 1, fiber 2, carbs 4, protein 1

Tomato Stew

Preparation time: 10 minutes
Cooking time: 10 minutes
Servings: 4

Ingredients:
- 1 tablespoon olive oil
- 2 garlic cloves, minced
- 1 pound green beans
- A pinch of sea salt
- 14 ounces canned tomatoes, chopped
- 1 tablespoon basil, chopped

Directions:
Set the instant pot on Sauté mode, add oil, heat it up, add garlic, stir and cook for 2 minutes. Add tomatoes, green beans and salt, cover pot and cook on High for 5 minutes. Sprinkle basil, toss, divide among plates and serve. Enjoy!

Nutrition: calories 60, fat 3, fiber 1, carbs 3, protein 6

Colored Tomato And Zucchini

Preparation time: 10 minutes
Cooking time: 10 minutes
Servings: 3

Ingredients:

- 1 tablespoon olive oil
- 1 pound colored cherry tomatoes, halved
- 2 yellow onions, chopped
- 1 cup tomato puree
- A pinch of salt and black pepper
- 2 garlic cloves, minced
- 6 zucchinis, roughly chopped
- A drizzle of olive oil
- 1 bunch basil, chopped

Directions:

Set your instant pot on Sauté mode, add the oil, heat it up, add onions, stir and cook for 5 minutes. Add zucchini, tomatoes, salt, pepper and tomato puree, stir, cover and cook on High for 5 minutes. Add garlic and basil, drizzle some olive oil, toss to coat, divide among plates and serve. Enjoy!

Nutrition: calories 70, fat 1, fiber 2, carbs 6, protein 7

Easy And Delicious Zucchini Pasta

Preparation time: 10 minutes
Cooking time: 20 minutes
Servings: 5

Ingredients:

- 15 ounces zucchini noodles
- 1 yellow onion, chopped
- 2 garlic cloves, minced
- 12 mushrooms, sliced
- 1 shallot, chopped
- A pinch of basil, dried
- A pinch of oregano, dried
- A pinch of salt and black pepper
- 1 tablespoon olive oil
- 1 cup veggie stock
- 2 cups water
- 5 ounces tomato paste
- 2 tablespoons coconut aminos

Directions:

Set your instant pot on Sauté mode, add oil, heat it up, add shallot, garlic, onion, a pinch of salt and pepper, stir and cook for 4 minutes. Add mushrooms, basil and oregano, stir and cook 1 more minute. Add veggie stock, water, tomato paste and aminos, stir, cover and cook on High for 5 minutes Divide zucchini noodles on plates, add mushroom mix on top and serve. Enjoy!

Nutritional value: calories 150, fat 1, fiber 1, carbs 4, protein 3

Easy And Delicious Salad

Preparation time: 10 minutes
Cooking time: 30 minutes
Servings: 4

Ingredients:
- 4 beets
- 1 cup water
- 2 tablespoons balsamic vinegar
- A bunch of parsley, chopped
- A pinch of salt and black pepper
- 1 tablespoon olive oil
- 1 garlic clove, minced
- 2 tablespoons capers, drained

Directions:
Put the water in your instant pot, add the steamer basket, place beets inside, cover and cook on High for 15 minutes. Transfer beets to a cutting board, cool them down, peel and cube them. In a bowl, mix parsley with garlic, salt, pepper, olive oil and capers and stir. Add beets and vinegar, toss and serve. Enjoy!

Nutrition: calories 50, fat 2, fiber 1, carbs 2, protein 1

Shrimp Delight

Preparation time: 5 minutes
Cooking time: 3 minutes
Servings: 4

Ingredients:
- 1 cup water
- 1 teaspoon olive oil
- 1 pound shrimp, peeled and deveined
-
- 1 bunch asparagus spears, trimmed
- ½ tablespoon Italian seasoning

Directions:
Put the water in your instant pot, add the steamer basket, add asparagus and shrimp inside, drizzle oil, sprinkle Italian seasoning, cover and cook on High for 3 minutes. Divide everything between plates and serve. Enjoy!

Nutrition: calories 142, fat 1, fiber 2, carbs 4, protein 6

Easy Asparagus And Prosciutto Dish

Preparation time: 5 minutes
Cooking time: 4 minutes
Servings: 4

Ingredients:
- 1 pound asparagus spears, trimmed
- 8 ounces prosciutto slices
- 2 cups water
- A pinch of salt

Directions:
Wrap each asparagus spears in prosciutto slices. Put 2 cups water in your instant pot, add the steamer basket, arrange wrapped asparagus inside, season with a pinch of salt, cover and cook at High for 4 minutes. Divide wrapped asparagus on plates and serve. Enjoy!

Nutrition: calories 65, fat 1, fiber 1, carbs 2, protein 2

Special Artichokes

Preparation time: 10 minutes
Cooking time: 18 minutes
Servings: 2

Ingredients:
- 2 artichokes, washed and trimmed
- 1 bay leaf
- 1 cup water
- 2 garlic cloves, minced
- 1 lemon, halved
- ¼ cup coconut oil
- ¼ cup extra virgin olive oil
- 3 anchovy fillets
- 3 garlic cloves

For the sauce:

Directions:
Put the water in your instant pot, add the steamer basket, place artichokes, lemon halves, 2 minced garlic cloves and bay leaf inside, cover and cook on High for 18 minutes. In your food processor, mix coconut oil with anchovy, 3 garlic cloves and olive oil and pulse well. Divide artichokes and lemon halves on plates, drizzle the anchovy mix you've just made and serve. Enjoy!

Nutrition: calories 232, fat 1, fiber 3, carbs 6, protein 12

Shrimp Surprise

Preparation time: 10 minutes
Cooking time: 4 minutes
Servings: 4

Ingredients:
- 1 pound shrimp, cooked, peeled and deveined
- 2 tablespoons olive oil
- 1 garlic clove, minced
- ¼ teaspoon oregano, dried
- 1 tablespoon parsley, chopped
- 1/3 cup water
- 10 ounces canned tomatoes, chopped
- 1/3 cup tomato paste

Directions:
Set your instant pot on Sauté mode, add oil, heat it up, add garlic, stir and brown for 2 minutes. Add shrimp, tomato paste, tomatoes, water, oregano and parsley, stir, cover and cook at High for 3 minutes. Divide among plates and serve with a side salad. Enjoy!

Nutrition: calories 232, fat 3, fiber 0, carbs 0, protein 7

Simple Artichoke Dish

Preparation time: 30 minutes
Cooking time: 10 minutes
Servings: 4

Ingredients:
- 4 big artichokes, washed and trimmed
- 2 cups water
- A pinch of sea salt and black pepper
- 2 tablespoons lemon juice
- ¼ cup olive oil
- 2 teaspoons balsamic vinegar
- 1 teaspoon oregano, dried
- 2 garlic cloves, minced

Directions:
Put 2 cups water in your instant pot, add the steamer basket, add artichokes inside, cover and cook on High for 10 minutes. In a bowl, mix lemon juice with vinegar, oil, salt, pepper, garlic and oregano and whisk very well. Divide artichokes on plates, drizzle the vinegar dressing all over and leave aside for 30 minutes before serving. Enjoy!

Nutrition: calories 132, fat 2, fiber 1, carbs 2, protein 5

Snacks And Appetizers Recipes

Special Party Spread

Preparation time: 10 minutes
Cooking time: 40 minutes
Servings: 4

Ingredients:
- 4 tablespoons sesame seeds paste
- 5 tablespoons olive oil
- 1 cup veggie stock
- 1 cauliflower head, florets separated
- 1 small eggplant, chopped
- 1 red bell pepper, chopped
- 4 tablespoons lemon juice
- 1 teaspoon garlic powder
- Black pepper to the taste
- ½ teaspoon cumin, ground

Directions:
Set your instant pot on sauté mode, add oil, heat it up, add cauliflower, eggplant and bell pepper, stir and sauté for 4 minutes. Add stock, cumin, garlic powder and black pepper, stir, cover and cook on High for 6 minutes. Transfer veggies to a blender, leave them to cool down a bit, add lemon juice and sesame seeds paste and pulse really well. Transfer to small bowls and serve with veggie matchsticks on the side. Enjoy!

Nutrition: calories 90, fat 1, fiber 2, carbs 4, protein 3

Red Pepper Spread

Preparation time: 10 minutes
Cooking time: 15 minutes
Servings: 8

Ingredients:
- 4 cups water
- 6 big red bell peppers, deseeded
- A pinch of salt
- 2 garlic cloves, roasted and minced
- 3 tablespoons olive oil
- A pinch of cumin, ground
- ½ cup lemon juice
- 1 cup sesame seeds, toasted

Directions:
Put bell peppers in your instant pot, add the water, cover and cook on High for 15 minutes. Drain, transfer them to your blender, add a pinch of salt, garlic, oil, cumin, lemon juice and sesame seeds and pulse really well. Divide into bowls and serve as a party spread. Enjoy!

Nutrition: calories 80, fat 1, fiber 2, carbs 2, protein 2

Onions Delight

Preparation time: 10 minutes
Cooking time: 25 minutes
Servings: 6

Ingredients:

- 12 red onions, peeled, tops cut off and insides scooped out
- 2 cups veggie stock
- 4 cups water
- 5 sweet potatoes, chopped
- 1 tablespoon flaxseed mixed well with 2 tablespoons water
- 3 tablespoons thyme, chopped
- A pinch of sea salt and black pepper

Directions:
Put sweet potatoes in your instant pot, add 2 water, cover, cook on High for 15 minutes, drain, transfer them to a bowl and mash well. Add flaxseed, salt, pepper and thyme, stir and stuff each onion with this mix. Add the rest of the water and the stock to your instant pot, add steamer basket as well and arrange stuffed onions inside. Cover and cook on High for 10 minutes more. Divide among a platter and serve as an appetizer. Enjoy!

Nutrition: calories 110, fat 1, fiber 2, carbs 2, protein 4

Special And Delicious Snack

Preparation time: 10 minutes
Cooking time: 5 minutes
Servings: 4

Ingredients:

- 1 and ½ pounds Brussels sprouts, halved
- 1 tablespoon white pepper
- 3 tablespoons coconut aminos
- 2 tablespoons balsamic vinegar
- 2 tablespoons olive oil
- 2 garlic cloves, minced

Directions:
Set your instant pot on Sauté mode, add the oil, heat it up, add the garlic, stir and cook for 1 minute. Add Brussels sprouts, coconut aminos, vinegar and the white pepper, toss to coat, cover and cook on High for 5 minutes. Transfer sprouts to a bowl and serve as a snack. Enjoy!

Nutritional value: calories 50, fat 0, fiber 3, carbs 3, protein 4

Carrot Snack

Preparation time: 5 minutes
Cooking time: 5 minutes
Servings: 6

Ingredients:

- 2 pounds carrots, halved and sliced
- 1 tablespoon maple syrup
- 1 tablespoon olive oil
- 1 cup water
- Black pepper to the taste
- ¼ cup raisins

Directions:
Put the carrots, raisins and the water in your instant pot, cover and cook on Low for 5 minutes. Drain carrots, transfer them to a bowl, add maple syrup, black pepper and oil, toss and serve as a snack. Enjoy!

Nutritional value: calories 40, fat 1, fiber 2, carbs 3, protein 3

Crab Appetizer

Preparation time: 5 minutes
Cooking time: 4 minutes
Servings: 4

Ingredients:

- 4 pounds crab legs, halved
- 3 lemon wedges
- ¼ cup ghee, melted
- 1 cup water

Directions:
Put the water in your instant pot, add the steamer basket, add crab legs, cover and cook on High for 4 minutes. Transfer crab legs to a platter, drizzle melted ghee and serve as an appetizer with lemon wedges on the side. Enjoy!

Nutrition: calories 40, fat 1, fiber 0, carbs 0, protein 3

Appetizer Meatballs

Preparation time: 10 minutes
Cooking time: 15 minutes
Servings: 4

Ingredients:

- 1 and ½ pounds beef, ground
- 1 egg, whisked
- 2 garlic cloves, minced
- 16 ounces tomatoes, crushed
- 14 ounces tomato puree
- ¼ cup parsley, chopped
- 1 yellow onion, chopped
- Black pepper to the taste

Directions:
In a bowl, mix beef with egg, parsley, garlic, black pepper and onion, stir and shape 16 meatballs. Put tomato puree and crushed tomatoes in your instant pot, add meatballs, cover and cook on High for 15 minutes. Arrange them on a platter and serve as an appetizer. Enjoy!

Nutrition: calories 130, fat 3, fiber 2, carbs 6, protein 6

Chicken Appetizer

Preparation time: 10 minutes
Cooking time: 15 minutes
Servings: 6

Ingredients:

- 2 tablespoons garlic, minced
- 3 pounds chicken wings
- 3 tablespoons coconut aminos
- 2 and ¼ cups pineapple juice
- 1 teaspoon olive oil
- 2 tablespoons almond flour
- 1 tablespoon ginger, grated
- A pinch of sea salt
- A pinch of red pepper flakes, crushed
- 2 tablespoons 5 spice powder
- Sesame seeds, toasted for serving

Directions:
Put 2 cups pineapple juice in your instant pot, add oil, a pinch of salt, coconut aminos, ginger and garlic and whisk well. In a bowl, mix almond flour with the rest of the pineapple juice, whisk and also add to your instant pot. Add chicken wings, a pinch of red pepper flakes and 5 spice, stir, cover and cook on High for 15 minutes. Transfer chicken wings to a platter, sprinkle sesame seeds on top and serve as an appetizer with the juices from the pot on the side Enjoy!

Nutrition: calories 200, fat 4, fiber 3, carbs 4, protein 12

Fish Delight

Preparation time: 10 minutes
Cooking time: 10 minutes
Servings: 4

Ingredients:

- 2 eggs, whisked
- 1 pound cod fillets, cut into medium strips
- 2 cups almond flour
- A pinch of sea salt and black pepper
- ¼ teaspoon paprika
- 1 cup water

Directions:

In a bowl, mix flour with salt, pepper and paprika and stir. Put the eggs in another bowl. Dip fish strips in the eggs and flour mix. Add the water to your instant pot, add the steamer basket, place fish strips inside, cover and cook on High for 10 minutes. Arrange on a platter and serve them. Enjoy!

Nutrition: calories 120, fat 2, fiber 4, carbs 3, protein 7

Great Green Dip

Preparation time: 10 minutes
Cooking time: 3 minutes
Servings: 4

Ingredients:

- 1 cup almond milk
- 2 garlic cloves, minced
- 28 ounces artichokes, canned, drained and chopped
- 1 cup cashews, soaked for 2 hours and drained
- 8 ounces canned water chestnuts, drained
- 2 tablespoons lemon juice
- 2 teaspoons mustard
- 8 ounces spinach
- Black pepper to the taste
- 1 tablespoon Paleo mayonnaise

Directions:

In your food processor, mix cashews with garlic, almond milk, mustard and lemon juice, blend well and transfer to your instant pot. Add chestnuts, spinach, black pepper and artichokes, stir, cover and cook on high for 3 hours. Transfer to a bowl, cool down, add mayo, stir and serve as a party dip. Enjoy!

Nutrition: calories 130, fat 4, fiber 2, carbs 3, protein 4

Carrot Snack

Preparation time: 10 minutes
Cooking time: 6 minutes
Servings: 14

Ingredients:

- ½ teaspoon cinnamon powder
- 1 cup water
- 1 egg white, whisked
- 1 cup baby carrots, grated
- ¾ cup pecans, chopped
- 1 tablespoon honey
- 2 tablespoons coconut flour
- 2 tablespoons flax meal

Directions:

In a bowl, mix baby carrots with egg white, cinnamon, pecans, honey, flax meal and coconut flour, stir well and shape 14 balls out of this mix. Add the water to your instant pot, add the steamer basket, add carrot balls, cover and cook on High for 6 minutes. Arrange carrot balls on a platter and serve. Enjoy!

Nutrition: calories 120, fat 2, fiber 1, carbs 2, protein 3

Mushroom Appetizer

Preparation time: 10 minutes
Cooking time: 12 minutes
Servings: 4

Ingredients:

- 1 pound chorizo, chopped
- 1 pound big white mushroom caps, stems separated and chopped
- 2 tablespoons olive oil
- 1 cup water
- 1 yellow onion, chopped
- A pinch of black pepper

Directions:

Set your instant pot on sauté mode, add oil, heat it up, add mushrooms stems, onion and a pinch of black pepper, stir and sauté for 5 minutes. Add chorizo, stir, transfer to a bowl, cool down and stuff mushrooms with this mix. Clean your instant pot, add the water, add the steamer basket, place stuffed mushrooms inside, cover and cook on High for 7 minutes. Arrange on a platter and serve as an appetizer. Enjoy!

Nutrition: calories 135, fat 2, fiber 2, carbs 4, protein 12

Zucchini Appetizer

Preparation time: 10 minutes
Cooking time: 5 minutes
Servings: 4

Ingredients:

- 3 zucchinis, thinly sliced lengthwise
- 14 bacon slices
- 1 cup water
- ½ cup sun dried tomatoes, chopped
- 4 tablespoons balsamic vinegar
- ½ cup basil, chopped
- Black pepper to the taste

Directions:

Put zucchini slices in a bowl, add vinegar, toss a bit and leave aside for 10 minutes. Drain and arrange zucchini slices on a cutting board. Divide bacon slices, basil and sundried tomatoes into each zucchini slices, season with a pinch of black pepper, wrap and secure with toothpicks. Add the water to your instant pot, add the steamer basket, add zucchini rolls, cover and cook on High for 5 minutes. Arrange on a platter and serve. Enjoy!

Nutrition: calories 143, fat 2, fiber 3, carbs 5, protein 3

Crazy And Unique Appetizer

Preparation time: 10 minutes
Cooking time: 10 minutes
Servings: 2

Ingredients:

- 3 tablespoons curry powder
- 1 cup almond flour
- 1 cup water
- 3 chicken breasts, boneless, skinless and cut into thin strips
- 2 teaspoons turmeric powder
- 1 tablespoon cumin, ground
- 1 tablespoon garlic powder
- Black pepper to the taste

Directions:

In a bowl, mix curry powder with flour, turmeric, cumin, garlic powder and black pepper, stir well, add chicken strips and toss to coat. Put the water in your instant pot, add the steamer basket, add chicken strips, cover and cook on High for 10 minutes. Arrange on a platter and serve. Enjoy!

Nutrition: calories 100, fat 2, fiber 3, carbs 4, protein 2

Almonds Surprise

Preparation time: 10 minutes
Cooking time: 10 minutes
Servings: 10

Ingredients:
- 3 tablespoons cinnamon powder
- 3 tablespoons stevia
- 4 and ½ cups almonds, raw
- 2 cups water
- 2 teaspoons vanilla extract

Directions:
In a bowl, mix 1 cup water with vanilla extract and whisk. In another bowl, mix cinnamon with stevia and stir. Di almonds in water, then in cinnamon mix and place them in a heatproof dish. Add the rest of the water to you instant pot, add the steamer basket, add the dish inside, cover and cook on High for 10 minutes. Transfe almond to a bowl and serve them as a snack. Enjoy!

Nutrition: calories 100, fat 3, fiber 4, carbs 3, protein 4

Sweet Potato Spread

Preparation time: 10 minutes
Cooking time: 12 minutes
Servings: 6

Ingredients:
- 2 cups sweet potatoes, peeled and chopped
- ¼ cup sesame seeds paste
- 2 tablespoons lemon juice
- 5 garlic cloves, minced
- 1 tablespoon olive oil
- ½ teaspoon cumin, ground
- 2 cups water+ 2 tablespoons water
- A pinch of salt

Directions:
Put 2 cups water in your instant pot, add the steamer basket, add potatoes, cover and cook on High for 12 minutes. Transfer potatoes to your food processor, add 2 tablespoons water, sesame seeds paste, lemon juice, garlic, oil, cumin and a pinch of salt and pulse really well. Divide into bowls and serve as an appetizer. Enjoy!

Nutrition: calories 130, fat 3, fiber 1, carbs 4, protein 7

Mint Dip

Preparation time: 10 minutes
Cooking time: 4 minutes
Servings: 4

Ingredients:
- 1 bunch spinach, chopped
- ½ cup water
- 2 tablespoons mint, chopped
- 1 scallion, sliced
- ¾ cup coconut cream
- Black pepper to the taste

Directions:
Put spinach and water in your instant pot, cover and cook on High for 4 minutes. Drain spinach well, transfer it to a bowl, add mint, scallion, cream and black pepper and stir really well. Leave this dip aside for 10 minutes before serving it. Enjoy!

Nutrition: calories 140, fat 3, fiber 3, carbs 3, protein 3

Popular Shrimp Appetizer

Preparation time: 10 minutes
Cooking time: 2 minutes
Servings: 8

Ingredients:
- 2 pounds big shrimp, deveined
- 4 cup water
- 1 lemon, halved
- 2 bay leaves
- 1 medium lemon, sliced for serving
- ¾ cup tomato paste
- 2 and ½ tablespoons horseradish, prepared
- ¼ teaspoon hot pepper sauce
- 2 tablespoons lemon juice

Directions:
Put the water in your instant pot, add halved lemon and bay leaves. Add shrimp, cover and cook on High for 2 minutes. Transfer shrimp to a bowl filled with ice water, cool it down and transfer to smaller bowls filled with ice. In a separate bowl, mix hot sauce with tomato paste, lemon juice and horseradish and whisk. Serve your shrimp with the sauce you made and lemon slices on the side. Enjoy!

Nutrition: calories 140, fat 1, fiber 3, carbs 5, protein 2

Incredible Scallops

Preparation time: 5 minutes
Cooking time: 6 minutes
Servings: 4

Ingredients:
- 1 jalapeno pepper, seedless and minced
- ¼ cup extra virgin olive oil
- ¼ cup rice vinegar
- ¼ teaspoon mustard
- Black pepper to the taste
- A pinch cayenne pepper
- 1 tablespoon vegetable oil
- 12 big sea scallops
- 2 oranges, sliced

Directions:
In your blender, mix jalapeno with olive oil, mustard, black and vinegar and pulse really well. Season scallops with cayenne pepper. Heat up a pan with the vegetable oil over high temperature, add scallops and cook them for 3 minutes on each side. Divide scallops on plates, place orange slices on top and drizzle the jalapeno vinaigrette. Enjoy!

Broiled Lobster Tails

Preparation time: 10 minutes
Cooking time: 10 minutes
Servings: 2

Ingredients:
- 2 big whole lobster tails
- ½ teaspoon paprika
- ½ cup coconut butter
- White pepper to the taste
- 1 lemon cut into wedges

Directions
Place lobster tails on a baking sheet, cut top side of lobster shells and pull them apart Season with white pepper and paprika. Add butter and toss gently Introduce lobster tails in preheated broiler and broil for 10 minutes. Divide among plates, garnish with lemon wedges and serve right away! Enjoy!

Nutrition: calories 140, fat 2, fiber 2, carbs 6, protein 6

Delightful Herring Appetizer

Preparation time: 10 minutes
Cooking time: 5 minutes
Servings: 4

Ingredients:
- 10 pieces herring roe, soaked in water for half a day and drained
- 3 cups water
- 2 tablespoons stevia
- 3 tablespoons coconut aminos
- 1 handful mild chili flakes

Directions:
In your instant pot, mix water with stevia, aminos, chili flakes and herring roe. Cover, cook on High for 2 minutes, divide into bowls and serve as an appetizer. Enjoy!

Nutrition: calories 140, fat 2, fiber 1, carbs 2, protein 3

Salmon Patties

Preparation time: 10 minutes
Cooking time: 10 minutes
Servings: 4

Ingredients:

- 1 pound salmon, ground
- 2 tablespoons lemon zest
- Black pepper to the taste
- A pinch of sea salt
- 1 teaspoon olive oil
- ½ cup flax meal

Directions:

In your food processor, mix salmon with flax meal, salt, pepper and lemon zest, pulse well, shape 4 patties out of this mix and place them on a plate. Set your instant pot on Sauté mode, add the oil and heat it up. Add patties, cover pot and cook on High for 10 minutes. Arrange patties on a platter and serve. Enjoy!

Nutrition: calories 142, fat 3, fiber 2, carbs 3, protein 4

Clams And Mussels Appetizer

Preparation time: 10 minutes
Cooking time: 15 minutes
Servings: 4

Ingredients:

- 2 chorizo links, chopped
- 15 clams
- 30 mussels, scrubbed
- 10 ounces veggies stock
- 1 yellow onion, chopped
- 1 teaspoon olive oil
- 2 tablespoons parsley, chopped
- Lemon wedges

Directions:

Put the oil in your instant pot, set it on Sauté mode, heat it up, add onions and chorizo, stir and cook for 4 minutes. Add clams, mussels and stock, stir, cover and cook on High for 10 minutes. Release pressure, add parsley, stir, divide into bowls and serve with lemon wedges on the side. Enjoy!

Nutrition: calories 142, fat 2, fiber 2, carbs 3, protein 6

Special Shrimp Appetizer

Preparation time: 5 minutes
Cooking time: 4 minutes
Servings: 4

Ingredients:

- 2 tablespoons coconut aminos
- 1 pound shrimp, peeled and deveined
- 1 cup chicken stock
- 3 tablespoon stevia
- 3 tablespoons balsamic vinegar
- ¾ cup pineapple juice

Directions:

In your instant pot, mix shrimp with aminos, stock, vinegar, pineapple juice and stevia, stir everything well, cover pot and cook on High for 4 minutes. Divide into bowls and serve as an appetizer. Enjoy!

Nutrition: calories 132, fat 2, fiber 2, carbs 3, protein 5

Stuffed Squid

Preparation time: 10 minutes
Cooking time: 20 minutes
Servings: 4

Ingredients:

- 14 ounces veggie stock
- 3 tablespoons coconut aminos
- 4 squid, tentacles separated and chopped
- 1 cup cauliflower rice
- 2 tablespoon water
- 2 tablespoons stevia

Directions:

In a bowl, mix tentacles with cauliflower rice, stir and stuff squid with this mix. Place stuffed squid in your instant pot, add aminos, stock, stevia and water stir, cover and cook on High for 15 minutes. Arrange on a platter and serve as an appetizer. Enjoy!

Nutrition: calories 162, fat 3, fiber 2, carbs 3, protein 6

Exotic Anchovies

Preparation time: 10 minutes
Cooking time: 4 minutes
Servings: 2

Ingredients:
- 2 garlic cloves, minced
- 1 tablespoon water
- 1 tablespoon stevia
- 1 cup anchovies, dried
- 1 and ½ tablespoons olive oil
- Black sesame seeds for serving
- Roasted sesame seeds for serving

Directions:
In a bowl, mix water with garlic and stevia, stir and leave aside for a couple of minutes. Set your instant pot on Sauté mode, add anchovies, stir, cook them for 1 minute and transfer to a bowl Add oil, heat up for 1 minute, add garlic mixture and anchovies, cover, cook on High for 2 minutes and transfer to bowls. Add black sesame seeds and roasted ones, toss and serve as an appetizer. Enjoy!

Nutrition: calories 132, fat 3, fiber 3, carbs 5, protein 5

Appetizer Salad

Preparation time: 10 minutes
Cooking time: 8 minutes
Servings: 4

Ingredients:
- ½ pounds mushrooms, roughly sliced
- 1 tablespoon olive oil
- 3 garlic cloves, minced
- 1 tomato, roughly chopped
- 1 teaspoon basil, dried
- 1 tablespoon coriander, chopped
- Black pepper to the taste
- 3 tablespoons lemon juice
- ½ cup water

Directions:
Set your instant pot on sauté mode, add oil, heat it up, add garlic and mushrooms, stir and sauté for 3 minutes. Add basil, water, tomato, lemon juice and black pepper, stir, cover and cook on High for 5 minutes. Divide into small bowls, sprinkle coriander on top and serve. Enjoy!

Nutrition: calories 90, fat 2, fiber 1, carbs 2, protein 3

Carrot Appetizer

Preparation time: 10 minutes
Cooking time: 9 minutes
Servings: 4

Ingredients:

- ¼ yellow onion, chopped
- 1 tablespoon olive oil
- ½ cup water
- 4 carrots, cut into thin matchsticks
- 1 garlic clove, minced
- 6 ounces canned white tuna, drained and flaked
- 1 tablespoon Dijon mustard
- 1 tablespoon balsamic vinegar
- A pinch of salt and black pepper
- 1 tablespoon lemon juice

Directions:

In a bowl, mix vinegar with salt, pepper, mustard and lemon juice, whisk well and leave aside. Set your instant pot on sauté mode, add the oil, heat it up, add onion and garlic, stir and sauté for 4 minutes. Add carrots and water, stir, cover and cook on High for 5 minutes. Transfer carrots to a salad bowl, add tuna and the salad dressing, toss to coat and keep in the fridge until you serve it as an appetizer. Enjoy!

Nutrition: calories 100, fat 3, fiber 3, carbs 6, protein 8

Salmon Cakes

Preparation time: 10 minutes
Cooking time: 6 minutes
Servings: 4

Ingredients:

- 28 ounces canned salmon, drained, skinless and flaked
- 1 and ¼ coconut flour
- 3 tablespoons capers
- 1 egg, whisked
- 1 tablespoon lemon juice
- 2 tablespoons parsley, chopped
- 1 tablespoon coconut aminos
- 1 and ½ teaspoons tarragon, chopped
- ½ cup water
- A pinch of sea salt and black pepper
- 2 tablespoons olive oil

Directions:

In a bowl, mix salmon with egg, ½ cup flour, aminos, tarragon, capers, salt and pepper, stir, shape 12 patties and place them on a plate. Put the rest of the flour in a bowl, add salmon patties and dredge them well. Set your instant pot on sauté mode, add the oil, heat it up, add patties, cook them for 2 minutes on each side and transfer to a plate. Clean the pot, add the water, add the steamer basket, place salmon cakes inside, cover, cook on High for 3 minutes more, arrange them on a platter and serve with parsley sprinkled on top and lemon juice drizzled at the end. Enjoy!

Nutrition: calories 142, fat 3, fiber 2, carbs 3, protein 5

Simple Beef Party Patties

Preparation time: 10 minutes
Cooking time: 35 minutes
Servings: 6

Ingredients:

- ½ cup flax meal
- 1 and ½ pound beef, ground
- 1 egg
- A pinch of salt and black pepper
- 10 ounces veggie stock
- 1 tablespoon coconut flour
- ¼ cup tomato paste
- ½ teaspoon mustard powder
- ¼ cup water

Directions:

In a bowl, mix 1/3 cup stock with beef, salt, pepper, egg and flax meal, shape 6 patties and leave them aside. Set your instant pot on Sauté mode, add beef patties, brown them for a few minutes and transfer to a plate. Add the rest of the stock, flour, water, tomato paste and mustard powder to your instant pot, stir, add patties, cover and cook on High for 10 minutes. Divide patties on a platter, drizzle the sauce over them and serve. Enjoy!

Nutrition: calories 214, fat 3, fiber 1, carbs 4, protein 13

Hearty Eggplants Appetizer

Preparation time: 10 minutes
Cooking time: 12 minutes
Servings: 4

Ingredients:

- 4 small eggplants, halved and insides scooped out
- A pinch of and black pepper to the taste
- 3 tablespoons olive oil
- 1 cup water
- 1 yellow onion, chopped
- 1 tablespoon garlic, minced
- 2 and ½ pounds tomatoes, peeled and grated
- 1 green bell pepper, chopped
- ½ cup cauliflower, chopped
- 1 teaspoon oregano, chopped
- ½ cup parsley, chopped

Directions:

Set your instant pot on sauté mode, add oil, heat it up, add onion, stir and sauté for 3 minutes. Add bell pepper, garlic and cauliflower, stir, cook for 2 minutes more, transfer to a bowl and mix with parsley, tomato, salt, pepper and oregano, stir and stuff eggplants with the veggie mix. Put the water in your instant pot, add the steamer basket, place stuffed eggplants, cover and cook on High for 6 minutes. Arrange them on a platter and serve as an appetizer. Enjoy!

Nutrition: calories 140, fat 4, fiber, 2, carbs 3, protein 2

Elegant Scallops Salad

Preparation time: 10 minutes
Cooking time: 4 minutes
Servings:

Ingredients:
- 1 pound bay scallops
- 2 teaspoons cayenne pepper
- 3 tablespoons lemon juice
- 1 tablespoon Paleo mayo
- 1 teaspoon mustard
- ½ cup olive oil+ 2 tablespoons
- 1 garlic clove, minced
- 2 handfuls mixed salad greens
- 1 avocado, pitted, peeled and cubed
- 1 red bell pepper, cut into thin strips
- 1 cup water

Directions:
In a salad bowl, mix salad greens with avocado and bell pepper and leave aside for now. In another bowl, mix lemon juice with mustard, garlic, mayo, 2 tablespoons oil and a pinch of cayenne, whisk well and also leave aside. Put in another bowl, add 2 teaspoons cayenne and toss to coat. Set your instant pot on sauté mode, add ½ cup oil, heat it up, add scallops and cook for 1 minute on each side. Clean your instant pot, add the water, add the steamer basket, add scallops, cover and cook on High for 2 minutes. Add scallops over mixed salad, drizzle the mustard and mayo dressing, toss gently, divide among appetizer plates and serve. Enjoy!

Nutrition: calories 145, fat 2, fiber 2, carbs 6, protein 6

Special Spinach Appetizer Salad

Preparation time: 10 minutes
Cooking time: 20 minutes
Servings: 4

Ingredients:
- 2 red onions, cut into medium wedges
- 1 butternut squash, cut into medium wedges
- 1 cup water
- 6 cups spinach
- 4 parsnips, roughly chopped
- A pinch of black pepper
- 2 tablespoons balsamic vinegar
- 1/3 cup nuts, roasted
- 1 teaspoon Dijon mustard
- ½ tablespoons oregano, dried
- 1 garlic clove, minced
- 6 tablespoons olive oil

Directions:
In a bowl, mix squash with onions, parsnips, half of the oil, oregano and a pinch of black pepper and toss well. Add the water to your instant pot, add the steamer basket, add veggies inside, cover and cook on High for 12 minutes. In a bowl, mix vinegar with the rest of the oil, garlic, mustard and pepper to the taste and whisk very well. Put spinach in a salad bowl, add roasted veggies, add dressing, sprinkle nuts, toss to coat, divide among appetizer plates and serve. Enjoy!

Nutrition: calories 131, fat 1, fiber 2, carbs 3, protein 4

Textured Appetizer Salad

Preparation time: 10 minutes
Cooking time: 17 minutes
Servings: 4

Ingredients:
- 1 pound beef steak, cut into strips
- ½ cup water
- 3 cups broccoli, florets separated
- 8 cups baby salad greens
- 1 red onion, sliced
- 1 red bell pepper, sliced
- 1 tablespoon ginger, minced
- Black pepper to the taste
- ½ cup olive oil
- 2 tablespoons lime juice
- 1 tablespoon balsamic vinegar
- 2 tablespoons shallots, finely chopped

Directions:
In a bowl, mix ginger with oil, lime juice, vinegar, shallots and pepper to the taste and whisk. Set your instant pot on sauté mode, add 2 tablespoons of the vinaigrette, heat it up, add broccoli and beef, stir and sauté for 3 minutes. Add water, cover and cook on High for 14 minutes. Transfer beef and broccoli to a salad bowl, add salad greens, onion and bell pepper Add black pepper, drizzle the rest of the vinaigrette, toss to coat and serve. Enjoy!

Nutrition: calories 140, fat 4, fiber 2, carbs 5, protein 6

Incredible Chicken Appetizer

Preparation time: 10 minutes
Cooking time: 10 minutes
Servings: 2

Ingredients:
- 2 teaspoons parsley
- 2 chicken breasts, skinless and boneless
- ½ teaspoon onion powder
- 1 cup water
- 2 teaspoons sweet paprika
- ½ cup lemon juice
- A pinch of sea salt and black pepper
- 5 cups baby spinach
- 8 strawberries, sliced
- 1 small red onion, sliced
- 1 avocado, pitted, peeled and cut into small chunks
- ¼ cup olive oil
- 1 tablespoon tarragon, chopped
- 2 tablespoons balsamic vinegar

Directions:
Put chicken in a bowl, add lemon juice, parsley, onion powder and paprika and toss to coat. Put the water in your instant pot, add the steamer basket, add chicken breasts, cover and cook on High for 10 minutes. Transfer chicken to a cutting board, cool down, shred and transfer to a salad bowl. Add spinach, onion, strawberries and avocado and toss. In a bowl, mix oil with vinegar, salt, pepper and tarragon, whisk well add to the salad, toss, divide among appetizer plates and serve. Enjoy!

Nutrition: calories 140, fat 1, fiber 3, carbs 3, protein 3

Special Bell Peppers Appetizer

Preparation time: 10 minutes
Cooking time: 17 minutes
Servings: 4

Ingredients:
- 1 tablespoon olive oil
- 1 teaspoon ghee
- ½ cup veggie stock
- 2 red bell peppers, cut into big strips
- 2 red onions, cut into strips
- Black pepper to the taste
- 1 teaspoon basil, dried

Directions:
Set your instant pot on sauté mode, add ghee and oil, heat it up, add onion and bell peppers, stir and sauté for 10 minutes. Add stock, basil and black pepper, cover and cook on Low for 7 minutes. Transfer to small bowls and serve. Enjoy!

Nutrition: calories 47, fat 4, fiber 1, carbs 1, protein 4

Red Chard Wonder

Preparation time: 10 minutes
Cooking time: 7 minutes
Servings: 4

Ingredients:
- 2 tablespoons olive oil
- 1 yellow onion, chopped
- ½ cup veggie stock
- 2 tablespoons capers
- 2 tablespoons kalamata olives, pitted and sliced
- Juice of 1 lemon
- Black pepper to the taste
- 1 teaspoon stevia
- 2 bunches red chard, chopped

Directions:
Set your instant pot on sauté mode, add oil, heat it up, add onions, stir and sauté for 3 minutes. Add stevia, chard, olives, lemon juice, capers, black pepper and stock, stir, cover and cook on High for 4 minutes. Divide into small bowls and serve as an appetizer. Enjoy!

Nutrition: calories 89, fat 1, fiber 1, carbs 2, protein 2

Special Olives Snack

Preparation time: 10 minutes
Cooking time: 20 minutes
Servings: 6

Ingredients:
- 1 cup black olives, pitted
- 1 cup kalamata olives, pitted
- 1 cup green olives, stuffed with almonds
- 10 garlic cloves
- 2 tablespoons olive oil
- ½ cup water
- 1 tablespoon Italian herbs, dried
- 1 teaspoon lemon zest, grated
- Black pepper to the taste
- 1 tablespoon thyme for serving

Directions:
In a bowl, mix black, kalamata and green olives with oil, garlic and herbs, toss to coat and transfer to a small baking dish. Put the water in your instant pot, add the steamer basket, place the baking dish inside, cover and cook on High for 6 minutes. Transfer olives to a bowl, sprinkle lemon zest, black pepper and thyme on top, toss to coat and serve as a snack. Enjoy!

Nutrition: calories 100, fat 2, fiber 2, carbs 3, protein 1

Tasty Turnip Sticks

Preparation time: 10 minutes
Cooking time: 5 minutes
Servings: 4

Ingredients:
- 2 pounds turnips, peeled and cut intoto sticks
- Black pepper to the taste
- 2 tablespoons olive oil
- ½ cup water
- 2 tablespoons chili powder
- 1 teaspoon onion powder
- 1 teaspoon garlic powder
- ½ teaspoon oregano, dried
- 1 and ½ tablespoons cumin, ground

Directions:
In a bowl, mix chili powder with onion powder, garlic powder, oregano, cumin and parsnip sticks and toss. Season with black pepper, drizzle the oil and toss to coat well. Add the water to your instant pot, add the steamer basket, add turnip sticks, cover and cook on High for 5 minutes. Transfer parsnips stick to a bowl and serve as a snack. Enjoy!

Nutrition: calories 112, fat 1, fiber 1, carbs 1, protein 3

Yummy Mushrooms Snack

Preparation time: 10 minutes
Cooking time: 30 minutes
Servings: 4

Ingredients:
- 2 tablespoons olive oil
- ½ cup water
- 16 ounces baby mushrooms
- Black pepper to the taste
- 3 tablespoons onion, dried
- 3 tablespoons parsley flakes
- 1 teaspoon garlic powder

Directions:
In a bowl, mix parsley flakes with onion, pepper, garlic powder, mushrooms and oil and toss. Put the water in your instant pot, add the steamer basket, add mushrooms, cover and cook on High for 10 minutes. Divide into small bowls and serve as a snack. Enjoy!
Nutrition: calories 98, fat 2, fiber 2, carbs 3, protein 4

Cauliflower Dip

Preparation time: 10 minutes
Cooking time: 6 minutes
Servings: 14

Ingredients:
- 1 and ½ cups veggie stock
- 1 cauliflower head, florets separated
- ¼ cup Paleo mayonnaise
- ½ cup yellow onion, chopped
- ¾ cup cashew cheese
- ½ teaspoon garlic powder
- ½ teaspoon chili powder
- ½ teaspoon cumin, ground
- Black pepper to the taste

Directions:
Put the stock in your instant pot, add onion, cauliflower, black pepper, chili powder, cumin and garlic powder, stir, cover and cook on High for 6 minutes. Add cashew cheese, stir and leave aside to cool down a bit. Add mayo, blend using an immersion blender, divide into bowls and keep in the fridge until your serve it with veggie matchsticks on the side. Enjoy!
Nutrition: calories 60, fat 1, fiber 1, carbs 1, protein 2

Wrapped Shrimp

Preparation time: 10 minutes
Cooking time: 4 minutes
Servings: 12

Ingredients:
- 2 tablespoons olive oil
- 1 cup water+ 2 tablespoons
- 12 big shrimp, cooked, peeled and deveined
- 1 tablespoons mint, chopped
- 2 tablespoons stevia
- 1/3 cup blackberries, pureed
- 12 prosciutto slices

Directions:
Put 1 cup water in your instant pot, add the steamer basket, wrap each shrimp in a prosciutto slice, drizzle the olive oil over them, add them to the steamer basket, cover and cook on High for 4 minutes. Meanwhile, heat up pan with ground blackberries over medium heat, add mint, stevia and 2 tablespoons water, stir, cook for 3 minutes and take off heat. Arrange wrapped shrimp on a platter, drizzle blackberries sauce all over and serve. Enjoy!
Nutrition: calories 142, fat 1, fiber 2, carbs 1, protein 6

Refreshing Zucchini Snack

Preparation time: 10 minutes
Cooking time: 3 minutes
Servings: 4

Ingredients:
- ½ cup tomato sauce
- 1 zucchini, sliced
- Black pepper to the taste
- A pinch of cumin

Directions:
Put tomato sauce in your instant pot, add zucchini slices, black pepper and a pinch of cumin, toss gently, cover and cook on High for 3 minutes. Arrange zucchini slices on a platter and serve them as a snack. Enjoy!
Nutrition: calories 100, fat 1, fiber 2, carbs 2, protein 3

Turkey Appetizer Meatballs

Preparation time: 10 minutes
Cooking time: 14 minutes
Servings: 12

Ingredients:
- 1 egg
- 1 pound turkey, ground
- A pinch of salt and black pepper
- ¼ cup almond flour
- ½ teaspoon garlic powder
- 1 cup water
- 2 tablespoons sun dried tomatoes, chopped
- 2 tablespoons olive oil
- 2 tablespoon basil, chopped

Directions:
In a bowl, mix turkey with salt, pepper, egg, flour, garlic powder, sun dried tomatoes and basil, stir well and shape 12 meatballs out of this mix. Set your instant pot on sauté mode, add the oil, heat it up, add meatballs brown them for 2 minutes on each side and transfer to a plate. Clean your instant pot, add the water, add the steamer basket, add meatballs inside, cover and cook on High for 12 minutes. Arrange turkey meatballs on a platter and serve. Enjoy!
Nutrition: calories 80, fat 1, fiber 3, carbs 2, protein 4

Tuna Patties

Preparation time: 10 minutes
Cooking time: 10 minutes
Servings: 12

Ingredients:
- 15 ounces canned tuna, drain and flaked
- 1 teaspoon parsley, chopped
- 1 teaspoon dill, chopped
- 1 teaspoon garlic powder
- ½ cup red onion, chopped
- A pinch of sea salt and black pepper
- 1 tablespoon olive oil
- ½ cup water
- 3 eggs

Directions:
In a bowl, mix tuna with salt, pepper, dill, parsley, onion, garlic powder and eggs, stir well, shape your patties and put them on a plate. Set your instant pot on sauté mode, add oil, heat it up, add patties, cook them for 2 minutes on each side and transfer them to a plate. Clean your instant pot, add the water, add the steamer basket, add tuna patties inside, cover and cook on High for 6 minutes, Arrange patties on a platter and serve them as an appetizer. Enjoy!
Nutrition: calories 120, fat 2, fiber 1, carbs 1, protein 3

Elegant Duck Appetizer

Preparation time: 10 minutes
Cooking time: 15 minutes
Servings: 4

Ingredients:
- 1 tablespoon stevia
- 1 shallot, chopped
- ¼ cup water
- ¼ cup balsamic vinegar
- ¼ cup olive oil
- 1 cup water
- ¾ cup raspberries
- 1 tablespoon Dijon mustard
- Black pepper to the taste
- 10 ounces baby spinach
- 2 duck legs
- ½ pint raspberries (for the salad)
- ½ cup pecans, halved

Directions:

In your blender, mix stevia with shallot, vinegar, water, oil, ¾ cup raspberries, mustard and black pepper, blend very well, strain into a bowl and leave aside. Put the water in your instant pot, season duck pieces with black pepper, add to the pot, cover and cook on High for 12 minutes. Discard bones from the meat, clean the pot, set it on sauté mode, add duck and cook it for 3 minutes on each side. Divide spinach on plates, add duck, sprinkle pecan halves and ½ pint raspberries Drizzle the raspberry vinaigrette on top and serve as an appetizer. Enjoy!

Nutrition: calories 215, fat 4, fiber 2, carbs 3, protein 12

Summer Lamb Appetizer

Preparation time: 10 minutes
Cooking time: 40 minutes
Servings: 4

Ingredients:
- 1 tablespoon olive oil
- 3 pounds leg of lamb, bone discarded
- 4 cups veggie stock
- Black pepper to the taste
- 1 teaspoon cumin, ground
- A pinch of thyme, dried
- 2 garlic cloves, minced

For the salad:
- ½ cup pecans, toasted
- 2 cups spinach
- 1 and ½ tablespoons lemon juice
- ¼ cup olive oil
- 1 cup mint, chopped

Directions:

Rub lamb really well with pepper, 1 tablespoon oil, thyme, cumin and minced garlic. Put the stock in your instant pot, add lamb, cover and cook on High for 40 minutes. Transfer lamb to a cutting board, cool it down, shred meat and transfer to a salad bowl. Add spinach, mint, ¼-cup olive oil, lemon juice, toasted pecans and pepper, toss to coat, divide among appetizer plates and serve. Enjoy!

Nutrition: calories 234, fat 3, fiber 3, carbs 5, protein 12

Great Veggie Appetizer

Preparation time: 10 minutes
Cooking time: 30 minutes
Servings: 6

Ingredients:

- 1 celery bunch, roughly chopped
- 3 tablespoons olive oil
- 1 yellow onion, chopped
- 4 garlic cloves, minced
- 1 parsley bunch, chopped
- 2 mint bunches, chopped
- 1 bunch green onion, chopped
- Black pepper to the taste
- 2 cups water

Directions:

Set your instant pot on Sauté mode, add oil and heat it up. Add green onions, onion and garlic, stir and sauté for 4 minutes. Add celery, black pepper and water, stir, cover pot and cook on High for 6 minutes Add parsley and mint, stir and cook for 2 minutes more. Divide into bowls and serve as an appetizer. Enjoy!

Nutrition: calories 100, fat 1, fiber 2, carbs 2, protein 6

Radish Snack

Preparation time: 10 minutes
Cooking time: 12 minutes
Servings: 2

Ingredients:

- 2 cups radishes, cut into quarters
- A pinch of salt and black pepper
- 2 tablespoons olive oil
- 1 tablespoon chives, chopped
- ½ cup water
- 1 tablespoon lemon zest

Directions:

In a bowl, mix radishes with salt, pepper, chives, lemon zest and oil and toss to coat. Add the water to your instant pot, add the steamer basket, add radishes, cover and cook on High for 12 minutes. Transfer to bowls and serve cold as a snack. Enjoy!

Nutrition: calories 122, fat 12, fiber 1, carbs 3, protein 14

Spinach And Chard Appetizer Salad

Preparation time: 10 minutes
Cooking time: 5 minutes
Servings: 4

Ingredients:

- 1 apple, cored and sliced
- 1 yellow onion, sliced
- 3 tablespoons olive oil
- ¼ cup raisins
- 6 garlic cloves, minced
- A pinch of sea salt and black pepper
- ¼ cup pine nuts, toasted
- ¼ cup balsamic vinegar
- 5 cups mixed spinach and chard
- ½ cup water
- A pinch of nutmeg

Directions:

Set your instant pot on sauté mode, add the oil, heat it up, add onion, stir and cook for 2 minutes. Add garlic, apple, vinegar and raisins, stir and cook for 4 minutes more. Add spinach and chard mix and the water, cover and cook on High for 4 minutes. Add nutmeg, pine nuts, a pinch of salt and pepper, stir, divide among small appetizer plates and serve as an appetizer salad. Enjoy!

Nutrition: calories 100, fat 1, fiber 1, carbs 2, protein 4

Side Dish Recipes

Cauliflower Risotto And Artichokes

Preparation time: 10 minutes
Cooking time: 10 minutes
Servings: 4

Ingredients:

- 1 tablespoon extra virgin olive oil
- 5 ounces cauliflower rice
- 2 garlic cloves, minced
- 1 and ¼ cups chicken stock
- 2 tablespoons flax meal
- 1 and ¼ cups water
- 15 ounces artichoke hearts, chopped
- 16 ounces cashew cheese
- 1 and ½ tablespoons thyme, chopped
- A pinch of sea salt and black pepper

Directions:

Set your instant pot on sauté mode, add the oil and cauliflower rice, stir and cook for 2 minutes. Add garlic, stir, cook for 1 minute, transfer to a heat proof dish and mix with flax meal, salt, pepper and stock. Put the water in your instant pot, add the steamer basket, put the dish with the cauliflower rice inside, cover and cook on High for 7 minutes. Add cashew cheese, artichoke hearts and thyme, stir, divide among plates and serve as a side dish. Enjoy!

Nutrition: calories 162, fat 2, fiber 2, carbs 4, protein 7

Cauliflower And Mushroom Risotto

Preparation time: 10 minutes
Cooking time: 13 minutes
Servings: 4

Ingredients:

- 2 cups cauliflower rice
- 4 cups chicken stock
- 2 garlic cloves, minced
- 2 ounces olive oil
- 1 yellow onion, chopped
- 8 ounces mushrooms, sliced
- 4 ounces coconut cream
- 4 ounces white vinegar
- 1 ounce basil, chopped

Directions:

Set your instant pot on sauté mode, add the oil and heat it up. Add onions, garlic and mushrooms, stir and cook for 3 minutes Add cauliflower rice, stock and vinegar, stir, cover and cook on High for 10 minutes. Add coconut cream and basil, stir, divide among plates and serve as a side dish. Enjoy!

Nutrition: calories 142, fat 2, fiber 1, carbs 2, protein 5

Pumpkin And Cauliflower Rice

Preparation time: 5 minutes
Cooking time: 10 minutes
Servings: 4

Ingredients:

- 2 ounces olive oil
- 1 yellow onion, chopped
- 2 garlic cloves, minced
- 12 ounces cauliflower rice
- 4 cups chicken stock
- 6 ounces pumpkin puree
- ½ teaspoon nutmeg, ground
- 1 teaspoon thyme chopped
- ½ teaspoon ginger, grated
- ½ teaspoon cinnamon powder
- ½ teaspoon allspice
- 4 ounces coconut cream

Directions:

Set your instant pot on sauté mode, add the oil, heat it up, add garlic and onion, stir and sauté for 3 minutes. Add cauliflower rice, stock, pumpkin puree, thyme, nutmeg, cinnamon, ginger and allspice, stir, cover and cook on High for 12 minutes. Add coconut cream, stir, divide among plates and serve as a side dish. Enjoy!

Nutrition: calories 152, fat 2, fiber 3, carbs 5, protein 6

Special Veggie Side Dish

Preparation time: 10 minutes
Cooking time: 12 minutes
Servings: 4

Ingredients:

- 2 cups cauliflower rice
- 1 cup mixed carrots and green beans
- 2 cups water
- ½ teaspoon green chili, minced
- ½ teaspoon ginger, grated
- 3 garlic cloves, minced
- 2 tablespoons ghee
- 1 cinnamon stick
- 1 tablespoon cumin seeds
- 2 bay leaves
- 3 whole cloves
- 5 black peppercorns
- 2 whole cardamoms
- 1 tablespoon stevia
- A pinch of sea salt

Directions:

Put water in your instant pot, add cauliflower rice, mixed veggies, green chili, grated ginger, garlic cloves, cinnamon stick, whole cloves and ghee and stir.. Also add cumin seeds, bay leaves, cardamoms, black peppercorns, salt and stevia, stir again, cover and cook on High for 12 minutes. Discard cinnamon stick, bay leaves, cloves and cardamom, divide among plates and serve as a side dish. Enjoy!

Nutrition: calories 152, fat 2, fiber 1, carbs 4, protein 6

Simple Glazed Carrots

Preparation time: 5 minutes
Cooking time: 7 minutes
Servings: 4

Ingredients:
- 16 ounces baby carrots
- 2 tablespoons olive oil
- 2 ounces water
- 2 ounces ghee
- 2 tablespoons dill, chopped
- A pinch of salt and black pepper

Directions:
Put carrots in your instant pot, add the ghee, water, salt and pepper, stir, cover and cook on High for 7 minutes. Drain carrots, transfer them to a bowl, add dill and the oil, toss and serve right away as a side dish. Enjoy!

Nutrition: calories 172, fat 3, fiber 3, carbs 5, protein 7

Great Broccoli Dish

Preparation time: 10 minutes
Cooking time: 12 minutes
Servings: 6

Ingredients:
- 31 oz broccoli florets
- 1 cup water
- 5 lemon slices
- A pinch of salt and black pepper

Directions:
Put the water in your instant pot, add the steamer basket, add broccoli florets and lemon slices, season with a pinch of salt and pepper, cover and cook on High for 12 minutes. Divide among plates and serve as a side dish. Enjoy!

Nutrition: calories 152, fat 2, fiber 1, carbs 2, protein 3

Brussels Sprouts Delight

Preparation time: 10 minutes
Cooking time: 8 minutes
Servings: 4

Ingredients:
- 2 tablespoons olive oil
- 2 garlic cloves, minced
- 2 tablespoons coconut aminos
- 1 and ½ pounds Brussels sprouts, halved
- 2 ounces water
- 1 and ½ teaspoon white pepper

Directions:
Put the oil in your instant pot, add garlic, Brussels sprouts, aminos, water and white pepper, stir, cover and cook on High for 8 minutes. Divide among plates and serve as a side dish. Enjoy!

Nutrition: calories 162, fat 2, fiber 1, carbs 2, protein 5

Special Sweet Potatoes

Preparation time: 10 minutes
Cooking time: 10 minutes
Servings: 8

Ingredients:
- 1 cup water
- 1 tablespoon lemon peel, grated
- 3 tablespoons stevia
- A pinch of sea salt
- 3 sweet potatoes, peeled and sliced
- ¼ cup ghee
- ¼ cup maple syrup
- 1 cup pecans, chopped
- 1 tablespoon arrowroot powder
- Whole pecans for garnish

Directions:
Pour the water in your instant pot, add lemon peel, stevia, sweet potatoes and salt, stir, cover, cook on High for 10 minutes and transfer them to a plate. Set your instant pot on Sauté mode, add the ghee and heat it up Add pecans, maple syrup arrowroot powder, stir very well and cook for 1 minutes, Divide sweet potatoes between plates, drizzle the pecans sauce all over, top with whole pecans and serve. Enjoy!

Nutrition: calories 162, fat 2, fiber 1, carbs 5, protein 6

Tasty Cauliflower And Mint Rice

Preparation time: 10 minutes
Cooking time: 5 minutes
Servings: 4

Ingredients:
- 1 cup cauliflower rice
- 2 tablespoons olive oil
- 1 small yellow onion, chopped
- 1 and ½ cups veggie stock
- 2 tablespoons mint, chopped
- A pinch of salt and black pepper

Directions:
Set your instant pot on sauté mode, add the oil, heat it up, add onion, stir and cook for 3 minutes. Add veggie stock, cauliflower rice, salt and pepper, stir, cover and cook on High for 5 minutes. Add mint, toss everything to coat, divide between plates and serve right away as a side dish. Enjoy!

Nutrition: calories 160, fat 3, fiber 2, carbs 6, protein 10

Special Collard Greens

Preparation time: 10 minutes
Cooking time: 5 minutes
Servings: 4

Ingredients:
- 1 tablespoons olive oil
- 16 ounces collard greens
- 1 cup yellow onion, chopped
- 2 garlic cloves, minced
- A pinch of sea salt and black pepper
- 14 ounces veggie stock
- 1 bay leaf
- 3 tablespoon balsamic vinegar

Directions:
Set your instant pot on sauté mode, add the oil, heat it up, add onion, stir and sauté for 3 minutes. Add collard greens, stir and sauté for 2 minutes more. Add garlic, salt, pepper, stock and bay leaf, stir, cover and cook on High for 5 minutes. Add vinegar, toss, divide among plates and serve. Enjoy!

Nutrition: calories 130, fat 1, fiber 2, carbs 3, protein 5

Amazing Carrots Side Dish

Preparation time: 10 minutes
Cooking time: 10 minutes
Servings: 12

Ingredients:
- 3 pounds carrots, peeled and cut into medium pieces
- A pinch of sea salt and black pepper
- ½ cup water
- ½ cup maple syrup
- 2 tablespoons olive oil
- ½ teaspoon orange rind, grated

Directions:
Put the oil in your instant pot, add the carrots and toss. Add maple syrup, water, salt, pepper and orange rind, stir, cover and cook on High for 10 minutes. Divide among plates and serve as a side dish. Enjoy!

Nutrition: calories 140, fat 2, fiber 1, carbs 2, protein 6

Rich Beets Side Dish

Preparation time: 10 minutes
Cooking time: 12 minutes
Servings: 6

Ingredients:
- 6 beets, peeled and cut into wedges
- A pinch of sea salt
- Black pepper to the taste
- 2 tablespoons lemon juice
- 2 tablespoons olive oil
- 2 tablespoons agave nectar
- 1 tablespoon cider vinegar
- ½ teaspoon lemon rind, grated
- 2 rosemary sprigs

Directions:
Put the beets in your slow cooker. Add a pinch of salt, black pepper, lemon juice, oil, agave nectar, rosemary and vinegar. Stir everything, cover and cook on Low for 8 hours. Add lemon rind, stir, divide among plates and serve. Enjoy!

Nutrition: calories 120, fat 1, fiber 2, carbs 6, protein 6

Green Beans Side Dish

Preparation time: 10 minutes
Cooking time: 14 minutes
Servings: 6

Ingredients:
- 5 cups water
- 1 tablespoon olive oil
- 2 tablespoons thyme, chopped
- 1 cup yellow onion, chopped
- 5 garlic cloves, minced
- 3 tablespoons balsamic vinegar
- ½ cup tomato paste
- ½ cup maple syrup
- 2 tablespoons coconut aminos
- 2 tablespoons red chili paste
- 2 tablespoons mustard
- 1 and ½ cups green beans
- A pinch of sea salt and black pepper

Directions:
Set your instant pot on sauté mode, add the oil, heat it up, add onion, stir and sauté for 3 minutes. Add garlic, thyme, vinegar and tomato paste, stir and cook for 1 minute more. Add green beans, water, maple syrup, mustard, chili paste, salt, pepper and aminos, stir, cover and cook on High for 10 minutes Divide among plates and serve as a side dish. Enjoy!

Nutrition: calories 160, fat 2, fiber 4, carbs 7, protein 8

Sweet Potatoes Side Dish

Preparation time: 10 minutes
Cooking time: 20 minutes
Servings: 6

Ingredients:

- 4 pounds sweet potatoes, peeled and sliced
- 2 tablespoons olive oil
- 1 cup water
- ½ cup orange juice
- 2 tablespoons maple syrup
- ½ teaspoon thyme, dried
- A pinch of sea salt and black pepper
- ½ teaspoon sage, dried

Directions:

Set your instant pot on sauté mode, add the oil, heat it up, add sweet potato slices and cook for 4 minutes. In a bowl, mix orange juice with honey, thyme, sage, a pinch of salt and black pepper and whisk well. Add this over potatoes, toss to coat, cover and cook on High for 16 minutes. Divide among plates and serve as a side dish. Enjoy!

Nutrition: calories 130, fat 3, fiber 2, carbs 5, protein 6

Wonderful And Special Side Dish

Preparation time: 10 minutes
Cooking time: 20 minutes
Servings: 12

Ingredients:

- 42 ounces veggie stock
- 1 cup carrot, shredded
- 2 and ½ cups cauliflower rice
- 2 tablespoons olive oil
- 2 teaspoons marjoram, dried
- 4 ounces mushrooms, sliced
- A pinch of sea salt and black pepper
- 2/3 cup cherries, dried
- ½ cup pecans, chopped
- 2/3 cup green onions, chopped

Directions:

Put the stock in your instant pot, add cauliflower rice, carrots, mushrooms, oil, salt, pepper and marjoram, stir, cover and cook on High for 12 minutes. Add cherries and green onions, stir, cover and cook for 5 minutes more. Divide among plates and serve as a side dish with chopped pecans on top. Enjoy!

Nutrition: calories 130, fat 2, fiber 3, carbs 4, protein 6

Mashed Sweet Potatoes

Preparation time: 10 minutes
Cooking time: 16 minutes
Servings: 12

Ingredients:

- 3 pounds sweet potatoes, peeled and cubed
- 1 cup coconut milk, hot
- 6 garlic cloves, minced
- 28 ounces veggie stock
- 1 bay leaf
- ¼ cup ghee, melted
- A pinch of sea salt and black pepper

Directions:

Put potatoes in your instant pot, add stock, garlic and bay leaf, stir, cover and cook on High for 16 minutes Drain potatoes, discard bay leaf, transfer them to a bowl, mash using a potato masher, mix with coconut milk and ghee and whisk really well. Season with a pinch of salt and pepper, stir well, divide among plates and serve as a side dish. Enjoy!

Nutrition: calories 135, fat 4, fiber 2, carbs 6, protein 4

Tasty Side Dish

Preparation time: 10 minutes
Cooking time: 10 minutes
Servings: 7

Ingredients:

- 2 tablespoons extra virgin olive oil
- ½ cup yellow onion, chopped
- ½ teaspoon saffron threads, crushed
- 2 tablespoons coconut milk, heated up
- 1 and ½ cups cauliflower rice
- 3 and ½ cups veggie stock
- A pinch of salt
- 1 tablespoon honey
- 1 cinnamon stick
- 1/3 cup almonds, chopped
- 1/3 cup currants, dried

Directions:

In a bowl, mix coconut milk with saffron and stir. Set your instant pot on Sauté mode, add oil, heat it up, add onions, stir and sauté them for 5 minutes. Add cauliflower rice, stock, saffron and milk, honey, salt, almonds, cinnamon stick and currants, stir, cover and cook on High for 5 minutes. Discard cinnamon stick, divide it between plates and serve as a side dish. Enjoy!

Nutrition: calories 243, fat 3, fiber 1, carbs 5, protein 5

Spinach Cauliflower Rice

Preparation time: 10 minutes
Cooking time: 10 minutes
Servings: 6

Ingredients:

- 2 garlic cloves, minced
- ¾ cup yellow onion, chopped
- 2 tablespoons extra virgin olive oil
- 1 and ½ cups cauliflower rice
- ½ cup water
- 12 ounces spinach, chopped
- 3 and ½ cups hot veggie stock
- A pinch of sea salt and black pepper
- 2 tablespoons lemon juice
- 1/3 cup pecans, toasted and chopped

Directions:

Set your instant pot on sauté mode, add the oil, heat it up, add garlic and onions, stir and sauté for 5 minutes. Add cauliflower rice and water, stir and cook for 1 minute more. Add 3 cups stock, cover the pot and cook on High for 4 minutes. Add spinach, stir, and set instant pot on Simmer mode, cook for 3 minutes and mix with the rest of the stock, salt, pepper and lemon juice. Stir; divide among plates, sprinkle pecans on top and serve as a side dish. Enjoy!

Nutrition: calories 243, fat 2, fiber 2, carbs 6, protein 12

Squash Puree

Preparation time: 10 minutes
Cooking time: 20 minutes
Servings: 4

Ingredients:

- ½ cup water
- 2 tablespoons ghee
- 2 acorn squash, halved
- A pinch of salt and black pepper
- ¼ teaspoon baking soda
- ½ teaspoon nutmeg, grated
- 2 tablespoons maple syrup

Directions:

Put the water in your instant pot, add the steamer basket, add squash halves inside, season with a pinch of salt, pepper and baking soda, rub a bit, cover and cook them on High for 20 minutes. Transfer squash to a plate, cool it down, scrape flesh, transfer to a bowl and mix with ghee, maple syrup and nutmeg. Mash using a potato masher, whisk well, divide among plates and serve as a side dish. Enjoy!

Nutrition: calories 143, fat 2, fiber 2, carbs 7, protein 2

Healthy Mushrooms and Green Beans

Preparation time: 10 minutes
Cooking time: 6 minutes
Servings: 4

Ingredients:

- 1 pound fresh green beans, trimmed
- 2 cups water
- 6 ounces bacon, chopped
- 1 small yellow onion, chopped
- 1 garlic clove, minced
- 8 ounces mushrooms, sliced
- A pinch of sea salt and black pepper
- A splash of balsamic vinegar

Directions:

Put the beans in your instant pot, add water to cover them, cover the pot, cook at High for 3 minutes, drain and leave them aside. Set your instant pot on Sauté mode, add bacon, brown it for 1 minute and mix with onion and garlic. Stir, cook 2 more minutes, add mushrooms, stir and cook until they are done. Return green beans to instant pot, add salt, pepper and a splash of vinegar, toss, divide among plates and serve as a side dish. Enjoy!

Nutrition: calories 123, fat 2, fiber 3, carbs 4, protein 3

Delicious Cauliflower Rice

Preparation time: 10 minutes
Cooking time: 20 minutes
Servings: 6

Ingredients:

- 2 cups cauliflower rice
- 2 cups water
- 1 small pineapple, peeled and chopped
- A pinch of sea salt and black pepper
- 2 teaspoons olive oil

Directions:

In your instant pot, mix cauliflower rice with pineapple, water, oil, salt and pepper, stir, cover and cook on Low for 20 minutes. Divide among plates and serve as a side dish. Enjoy!

Nutrition: calories 100, fat 2, fiber 2, carbs 6, protein 5

Lovely Mash

Preparation time: 10 minutes
Cooking time: 5 minutes
Servings: 4

Ingredients:

- 4 turnips, peeled and chopped
- 1 yellow onion, chopped
- ½ cup chicken stock
- A pinch of sea salt and black pepper
- ¼ cup coconut cream

Directions:

Put turnips, stock and onion in your instant pot, stir, cover and cook on High for 5 minutes Drain turnips, transfer them to a bowl, blend using an immersion blender, mix with a pinch of salt, pepper and coconut cream. Blend again, divide among plates and serve as a side dish. Enjoy!

Nutrition: calories 100, fat 2, fiber 2, carbs 6, protein 3

Carrot Puree

Preparation time: 5 minutes
Cooking time: 5 minutes
Servings: 4

Ingredients:
- 1 and ½ pounds carrots, chopped
- A pinch of salt and white pepper
- 1 tablespoon ghee, melted
- 1 teaspoon stevia
- 1 cup water
- 1 tablespoon honey

Directions:
Put carrots in your instant pot, add the water, cover, cook on High for 4 minutes, drain, transfer to a bowl and mash using an immersion blender. Add ghee, honey, a pinch of salt, pepper and stevia, blend again, divide among plates and serve. Enjoy!

Nutrition: calories 73, fat 2, fiber 2, carbs 4, protein 6

Apple Mash

Preparation time: 10 minutes
Cooking time: 15 minutes
Servings: 4

Ingredients:
- 1 cup water
- 2 apples, peeled, cored and sliced
- A pinch of sea salt
- 1 butternut squash, peeled and cut intoto medium chunks
- 2 tablespoons maple syrup
- 1 yellow onion, chopped
- ½ teaspoon apple pie spice

Directions:
Put the water in your instant pot, add the steamer basket inside, add squash pieces, onion and apple slices inside, cover and cook on High for 8 minutes/ Transfer squash, onion and apple to a bowl, mash using a potato masher, add a pinch of salt, maple syrup and pie spices, stir well, divide among plates and serve as a side dish. Enjoy!

Nutrition: calories 142, fat 2, fiber 3, carbs 5, protein 6

Simple Fennel Side Dish

Preparation time: 5 minutes
Cooking time: 6 minutes
Servings: 3

Ingredients:
- 2 fennel bulbs, sliced
- 1 tablespoon coconut flour
- 2 tablespoons olive oil
- A pinch of sea salt
- 2 cups coconut milk
- A pinch of nutmeg, ground

Directions:
Set your instant pot on Sauté mode, add ghee, heat it up, add fennel, brown for a couple of minutes and mix with salt, pepper, nutmeg, coconut milk and flour. Stir gently, cover and cook on Low for 6 minutes. Divide among plates and serve. Enjoy!

Nutrition: calories 152, fat 2, fiber 3, carbs 5, protein 6

Simple And Fast Side Dish

Preparation time: 10 minutes
Cooking time: 10 minutes
Servings: 4

Ingredients:
- 5 bok choy bunches
- 1 tablespoon olive oil
- 2 garlic cloves, minced
- 5 cups water
- 1 teaspoon ginger, grated
- A pinch of sea salt

Directions:
Put bok choy in your instant pot, add the water, cover, cook on High for 7 minutes, drain and transfer to a bowl. Clean the pot, set it on Sauté mode, add the oil and heat it up. Return bok choy to the pot, add a pinch of salt, garlic and ginger, stir and sauté for 3 minutes. Divide among plates and serve as a side dish. Enjoy!

Nutrition: calories 75, fat 1, fiber 1, carbs 3, protein 5

Mixed Veggies

Preparation time: 10 minutes
Cooking time: 10 minutes
Servings: 4

Ingredients:
- 2 yellow bell peppers, sliced
- 1 tablespoon olive oil
- ¼ cup water
- 2 red bell peppers, sliced
- 1 green bell pepper, sliced
- 2 garlic cloves, minced
- 2 tomatoes, chopped
- 1 red onion, chopped
- A pinch of salt and black pepper
- 1 bunch parsley, finely chopped

Directions:
Set your instant pot on Sauté mode, add the oil, heat it up, add onions, stir and cook for 3 minutes. Add red, yellow peppers, green peppers, tomatoes, the water, salt and pepper, stir, cover and cook on High for 7 minutes Transfer veggies to a bowl, add garlic and parsley, toss, divide among plates and serve as a side dish. Enjoy!

Nutrition: calories 152, fat 1, fiber 2, carbs 5, protein 6

Italian Side Dish

Preparation time: 10 minutes
Cooking time: 13 minutes
Servings: 4

Ingredients:
- 2 eggplants, cubed
- 1 garlic clove
- 1 bunch oregano, chopped
- A pinch of salt and black pepper
- 2 tablespoons olive oil
- A pinch of hot pepper flakes
- ½ cup water
- 2 anchovies, chopped

Directions:
Put eggplant cubes in a bowl, season with a pinch of salt, leave aside for 10 minutes, press well and transfer to another bowl. Set your instant pot on Sauté mode, add the oil, heat it up, add garlic, stir and cook for 1 minute. Discard garlic clove, add eggplant pieces, anchovies, oregano, salt, pepper and pepper flakes, stir and cook for 6 minutes. Add water, stir, cover the pot, cook at High for 3 minutes, divide among plates and serve as a side dish.
Enjoy!

Nutrition: calories 142, fat 2, fiber 2, carbs 6, protein 8

Artichokes Delight

Preparation time: 10 minutes
Cooking time: 20 minutes
Servings: 4

Ingredients:
- 4 artichokes, trimmed
- 2 cup chicken stock
- 1 tablespoon tarragon, chopped
- 1 lemon, sliced
- Juice and zest from 1 lemon
- 1 celery stalk, chopped
- ½ cup olive oil
- A pinch of sea salt

Directions:
Put artichokes in your instant pot, add stock and sliced lemon, season with a pinch of salt, cover and cook on High for 20 minutes. In your blender, mix tarragon with lemon zest and lemon juice, oil, celery and a pinch of salt and pulse really well. Divide artichokes on plates, drizzle lemon sauce all over and serve as a side dish. Enjoy!

Nutrition: calories 163, fat 4, fiber 6, carbs 8, protein 7

Beets Side Dish

Preparation time: 10 minutes
Cooking time: 7 minutes
Servings: 4

Ingredients:
- 1 and ½ pounds small beets, peeled and halved
- 2 tablespoons balsamic vinegar
- 2 teaspoons orange zest, grated
- 3 strips orange peel
- 2 tablespoons stevia
- ½ cup orange juice
- 2 scallions, chopped
- 2 teaspoons mustard

Directions:
In your instant pot, mix beets with orange peel strips, vinegar and orange juice, toss a bit, cover and cook on High for 7 minutes. Transfer beets to a bowl, discard orange peel, add stevia, mustard, grated orange zest, scallions and some cooking liquid from the beets, toss, divide among plates and serve as a side dish. Enjoy!

Nutrition: calories 152, fat 2, fiber 2, carbs 5, protein 6

Tomato Side Salad

Preparation time: 10 minutes
Cooking time: 20 minutes
Servings: 6

Ingredients:
- 2 and ½ cups water
- 8 small beets, trimmed
- 1 pint colored cherry tomatoes, halved
- 1 red onion, sliced
- 1 cup balsamic vinegar
- 1 tablespoon stevia
- A pinch of salt and black pepper
- 2 tablespoons olive oil
- 2 ounces pecans

Directions:
Put 1 and ½ cups water in your instant pot, add the steamer basket, add beets inside, cover and cook on High for 17 minutes. Leave beets to cool down, peel, cut them into medium cubes, transfer to a bowl, mix with tomatoes and onions, toss and leave aside. Clean the instant pot, set it on Simmer mode, add 1 cup water, vinegar, stevia, a pinch of salt and pepper, stir and cook for 2 minutes. In a bowl, mix 4 tablespoons of vinegar mix with the oil, whisk well, add to tomato salad and toss. Sprinkle pecans on top, toss to coat, divide among plates and serve as a side dish. Enjoy!

Nutrition: calories 152, fat 3, fiber 3, carbs 6, protein 8

Broccoli Side Dish

Preparation time: 10 minutes
Cooking time: 13 minutes
Servings: 4

Ingredients:
- 1 broccoli head, florets separated
- ½ cup water
- 6 garlic cloves, minced
- 1 tablespoon olive oil
- 1 tablespoon balsamic vinegar
- A pinch of black pepper

Directions:
Put the water in your instant pot, add the steamer basket, add broccoli florets inside, cover and cook on Low for 10 minutes. Transfer broccoli to a bowl filled with ice water, cool down, drain and transfer to a bowl. Clean your instant pot, set it on Sauté mode, add oil, heat it up, add garlic, stir and cook for 3 minutes. Add broccoli florets, a pinch of black pepper and the vinegar, stir, sauté for 1 minute more, divide among plates and serve. Enjoy!

Nutrition: calories 100, fat 2, fiber 0, carbs 1, protein 5

Light Brussels Sprouts Side Dish

Preparation time: 5 minutes
Cooking time: 5 minutes
Servings: 4

Ingredients:
- 1 pound Brussels sprouts
- 1 cup water
- Seeds from 1 pomegranate
- A pinch of sea salt and black pepper
- 1 tablespoon olive oil
- ¼ cup pine nuts, toasted

Directions:
Put the water in your instant pot, add the steamer basket, add Brussels sprouts inside, cover and cook on High for 5 minutes. Transfer sprouts to a bowl, add pomegranate seeds, pine nuts, salt, pepper and oil, toss, divide among plates and serve as a side dish. Enjoy!

Nutrition: calories 100, fat 1, fiber 2, carbs 2, protein 6

Perfect Side Dish

Preparation time: 4 minutes
Cooking time: 6 minutes
Servings: 4

Ingredients:

- 1 pound Brussels sprouts, halved
- 1 tablespoon mustard
- 1 cup chicken stock
- A pinch of sea salt and black pepper
- ½ cup bacon, chopped
- 1 tablespoon olive oil
- 2 tablespoons dill, chopped

Directions:

Set your instant pot on Sauté mode, add bacon, brown for a few minutes, add sprouts, salt, pepper, mustard and stock, stir, cover and cook on High for 5 minutes. Add oil and dill, toss, divide among plates and serve as a side dish. Enjoy!

Nutrition: calories 152, fat 3, fiber 3, carbs 6, protein 8

Unbelievable Cabbage Side Dish

Preparation time: 10 minutes
Cooking time: 10 minutes
Servings: 4

Ingredients:

- 1 cabbage, roughly shredded
- 1 tablespoon olive oil
- 2 carrots, grated
- ¼ cup balsamic vinegar
- 1 and ¼ cups water+2 teaspoons
- 1 teaspoon stevia
- A pinch of cayenne pepper
- A pinch of red pepper flakes
- 2 teaspoons arrowroot powder

Directions:

Set your instant pot on Sauté mode, add oil, heat it up, add cabbage, stir and sauté for 3 minutes. Add carrots, 1 and ¼ cups water, stevia, vinegar, cayenne and pepper flakes, stir, cover and cook at High for 5 minutes. Divide cabbage mix on plates and leave aside. Set the pot on Simmer mode, add arrowroot, the remaining water, stir, cook for 2 minutes, drizzle over cabbage and serve as a side dish. Enjoy!

Nutrition: calories 73, fat 2, fiber 3, carbs 7, protein 1

Special Flavored Side Dish

Preparation time: 10 minutes
Cooking time: 8 minutes
Servings: 8

Ingredients:
- 2 cups chicken stock
- 1 green cabbage head, chopped
- 3 tablespoons olive oil
- 3 bacon slices, chopped
- A pinch of black pepper

Directions:
Set your instant pot on Sauté mode, add bacon, stir, cook for 4 minutes. Add oil, cabbage, stock and pepper, stir, cover and cook at High for 3 minutes. Divide cabbage between plates and serve. Enjoy!

Nutrition: calories 100, fat 3, fiber 2, carbs 6, protein 5

Southern Side Dish

Preparation time: 10 minutes
Cooking time: 12 minutes
Servings: 6

Ingredients:
- 1 sweet onion, chopped
- 3 garlic cloves minced
- 2 tablespoons olive oil
- 2 and ½ pounds collard greens, roughly chopped
- A pinch of sea salt and black pepper
- 2 cups chicken stock
- 2 tablespoons balsamic vinegar
- 1 tablespoon stevia
- A pinch of red pepper, crushed
- ½ teaspoon smoked paprika

Directions:
Set your instant pot on Sauté mode, add oil, heat it up, add onions, stir and cook for 2 minutes. Add garlic, stock, greens, vinegar, salt, pepper, crushed red pepper, stevia and paprika, stir, cover and cook on High for 10 minutes. Divide among plates and serve as a side dish. Enjoy!

Nutrition: calories 100, fat 1, fiber 1, carbs 2, protein 3

French Endives Side Dish

Preparation time: 10 minutes
Cooking time: 7 minutes
Servings: 4

Ingredients:

- 4 endives, trimmed and halved
- 1 tablespoon ghee
- ½ cup water
- A pinch of sea salt and black pepper
- 1 tablespoon lemon juice

Directions:

Set your instant pot on Sauté mode, add ghee, heat it up, add endives, water, salt, pepper and lemon juice, toss, cover and cook on High for 7 minutes. Divide endives on plates, drizzle cooking juices all over and serve as a side dish. Enjoy!

Nutrition: calories 73, fat 2, fiber 1, carbs 1, protein 3

Fast Side Dish Delight

Preparation time: 10 minutes
Cooking time: 15 minutes
Servings: 4

Ingredients:

- 8 endives, trimmed
- A pinch of sea salt and black pepper
- 4 tablespoon ghee
- 1 teaspoon stevia
- Juice from ½ lemon
- ½ cup water
- 2 tablespoons parsley, chopped

Directions:

Put the endives in your instant pot, add 1 tablespoon ghee, lemon juice, water, stevia, salt and pepper, stir, cover, cook on High for 10 minutes, transfer to a plate and leave aside for now. Clean your instant pot, set it on Sauté mode, add the rest of the ghee, heat it up, return endives to the pot, add parsley, stir, sauté for 5 minutes, divide among plates and serve as a side dish. Enjoy!

Nutrition: calories 62, fat 1, fiber 2, carbs 2, protein 3

Delicious Okra

Preparation time: 10 minutes
Cooking time: 14 minutes
Servings: 3

Ingredients:
- 2 cups okra, sliced
- 2 teaspoons sweet paprika
- 4 bacon slices, chopped
- 1 cup tomatoes, chopped
- 2 and ¼ cups water
- Black pepper to the taste

Directions:
Set your instant pot on Sauté mode, add bacon, brown it for 2 minutes, add okra and paprika, stir and cook for 4 minutes more. Add black pepper, tomatoes and water, stir, cover and cook on High for 8 minutes. Divide among plates and serve as a side dish. Enjoy!

Nutrition: calories 93, fat 2, fiber 2, carbs 2, protein 6

Kale And Carrots Side Dish

Preparation time: 10 minutes
Cooking time: 10 minutes
Servings: 2

Ingredients:
- 10 ounces kale, chopped
- 1 yellow onion, chopped
- 3 carrots, sliced
- 1 tablespoon olive oil
- ½ cup chicken stock
- A pinch of black pepper
- 5 garlic cloves, minced
- A splash of balsamic vinegar
- ¼ teaspoon red pepper flakes

Directions:
Set your instant pot on Sauté mode, add the oil, heat it up, add onion and carrots, stir and cook for 2 minutes. Add garlic, kale, stock and pepper, stir, cover and cook at High for 7 minutes. Add vinegar and pepper flakes, toss to coat, divide among plates and serve as a side dish. Enjoy!

Nutrition: calories 73, fat 1, fiber 2, carbs 2, protein 3

Sweet Potatoes

Preparation time: 10 minutes
Cooking time: 16 minutes
Servings: 4

Ingredients:

- 2 pounds sweet potatoes, cut into medium wedges
- 5 tablespoons olive oil
- 5 garlic cloves, minced
- Black pepper to the taste
- 1 rosemary spring
- ½ cup stock

Directions:

Set your instant pot on Sauté mode, add oil, heat it up, add potatoes, rosemary and garlic, stir and brown them for 6 minutes. Add stock and pepper to the pot, cover and cook at High for 10 minutes. Discard rosemary, divide potatoes on plates and serve. Enjoy!

Nutrition: calories 73, fat 1, fiber 1, carbs 2, protein 2

Classic Indian Side Dish

Preparation time: 10 minutes
Cooking time: 18 minutes
Servings: 4

Ingredients:

- 20 ounces turnips, peeled and chopped
- 1 cup water
- 2 tablespoons olive oil
- 1 teaspoon garlic, minced
- 2 tomatoes, chopped
- 2 yellow onions, chopped
- 1 teaspoon ginger, grated
- 1 teaspoon stevia
- 2 green chilies, chopped
- 1 teaspoon cumin, ground
- 1 teaspoon coriander, ground
- ½ teaspoon turmeric powder
- 1 tablespoon coriander leaves, chopped

Directions:

Set your instant pot on Sauté mode, add the oil, heat it up, add green chilies, garlic and ginger, stir and cook for 1 minute. Add onions, tomatoes, cumin, coriander and turmeric, stir and sauté for 4 minutes more. Add turnips and water, stir, cover and cook on Low for 13 minutes. Add stevia and coriander, toss, divide among plates and serve as a side dish. Enjoy!

Nutrition: calories 100, fat 2, fiber 2, carbs 5, protein 7

Delicious Pumpkin Side Dish

Preparation time: 10 minutes
Cooking time: 11 minutes
Servings: 4

Ingredients:
- 2 tablespoons olive oil
- ½ cup water
- 2 garlic cloves, minced
- 3 tablespoons coconut aminos
- 1 inch ginger, grated
- ½ teaspoons red pepper flakes
- 4 bok choy bunches,, cut into quarters
- 1 small pumpkin, peeled, seeded and chopped
- 1 tablespoon sesame seeds, toasted

Directions:
Set your instant pot on Sauté mode, add the oil, heat it up, add garlic, ginger, aminos and pepper flakes, stir and sauté for 1 minutes. Add pumpkin, bok choy and water, stir gently, cover and cook on High for 10 minutes. Divide among plates, sprinkle sesame seeds on top and serve as a side dish. Enjoy!

Nutrition: calories 119 fat 2, fiber 2, carbs 3 protein 6

Healthy Broccoli Side Dish

Preparation time: 10 minutes
Cooking time: 7 minutes
Servings: 4

Ingredients:
- 8 garlic cloves, minced
- 2 tablespoons olive oil
- 8 cups broccoli florets
- 1 cup water
- Zest from 1 lemon, grated
- ¼ cup parsley, chopped
- Black pepper to the taste

Directions:
Set your instant pot on sauté mode, add garlic, stir and cook for 1 minute. Add broccoli, lemon zest, water and black pepper, stir, cover and cook on High for 6 minutes. Add parsley, toss, divide among plates and serve as a side dish. Enjoy!

Nutrition: calories 120, fat 1, fiber 2, carbs 3, protein 6

Cauliflower And Leeks

Preparation time: 10 minutes
Cooking time: 8 minutes
Servings: 4

Ingredients:
- 1 and ½ cups leeks, chopped
- 1 and ½ cups cauliflower florets
- 1 and ½ cups artichokes
- 1 cup water
- 2 garlic cloves, minced
- 2 tablespoons olive oil
- Black pepper to the taste

Directions:
Set your instant pot on Sauté mode, add the oil, heat it up, add garlic, stir and sauté for 1 minute. Add leeks, cauliflower, artichokes and water, stir, cover and cook on High for 7 minutes. Divide among plates, sprinkle some black pepper on top and serve as a side dish. Enjoy!

Nutrition: calories 110, fat 2, fiber 2, carbs 6, protein 3

Tasty Squash Side Dish

Preparation time: 10 minutes
Cooking time: 11 minutes
Servings: 2

Ingredients:
- 1 tablespoon olive oil
- 1 butternut squash, peeled and cubed
- 1 cup water
- 2 garlic cloves, minced
- 12 ounces coconut milk
- 1 small yellow onion, chopped
- ½ cup cranberries, dried
- 1 teaspoon curry powder
- 1 teaspoon cinnamon powder

Directions:
Set your instant pot on Sauté mode, add the oil, heat it up, add garlic and onion, stir and cook for 2 minutes. Add squash, curry powder and cinnamon, stir, cover and cook on High for 6 minutes. Add coconut milk and cranberries, set the pot on simmer mode and cook for 3 minutes more. Divide among plates and serve as a side dish. Enjoy!

Nutrition: calories 100, fat 2, fiber 2, carbs 3, protein 2

Special Carrots Side Dish

Preparation time: 10 minutes
Cooking time: 6 minutes
Servings: 4

Ingredients:
- ½ cup water
- 1 tablespoon olive oil
- 1 pound baby carrots
- 2 tablespoons dill, chopped
- 1 tablespoon honey
- A pinch of black pepper

Directions:
Set your instant pot on sauté mode, add the oil and heat it up. Add carrots, stir and sauté them for 1 minute. Add honey, black pepper and water, cover and cook on High for 5 minutes. Add dill, stir, divide among plates and serve as a side dish. Enjoy!

Nutrition: calories 100, fat 2, fiber 3, carbs 3, protein 4

Nutritious Side Dish

Preparation time: 10 minutes
Cooking time: 7 minutes
Servings: 4

Ingredients:
- 3 ounces bacon, chopped
- 1 garlic clove, minced
- ½ cup veggie stock
- 1 bunch kale, roughly chopped
- 1 tablespoon lemon juice
- Black pepper to the taste

Directions:
Set your instant pot on Sauté mode, add bacon and brown for 3 minutes on each side. Add kale, stock, garlic, lemon juice and black pepper, stir, cover and cook on High for 4 minutes. Stir gently the whole mix, divide it between plates and serve as a side dish. Enjoy!

Nutrition: calories 100, fat 2, fiber 1, carbs 4, protein 5

Zucchini Side Dish

Preparation time: 10 minutes
Cooking time: 4 minutes
Servings: 4

Ingredients:
- 2 tablespoons mint, chopped
- 1 tablespoon olive oil
- ½ cup water
- 2 zucchinis, halved and roughly chopped
- ½ tablespoon dill, chopped
- A pinch of black pepper

Directions:
Set your instant pot on sauté mode, add the oil, heat it up, add zucchinis, stir and cook for 1 minute. Add water and black pepper, stir, cover and cook on High for 3 minutes. Add mint and dill, stir gently, divide among plates and serve as a side dish. Enjoy!

Nutrition: calories 30, fat 0, fiber 1, carbs 2, protein 2

Dessert Recipes

Almond Cream Cheese Cake

Preparation time: 10 minutes
Cooking time: 20 minutes
Servings: 12

Ingredients:
- 1 pound almond cream cheese
- 6 oz dates, soaked for 15 minutes and drained
- 2 ounces honey
- 4 eggs
- 2 ounces stevia
- Some vanilla extract
- 17 ounces water
- Orange juice and zest from ½ orange

Directions:
In a bowl, mix almond cream cheese with eggs, honey, stevia, vanilla, orange zest, orange juice and dates, stir well, pour into a heatproof dish and cover with tin foil. Put water in instant pot, add the trivet on the bottom, add the baking dish, cover and cook on Medium for 20 minutes. Leave cake to cool down, slice and serve it. Enjoy!

Nutrition: calories 200, fat 2, fiber 2, carbs 3, protein 3

Sweet Cauliflower Rice Pudding

Preparation time: 5 minutes
Cooking time: 14 minutes
Servings: 6

Ingredients:
- 1 tablespoon ghee
- 7 ounces cauliflower, riced
- 4 ounces water
- 16 ounces almond milk
- 2 tablespoons stevia
- 1 egg
- 1 tablespoon coconut cream
- 1 teaspoon vanilla
- Cinnamon to the taste

Directions:
Set your instant pot on Sauté mode, add ghee, melt it, add cauliflower rice and stir well. Add water, milk and stevia, stir, cover and cook on High for 8 minutes. In a bowl, mix cream with vanilla and eggs and stir well. Pour some of the liquid from the pot into the egg mixture, stir and add this to the pot, cover and cook on High for 4 minutes more. Divide into bowls, sprinkle cinnamon all over and serve. Enjoy!

Nutrition: calories 172, fat 2, fiber 2, carbs 3, protein 6

Great Pears Dessert

Preparation time: 10 minutes
Cooking time: 10 minutes
Servings: 4

Ingredients:
- 4 pears
- Zest and juice from 1 lemon
- 26 ounces natural grape juice
- 11 ounces natural and Paleo currant jelly
- 4 cloves
- ½ vanilla bean
- 4 peppercorns
- 2 rosemary sprigs

Directions:
Put currant jelly in your instant pot, add grape juice, orange zest and juice, cloves, peppercorns, rosemary and vanilla bean and stir well. Dip pears in this mix and wrap them in tin foil. Put the steamer basket into the pot, add wrapped pears inside, cover and cook on High for 10 minutes. Unwrap pears, divide them between plates, drizzle juices from the pot all over and serve. Enjoy!

Nutrition: calories 182, fat 3, fiber 1, carbs 2, protein 3

Pears And Special Sauce

Preparation time: 10 minutes
Cooking time: 10 minutes
Servings: 6

Ingredients:
- 6 green pears
- 1 vanilla pod
- 1 clove
- A pinch of cinnamon
- 7 oz stevia
- 1 glass natural red grape juice

Directions:
In your instant pot, mix red grapes juice with stevia and cinnamon and stir. Add the pears and clove, cover and cook on High for 10 minutes. Divide pears and grapes sauce on plates and serve. Enjoy!

Nutrition: calories 172, fat 2, fiber 2, carbs 3, protein 6

Tapioca Pudding

Preparation time: 10 minutes
Cooking time: 10 minutes
Servings: 4

Ingredients:
- 1 and ½ cups water
- 1/3 cup tapioca pearls
- 1 and ¼ cup coconut milk
- Zest from ½ lemon
- 3 tablespoons stevia

Directions:
Put tapioca pearls in a heat proof bowl, add milk, ½ cup water, lemon zest and stevia and stir well. Put 1 cup water in your instant pot, add the steamer basket, add the dish with tapioca pudding, cover and cook on High for 10 minutes. Divide into dessert cups and serve. Enjoy!

Nutrition: calories 162, fat 4, fiber 1, carbs 3, protein 3

Sweet Apples

Preparation time: 10 minutes
Cooking time: 10 minutes
Servings: 6

Ingredients:
- 6 apples
- 1 cup natural red grape juice
- ¼ cup raisins
- 1 teaspoon cinnamon powder
- 2 tablespoons stevia

Directions:

Put the apples in your instant pot, add grape juice, raisins, cinnamon and stevia, toss a bit, cover and cook on High for 10 minutes. Divide among small dessert plates and serve. Enjoy!

Nutrition: calories 130, fat 1, fiber 2, carbs 6, protein 1

Amazing Chocolate Dessert

Preparation time: 5 minutes
Cooking time: 2 minutes
Servings: 4

Ingredients:
- 2 cups water
- 3.5 ounces dark chocolate, chopped
- 3.5 ounces coconut milk

Directions:

In a ramekin, mix chocolate with coconut milk and whisk well. Put the water in your instant pot, add the steamer basket, add ramekin inside, cover and cook on High for 2 minutes. Stir chocolate mix well and serve. Enjoy!

Nutritional value: calories 110, fat 3, fiber 2, carbs 4, protein 2

Simple And Delicious Cake

Preparation time: 10 minutes
Cooking time: 35 minutes
Servings:

Ingredients:
- 1 and ¼ cup coconut flour
- ½ teaspoon baking powder
- ½ teaspoon baking soda
- ½ teaspoon cardamom, ground
- ½ cup almond milk
- 2 tablespoons stevia
- 2 tablespoons flax seeds
- 2 tablespoon coconut oil, melted
- 1 cup pear, chopped
- ½ cup cranberries, chopped
- 1 and ½ cups water

Directions:

In a bowl, mix flour with baking soda and powder and cardamom and stir. In another bowl, mix milk with flax seeds, stevia and oil and stir well. Combine the two mixtures, add cranberries and pear, stir and pour into a greased cake pan. Pour the water in your instant pot, add the steamer basket and place the pan inside, cover and cook on High for 35 minutes. Leave cake to cool down, slice and serve. Enjoy!

Nutrition: calories 160, fat 2, fiber 3, carbs 3, protein 4

Carrot Cake

Preparation time: 10 minutes
Cooking time: 30 minutes
Servings: 6

Ingredients:
- 5 ounces coconut flour
- ¾ teaspoon baking powder
- ½ teaspoon baking soda
- ½ teaspoon allspice
- ½ teaspoon cinnamon powder
- 3 tablespoons coconut cream
- ¼ teaspoon nutmeg, ground
- 1 tablespoon flaxseed mixed well with 2 tablespoons water
- 3 tablespoons stevia
- 1/3 cup carrots, grated
- ¼ cup pineapple juice
- 1/3 cup coconut flakes
- 4 tablespoons coconut oil, melted
- 1/3 cup pecans, toasted and chopped
- Cooking spray
- 2 cups water

Directions:

In a bowl, mix flour with baking soda and powder, salt, allspice, cinnamon and nutmeg and stir. Add flaxseed, cream, stevia, pineapple juice, oil, carrots, pecans and coconut flakes, stir and pour into a greased cake pan. Put 2 cups water in your instant pot, add the steamer basket, add cake pan, cover and cook on High for 32 minutes. Leave cake to cool down, slice and serve it. Enjoy!

Nutrition: calories 140, fat 3, fiber 2, carbs 3, protein 4

Simple Cobbler

Preparation time: 10 minutes
Cooking time: 12 minutes
Servings: 4

Ingredients:
- 3 apples, cored and cut into medium pieces
- 1 and ½ cups hot water
- 2 pears, cored and cut into chunks
- ¼ cup date syrup
- 3 tablespoons flax meal
- 1 teaspoon cinnamon powder

Directions:

Put apples and pears in your instant pot, add hot water, date syrup, flax meal and cinnamon, stir, cover and cook on High for 12 minutes. Divide into bowls and serve. Enjoy!

Nutrition: calories 143, fat 3, fiber 1, carbs 2, protein 3

Simple And Delicious Compote

Preparation time: 10 minutes
Cooking time: 3 minutes
Servings: 6

Ingredients:
- 8 peaches, stones removed and chopped
- ½ cup water
- 4 tablespoons stevia
- 1 teaspoon cinnamon powder
- 1 vanilla bean, scraped
- 1 teaspoon vanilla extract

Directions:
Put the peaches in your instant pot, add stevia, water, vanilla bean, vanilla extract and cinnamon, stir, cover and cook on High for 3 minutes. Divide into bowls and serve. Enjoy!

Nutrition: calories 100, fat 2, fiber 1, carbs 2, protein 3, protein 3

Delightful Peaches Surprise

Preparation time: 10 minutes
Cooking time: 4 minutes
Servings: 4

Ingredients:
- 6 peaches, tops cut off and insides removed
- ¼ cup coconut flour
- ¼ cup maple syrup
- 2 tablespoons coconut butter
- ½ teaspoon cinnamon powder
- 1 teaspoon almond extract
- 1 cup water

Directions:
In a bowl, mix flour with maple syrup, coconut butter, cinnamon and ½ teaspoon almond extract, stir well and stuff peaches with this mix. Add the water and the rest of the almond extract to your instant pot, add steamer basket, add peaches inside, cover and cook on High for 4 minutes. Divide among plates and serve. Enjoy!

Nutrition: calories 165, fat 3, fiber 1, carbs 2, protein 4

Carrots Dessert

Preparation time: 10 minutes
Cooking time: 14 minutes
Servings: 4

Ingredients:
- 1 tablespoon stevia
- 2 cups baby carrots
- ½ cup water
- ½ tablespoon ghee

Directions:
Set your instant pot on Sauté mode, add ghee, melt it up, mix with stevia and water and stir well. Add carrots, toss to coat, cover the pot and cook on High for 12 minutes. Divide into small bowls and serve. Enjoy!

Nutrition: calories 76, fat 1, fiber 1, carbs 2, protein 2

Elegant Dessert

Preparation time: 10 minutes
Cooking time: 7 minutes
Servings: 4

Ingredients:
- 1 cup red grapes juice
- 1 pound figs
- ½ cup pine nuts, toasted
- 2 tablespoons stevia

Directions:
Put grape juice in your instant pot, add the steamer basket, and add figs, cover, cook on High for 4 minutes, divide among plates and leave aside for now. Set the pot on Simmer mode, add stevia, stir well, cook for 1 minute and drizzle this over figs. Enjoy!
Nutrition: calories 73, fat 0, fiber 1, carbs 2, protein 2

Special Lemon Cream

Preparation time: 30 minutes
Cooking time: 5 minutes
Servings: 4

Ingredients:
- 1 cup coconut milk
- Zest from 1 lemon, grated
- 6 egg yolks
- 1 cup coconut cream
- 1 cup water
- 1 tablespoon stevia
- ½ cup fresh blackberries

Directions:
Heat up a pan over medium heat, add coconut milk, lemon zest and coconut cream, stir, bring to a boil, take off heat and leave aside for 30 minutes. In a bowl, mix egg yolks with stevia and cream mix, stir, divide into 4 ramekins and cover them with tin foil. Add the water to your instant pot, add the steamer basket, add ramekins inside, cover and cook on High 5 minutes. Serve with blackberries on top. Enjoy!
Nutrition: calories 132, fat 2, fiber 1, carbs 2, protein 2

Delicious Carrot Dessert

Preparation time: 10 minutes
Cooking time: 1 hour
Servings: 6

Ingredients:
- 1 and ½ cups water
- 2 tablespoons stevia
- 2 eggs
- ¼ cup molasses
- ½ cup coconut flour
- ½ teaspoon allspice
- ½ teaspoon baking soda
- ½ teaspoon cinnamon powder
- A pinch of nutmeg, ground
- ½ cup pecans, chopped
- ½ cup carrots, grated
- ½ cup raisins
- ½ cup flax meal

Directions:
In a bowl, mix molasses with eggs and stevia and stir. Add flour, carrots, nuts, raisins, flax meal, cinnamon, allspice, nutmeg and baking soda, stir everything, pour into a greased cake pan and cover with tin foil. Put the water in your instant pot, add the steamer basket, add cake pan inside, cover and cook on High for 1 hour. Leave cake to cool down, slice and serve it. Enjoy!
Nutrition: calories 200, fat 2, fiber 3, carbs 6, protein 7

Chocolate Cake

Preparation time: 10 minutes
Cooking time: 40 minutes
Servings: 6

Ingredients:

- ¾ cup cocoa powder
- ¾ cup almond flour
- ½ cup ghee, melted
- 1 cup water
- 4 tablespoons stevia
- ½ teaspoon baking powder
- 3 eggs, whites and yolks separated
- 1 teaspoon vanilla extract

Directions:

In a bowl, beat egg whites with your mixer. In another bowl, beat egg yolks with your mixer. In a third bowl, mix flour with baking powder, stevia, cocoa powder, egg white, egg yolks, ghee and vanilla extract, stir very well and pour into a greased and lined baking pan. Put the water in your instant pot, add the steamer basket, add cake pan, cook on Low for 40 minutes, and leave cake to cool down, slice and serve it. Enjoy!

Nutrition: calories 241, fat 2, fiber 2, carbs 3, protein 5

Simple And Delicious Compote

Preparation time: 10 minutes
Cooking time: 30 minutes
Servings: 8

Ingredients:

- 1/3 cup water
- 1 tablespoon mint, chopped
- 2 pounds rhubarb, chopped
- 3 tablespoon honey
- 1 pound strawberries, chopped

Directions:

Put rhubarb and water in your instant pot, add honey, mint and strawberries, stir cover and cook on High for 7 minutes. Switch instant pot to simmer mode and cook compote for 15 minutes more. Serve cold. Enjoy!

Nutrition: calories 74, fat 0, fiber 0, carbs 1, protein 2

Special Pudding

Preparation time: 15 minutes
Cooking time: 20 minutes
Servings: 8

Ingredients:

- 2 cups water
- 1 egg
- 1 and ¼ cups dates, chopped
- ¼ cup blackstrap molasses
- ¾ cup hot water
- 1 teaspoon baking powder
- 1 and ¼ cups coconut flour
- 2 tablespoons stevia
- 1/3 cup ghee, melted
- 1 teaspoon vanilla extract

Directions:

In a bowl, mix dates with hot water and molasses and stir, In another bowl, mix baking powder with flour and stir. In a third bowl, mix stevia with ghee, egg and vanilla and stir Add flour and dates mixtures to this mix, stir again and divide this into 8 small and greased ramekins. Put the water in your instant pot, add the steamer basket, add ramekins inside, cover and cook on Low for 20 minutes. Serve them warm. Enjoy!

Nutrition: calories 174, fat 1, fiber 3, carbs 6, protein 7

Fast Dessert

Preparation time: 10 minutes
Cooking time: 15 minutes
Servings: 6

Ingredients:

- 2 egg yolks
- 3 eggs
- 1 and ½ cups water
- 2 cups coconut milk, warm
- 2 tablespoons stevia
- ½ cup coconut cream
- 2 tablespoons hazelnut syrup
- 1 teaspoon vanilla extract

Directions:

In a bowl, mix eggs with yolks and stevia and whisk well. Add warm milk, hazelnut syrup, vanilla and coconut cream, stir, strain and pour into custard cups. Add the water to your instant pot, add the steamer basket, add custard cups, cover and cook on High for 6 minutes. Leave custard to cool down completely and serve. Enjoy!

Nutrition: calories 142, fat 1, fiber 2, carbs 2, protein 3

Cool Pudding

Preparation time: 10 minutes
Cooking time: 5 minutes
Servings: 8

Ingredients:

- 1 tablespoon coconut oil
- 1 and ½ cups water
- 1 cup cauliflower, riced
- 14 ounces coconut milk
- 2 eggs
- 3 tablespoons stevia
- ½ teaspoon vanilla extract
- 8 ounces canned pineapple, chopped

Directions:

In your instant pot, mix oil with water and cauliflower rice, stir, cover and cook at High for 3 minutes. Add stevia, coconut milk, eggs and vanilla, stir, set the pot on Simmer mode and bring to boil. Add pineapple, stir, divide into bowls and serve. Enjoy!

Nutrition: calories 112, fat 2, fiber 2, carbs 2, protein 3

Zucchini Dessert

Preparation time: 10 minutes
Cooking time: 25 minutes
Servings: 6

Ingredients:

- 1 cup natural applesauce
- 3 eggs, whisked
- 1 tablespoon vanilla extract
- 3 tablespoons stevia
- 2 cups zucchini, grated
- 2 and ½ cups coconut flour
- ½ cup cocoa powder
- 1 teaspoon baking soda
- ¼ teaspoon baking powder
- 1 teaspoon cinnamon powder
- ½ cup walnuts, chopped
- ½ cup dark chocolate chips
- 1 and ½ cups water

Directions:

In a bowl, mix zucchini with stevia, vanilla, eggs and applesauce and stir well. Add flour, cocoa, baking soda, baking powder, cinnamon, chocolate chips and walnuts, stir and pour into a greased cake pan. Add the water to your instant pot, add the steamer basket, add the pan, cover and cook on High for 25 minutes. Leave cake to cool down, slice and serve. Enjoy!

Nutrition: calories 200, fat 1, fiber 3, carbs 2, protein 6

Berry Compote

Preparation time: 10 minutes
Cooking time: 5 minutes
Servings: 8

Ingredients:
- 1 cup blueberries
- 2 cups strawberries, sliced
- 2 tablespoons lemon juice
- 2 tablespoons stevia
- 1 tablespoon arrowroot powder
- 1 tablespoon water

Directions:
In your instant pot, mix blueberries with lemon juice and stevia, stir, cover and cook at High for 3 minutes. Add arrowroot powder mixed with 1 tablespoon water, stir, set the pot on Simmer mode and cook for 2 minutes more. Serve cold. Enjoy!

Nutrition: calories 162, fat 2, fiber 2, carbs 3, protein 3

Refreshing Curd

Preparation time: 10 minutes
Cooking time: 5 minutes
Servings: 4

Ingredients:
- 3 tablespoons stevia
- 12 ounces raspberries
- 2 egg yolks
- 2 tablespoons lemon juice
- 2 tablespoons ghee

Directions:
Put raspberries in your instant pot, add stevia and lemon juice, stir, cover and cook on High for 2 minutes. Strain this into a bowl, add egg yolks, stir well and return to your pot. Set the pot on Simmer mode, cook for 2 minutes, add ghee, stir well, transfer to a container and serve cold. Enjoy!

Nutrition: calories 132, fat 1, fiber 0, carbs 2, protein 4

The Best Jam Ever

Preparation time: 10 minutes
Cooking time: 5 minutes
Servings: 6

Ingredients:
- 4 and ½ cups peaches, peeled and cubed
- 4 tablespoons stevia
- ¼ cup crystallized ginger, chopped

Directions:
Set your instant pot on Simmer mode, add peaches, ginger and stevia, stir, bring to a boil, cover and cook on High for 5 minutes. Divide into bowls and serve cold. Enjoy!

Nutrition: calories 53, fat 0, fiber 0, carbs 0, protein 2

Divine Pears

Preparation time: 10 minutes
Cooking time: 4 minutes
Servings: 12

Ingredients:
- 8 pears, cored and cut intoto quarters
- 1 teaspoon cinnamon powder
- 2 apples, peeled, cored and cut intoto quarters
- ¼ cup natural apple juice

Directions:
In your instant pot, mix pears with apples, cinnamon and apple juice, stir, cover and cook on High for 4 minutes. Blend using an immersion blender, divide into small jars and serve cold Enjoy!

Nutrition: calories 100, fat 0, fiber 0, carbs 0, protein 2

Berry Marmalade

Preparation time: 10 minutes
Cooking time: 20 minutes
Servings: 12

Ingredients:
- 1 pound cranberries
- 1 pound strawberries
- ½ pound blueberries
- 3.5 ounces black currant
- 4 tablespoons stevia
- Zest from 1 lemon
- A pinch of salt
- 2 tablespoon water

Directions:
In your instant pot, mix strawberries with cranberries, blueberries, currants, lemon zest, stevia and water, stir, cover and cook on High for 10 minutes. Divide into jars and serve cold. Enjoy!

Nutrition: calories 87, fat 2, fiber 0, carbs 1, protein 2

Orange Delight

Preparation time: 10 minutes
Cooking time: 25 minutes
Servings: 8

Ingredients:
- Juice from 2 lemons
- 6 tablespoons stevia
- 1 pound oranges, peeled and halved
- 1-pint water

Directions:
In your instant pot, mix lemon juice with orange juice and orange segments, water and stevia, cover and cook on High for 15 minutes. Divide into jars and serve cold.
Nutrition: calories 75, fat 0, fiber 0, carbs 2, protein 2

Simple Squash Pie

Preparation time: 10 minutes
Cooking time: 14 minutes
Serving: 8

Ingredients:

- 2 pounds butternut squash, peeled and chopped
- 2 eggs
- 2 cups water
- 1 cup coconut milk
- 2 tablespoons honey
- 1 teaspoon cinnamon powder
- ½ teaspoon ginger powder
- ¼ teaspoon cloves, ground
- 1 tablespoon arrowroot powder
- Chopped pecans

Directions:

Put 1 cup water in your instant pot, add the steamer basket, add squash pieces, cover, cook on High for 4 minutes, drain, transfer to a bowl and mash. Add honey, milk, eggs, cinnamon, ginger and cloves, stir very well and pour into ramekins. Add the rest of the water to your instant pot, add the steamer basket, add ramekins inside, cover and cook on High for 10 minutes. Garnish with chopped pecans and serve. Enjoy!

Nutrition: calories 132, fat 1, fiber 2, carbs 2, protein 3

Winter Pudding

Preparation time: 10 minutes
Cooking time: 40 minutes
Servings: 4

Ingredients:

- 4 ounces dried cranberries, soaked for a few hours and drained
- 2 cups water
- 4 ounces apricots, chopped
- 1 cup coconut flour
- 3 teaspoons baking powder
- 3 tablespoons stevia
- 1 teaspoon ginger powder
- A pinch of cinnamon powder
- 15 tablespoons ghee
- 3 tablespoons maple syrup
- 4 eggs
- 1 carrot, grated

Directions:

In a blender, mix flour with baking powder, stevia, cinnamon and ginger and pulse a few times. Add ghee, maple syrup, eggs, carrots, cranberries and apricots, stir and spread into a greased pudding pan. Add the water to your instant pot, add the steamer basket, add the pudding, cover and cook on High for 30 minutes. Leave pudding to cool down before serving. Enjoy!

Nutrition: calories 213, fat 2, fiber 1, carbs 3, protein 3

Banana Dessert

Preparation time: 10 minutes
Cooking time: 30 minutes
Servings: 6

Ingredients:
- 2 tablespoons stevia
- 1/3 cup ghee, soft
- 1 teaspoon vanilla
- 1 egg
- 2 bananas, mashed
- 1 teaspoon baking powder
- 1 and ½ cups coconut flour
- ½ teaspoons baking soda
- 1/3 cup coconut milk
- 2 cups water
- Cooking spray

Directions:
In a bowl, mix milk stevia, ghee, egg, vanilla and bananas and stir everything. In another bowl, mix flour with salt, baking powder and soda. Combine the 2 mixtures, stir well and pour into a greased cake pan. Add the water to your pot, add the steamer basket, add the cake pan, cover and cook at High for 30 minutes. Leave cake to cool down, slice and serve. Enjoy!

Nutrition: calories 243, fat 1, fiber 1, carbs 2, protein 4

Apple Cake

Preparation time: 10 minutes
Cooking time: 1 hour and 10 minutes
Servings: 6

Ingredients:
- 3 cups apples, cored and cubed
- 1 cup water
- 3 tablespoons stevia
- 1 tablespoon vanilla
- 2 eggs
- 1 tablespoon apple pie spice
- 2 cups coconut flour
- 1 tablespoon baking powder
- 1 tablespoon ghee

Directions:
In a bowl mix eggs with ghee, apple pie spice, vanilla, apples and stevia and stir using your mixer. In another bowl, mix baking powder with flour, stir, add to apple mix, stir again well and transfer to a cake pan. Add 1 cup water to your instant pot, add the steamer basket, add cake pan, cover and cook at High for 1 hour and 10 minutes. Cool cake down, slice and serve it. Enjoy!

Nutrition: calories 100, fat 2, fiber 1, carbs 2, protein 2

Special Vanilla Dessert

Preparation time: 10 minutes
Cooking time: 10 minutes
Servings: 4

Ingredients:

- 1 cup almond milk
- 4 tablespoons flax meal
- 2 tablespoons coconut flour
- 2 and ½ cups water
- 2 tablespoons stevia
- 1 teaspoon espresso powder
- 2 teaspoons vanilla extract
- Coconut cream for serving

Directions:

In your instant pot, mix flax meal with flour, water, stevia, milk and espresso powder, stir, cover and cook on high for 10 minutes. Add vanilla extract, stir well, leave aside for 5 minutes, divide into bowls and serve with coconut cream on top. Enjoy!
Nutrition: calories 182, fat 2, fiber 1, carbs 3, protein 4

Tasty And Amazing Pear Dessert

Preparation time: 10 minutes
Cooking time: 6 minutes
Servings: 4

Ingredients:

- 1 cup water
- 2 cups pear, peeled and cubed
- 2 cups coconut milk
- 1 tablespoon ghee
- ¼ cups brown stevia
- ½ teaspoon cinnamon powder
- 4 tablespoons flax meal
- ½ cup walnuts, chopped
- ½ cup raisins

Directions:

In a heat proof dish, mix milk with stevia, ghee, flax meal, cinnamon, raisins, pears and walnuts and stir. Put the water in your instant pot, add the steamer basket, place heat proof dish inside, cover and cook on High for 6 minutes. Divide this great dessert into small cups and serve cold. Enjoy!
Nutrition: calories 162, fat 3, fiber 1, carbs 2, protein 6

Cranberries Jam

Preparation time: 10 minutes
Cooking time: 15 minutes
Servings: 12

Ingredients:

- 16 ounces cranberries
- 4 ounces raisins
- 3 ounces water+ ¼ cup water
- 8 ounces figs
- 16 ounces strawberries, chopped
- Zest from 1 lemon

Directions:

Put figs in your blender, add ¼ cup water, pulse well and strain into a bowl. In your instant pot, mix strawberries with cranberries, lemon zest, raisins, 3 ounces water and figs puree, stir, cover the pot, cook at High for 15 minutes, divide into small jars and serve.
Nutrition: calories 73, fat 1, fiber 1, carbs 2, protein 3

Lemon Jam

Preparation time: 10 minutes
Cooking time: 12 minutes
Servings: 8

Ingredients:
- 2 pounds lemons, sliced
- 2 cups dates
- 1 cup water
- 1 tablespoon vinegar

Directions:
Put dates in your blender, add water and pulse really well. Put lemon slices in your instant pot, add dates paste and vinegar, stir, cover and cook on High for 12 minutes. Stir, divide into small jars and serve. Enjoy!

Nutrition: calories 72, fat 2, fiber 1, carbs 2, protein 6

Special Dessert

Preparation time: 10 minutes
Cooking time: 25 minutes
Servings: 4

Ingredients:
- 1 tablespoon cinnamon, ground
- 2 cups cauliflower, riced
- 2 apples, diced
- 1 teaspoon cloves, ground
- 1 teaspoon turmeric, ground
- A drizzle of honey
- 3 cups rooibos tea

Directions:
Put cauliflower rice in your instant pot, add tea, stir, cover and cook at High for 10 minutes Add cinnamon, apples, turmeric and cloves, stir, cover and cook at High for 10 minutes mode. Divide into bowls, drizzle honey on top and serve. Enjoy!

Nutrition: calories 152, fat 2, fiber 1, carbs 5, protein 6

Superb Banana Dessert

Preparation time: 10 minutes
Cooking time: 30 minutes
Servings: 4

Ingredients:
- Juice from ½ lemon
- 2 tablespoons stevia
- 3 ounces water
- 1 tablespoon coconut oil
- 4 bananas, peeled and sliced
- ½ teaspoon cardamom seeds

Directions:
Put bananas, stevia, water, oil, lemon juice and cardamom in your instant pot, stir a bit, cover and cook on High for 30 minutes, shaking the pot from time to time. Divide into bowls and serve. Enjoy!

Nutrition: calories 87, fat 1, fiber 2, carbs 3, protein 3

Rhubarb Dessert

Preparation time: 10 minutes
Cooking time: 5 minutes
Servings: 4

Ingredients:
- 5 cups rhubarb, chopped
- 2 tablespoons ghee, melted
- 1/3 cup water
- 1 tablespoon stevia
- 1 teaspoon vanilla extract

Directions:
Put rhubarb, ghee, water, stevia and vanilla extract in your instant pot, cover and cook on High for 5 minutes. Divide into small bowls and serve cold. Enjoy!

Nutrition: calories 83, fat 2, fiber 1, carbs 2, protein 2

Plum Delight

Preparation time: 10 minutes
Cooking time: 5 minutes
Servings: 10

Ingredients:
- 4 pounds plums, stones removed and chopped
- 1 cup water
- 2 tablespoons stevia
- 1 teaspoon cinnamon, powder
- ½ teaspoon cardamom, ground

Directions:
Put plums, water, stevia, cinnamon and cardamom in your instant pot, cover and cook on High for 5 minutes. Stir well, pulse a bit using an immersion blender, divide into small jars and serve. Enjoy!

Nutrition: calories 83, fat 0, fiber 1, carbs 2, protein 5

Refreshing Fruits Dish

Preparation time: 10 minutes
Cooking time: 10 minutes
Servings: 4

Ingredients:
- 1 and ½ pounds plums, stones removed and halved
- 2 tablespoons stevia
- 1 tablespoon cinnamon powder
- 2 apples, cored, peeled and cut into wedges
- 2 tablespoons lemon zest, grated
- 2 teaspoons balsamic vinegar
- 1 cup hot water

Directions:
Put plums, water, apples, stevia, cinnamon, lemon zest and vinegar in your instant pot, cover and cook on High for 10 minutes. Stir again well, divide into small cups and serve cold.

Nutrition: calories 73, fat 0, fiber 1, carbs 2, protein 4

Dessert Stew

Preparation time: 10 minutes
Cooking time: 6 minutes
Servings: 6

Ingredients:

- 14 plums, stones removed and halved
- 2 tablespoons stevia
- 1 teaspoon cinnamon powder
- ¼ cup water
- 2 tablespoons arrowroot powder

Directions:

Put plums, stevia, cinnamon, water and arrowroot in your instant pot, cover and cook on High for 6 minutes. Divide into small jars and serve cold. Enjoy!

Nutrition: calories 83, fat 0, fiber 1, carbs 2, protein 2

Original Fruits Dessert

Preparation time: 10 minutes
Cooking time: 10 minutes
Servings: 10

Ingredients:

- 3 cups canned pineapple chunks, drained
- 3 cups canned cherries, drained
- 2 cups canned apricots, halved and drained
- 2 cups canned peach slices, drained
- 3 cups natural applesauce
- 2 cups canned mandarin oranges, drained
- 2 tablespoons stevia
- 1 teaspoon cinnamon powder

Directions:

Put pineapples, cherries, apricots, peaches, applesauce, oranges, cinnamon and stevia in your instant pot, cover and cook on High for 10 minutes. Divide into small bowls and serve cold. Enjoy!

Nutrition: calories 120, fat 1, fiber 2, carbs 3, protein 2

Delicious Apples And Cinnamon

Preparation time: 10 minutes
Cooking time: 10 minutes
Servings: 8

Ingredients:

- 1 teaspoon cinnamon powder
- 12 ounces apples, cored and chopped
- 2 tablespoons flax seed meal mixed with 1 tablespoon water
- ½ cup coconut cream
- 3 tablespoons stevia
- ½ teaspoon nutmeg
- 2 teaspoons vanilla extract
- 1/3 cup pecans, chopped

Directions:

In your instant pot, mix flax seed meal with coconut cream, vanilla, nutmeg, stevia, apples and cinnamon, stir a bit, cover and cook on High for 10 minutes. Divide into bowls, sprinkle pecans on top and serve. Enjoy!

Nutrition: calories 120, fat 3, fiber 2, carbs 3, protein 3

Crazy Delicious Pudding

Preparation time: 10 minutes
Cooking time: 35 minutes
Servings: 6

Ingredients:

- 1 mandarin, sliced
- Juice from 2 mandarins
- 3 tablespoons stevia
- 4 ounces ghee, melted
- ½ cup water
- 2 tablespoons flax meal
- ¾ cup coconut flour
- 1 teaspoon baking powder
- ¾ cup almonds, ground
- Olive oil cooking spray

Directions:

Grease a loaf pan, arrange sliced mandarin on the bottom and leave aside. In a bowl, mix ghee with stevia, flax meal, almonds, mandarin juice, flour and baking powder, stir and spread this over mandarin slices. Add the water to your instant pot, place the trivet on top, add loaf pan, cover and cook on High for 35 minutes. Leave aside to cool down, slice and serve. Enjoy!

Nutrition: calories 200, fat 2, fiber 2, carbs 3, protein 4

Wonderful Berry Pudding

Preparation time: 10 minutes
Cooking time: 35 minutes
Servings: 6

Ingredients:

- 1 cup almond flour
- 2 tablespoons lemon juice
- 2 cups blueberries
- 2 teaspoons baking powder
- ½ teaspoon nutmeg, ground
- ½ cup coconut milk
- 3 tablespoons stevia
- 1 tablespoon flax meal mixed with 1 tablespoon water
- 3 tablespoons ghee, melted
- 1 teaspoon vanilla extract
- 1 tablespoon arrowroot powder
- 1 cup cold water

Directions:

In a greased heat proof dish, mix blueberries and lemon juice, toss a bit and spread on the bottom. In a bowl, mix flour with nutmeg, stevia, baking powder, vanilla, ghee, flaxseed meal, arrowroot and milk, stir well again and spread over blueberries. Put the water in your instant pot, add the trivet, and the heatproof dish, cover and cook on High for 35 minutes. Leave pudding to cool down, transfer to dessert bowls and serve. Enjoy!

Nutrition: calories 220, fat 4, fiber 4, carbs 9, protein 6

Winter Fruits Dessert

Preparation time: 10 minutes
Cooking time: 15 minutes
Servings: 6

Ingredients:
- 1-quart water
- 2 tablespoons stevia
- 1 pound mixed apples, pears and cranberries
- 5-star anise
- A pinch of cloves, ground
- 2 cinnamon sticks
- Zest from 1 orange, grated
- Zest from 1 lemon, grated

Directions:
Put the water, stevia, apples, pears, cranberries, star anise, cinnamon, orange and lemon zest and cloves in your instant pot, cover and cook on High for 15 minutes. Serve cold. Enjoy!

Nutrition: calories 98, fat 0, fiber 0, carbs 0, protein 2

Different Dessert

Preparation time: 10 minutes
Cooking time: 4 minutes
Servings: 2

Ingredients:
- 2 cups orange juice
- 4 pears, peeled, cored and cut into medium chunks
- 5 cardamom pods
- 2 tablespoons stevia
- 1 cinnamon stick
- 1 small ginger piece, grated

Directions:
Place pears, cardamom, orange juice, stevia, cinnamon and ginger in your instant pot, cover and cook on High for 4 minutes. Divide into small bowls and serve cold. Enjoy!

Nutrition: calories 100, fat 0, fiber 1, carbs 1, protein 2

Orange Dessert

Preparation time: 10 minutes
Cooking time: 30 minutes
Servings: 4

Ingredients:
- 1 and ¾ cup water
- 1 teaspoon baking powder
- 1 cup coconut flour
- 2 tablespoons stevia
- ½ teaspoon cinnamon powder
- 3 tablespoons coconut oil, melted
- ½ cup coconut milk
- ½ cup pecans, chopped
- ½ cup raisins
- ½ cup orange peel, grated
- ¾ cup orange juice

Directions:
In a bowl, mix flour with stevia, baking powder, cinnamon, 2 tablespoons oil, milk, pecans and raisins, stir and transfer to a greased heat proof dish. Heat up a small pan over medium high heat, mix ¾ cup water with orange juice, orange peel and the rest of the oil, stir, bring to a boil and pour over the pecans mix. Put 1 cup water in your instant pot, add the trivet, add heat proof dish, cover and cook on High for 30 minutes. Serve cold. Enjoy!

Nutrition: calories 142, fat 3, fiber 1, carbs 3, protein 3

Great Pumpkin Dessert

Preparation time: 10 minutes
Cooking time: 30 minutes
Servings: 10

Ingredients:
- 1 and ½ teaspoons baking powder
- 2 cups coconut flour
- ½ teaspoon baking soda
- ¼ teaspoon nutmeg, ground
- 1 teaspoons cinnamon powder
- ¼ teaspoon ginger, grated
- 1 tablespoon coconut oil, melted
- 1 egg white
- 1 tablespoon vanilla extract
- 1 cup pumpkin puree
- 2 tablespoons stevia
- 1 teaspoon lemon juice
- 1 cup water

Directions:
In a bowl, flour with baking powder, baking soda, cinnamon, ginger, nutmeg, oil, egg white, ghee, vanilla extract, pumpkin puree, stevia and lemon juice, stir well and transfer this to a greased cake pan. Put the water in your instant pot, add trivet, add cake pan, cover and cook on High for 30 minutes. Leave cake to cool down, slice and serve. Enjoy!

Nutrition: calories 180, fat 3, fiber 2, carbs 3, protein 4

Breakfast Recipes

Eggplant Breakfast Spread

Preparation time: 5 minutes
Cooking time: 10 minutes
Servings: 6

Ingredients:

- 4 tablespoons olive oil
- 2 pounds eggplants, peeled and roughly chopped
- 4 garlic cloves, minced
- A pinch of salt and black pepper
- 1 cup water
- ¼ cup lemon juice
- 1 tablespoon sesame seeds paste
- ¼ cup black olives, pitted
- A few sprigs thyme, chopped
- A drizzle of olive oil

Directions:

Set your instant pot on sauté mode, add oil, heat it up, add eggplant pieces, stir and sauté for 5 minutes Add garlic, salt, pepper and the water, stir gently, cover and cook on High for 5 minutes. Discard excess water, add sesame seeds paste, lemon juice and olives and blend using an immersion blender. Transfer to a bowl, sprinkle chopped thyme, drizzle some oil and serve for a fancy breakfast. Enjoy!

Nutrition: calories 163, fat 2, fiber 1, carbs 5, protein 7

Chicken Liver Breakfast Spread

Preparation time: 5 minutes
Cooking time: 10 minutes
Servings: 8

Ingredients:

- 1 teaspoon olive oil
- ¾ pound chicken livers
- 1 yellow onion, chopped
- ¼ cup water
- 1 bay leaf
- 2 anchovies
- 1 tablespoons capers
- 1 tablespoon ghee
- A pinch of salt and black pepper

Directions:

Put the olive oil in your instant pot, add onion, salt, pepper, chicken livers, water and the bay leaf, stir, cover and cook on High for 10 minutes. Discard bay leaf, add anchovies, capers and the ghee and pulse everything using your immersion blender. Add salt and pepper, blend again, divide into bowls and serve for breakfast. Enjoy!

Nutrition: calories 152, fat 4, fiber 2, carbs 5, protein 7

Mushroom Spread

Preparation time: 10 minutes
Cooking time: 14 minutes
Servings: 6

Ingredients:
- 1 ounce porcini mushrooms, dried
- 1 pound button mushrooms, sliced
- 1 cup hot water
- 1 tablespoon ghee
- 1 tablespoon olive oil
- 1 shallot, chopped
- ¼ cup cold water
- A pinch of salt and pepper
- 1 bay leaf

Directions:
Put porcini mushrooms in a bowl, add 1 cup hot water and leave aside for now. Set your instant pot on Sauté mode, add ghee and oil and heat it up. Add shallot, stir and sauté for 2 minutes Add porcini mushrooms and their liquid, fresh mushrooms, cold, salt, pepper and bay leaf, stir, cover and cook on High for 12 minutes, Discard bay leaf and some of the liquid and blend mushrooms mix using an immersion blender. Transfer to small bowls and serve as a breakfast spread. Enjoy!

Nutrition: calories 163, fat 2, fiber 1, carbs 5, protein 7

Breakfast Chia Pudding

Preparation time: 2 hours
Cooking time: 3 minutes
Servings: 4

Ingredients:
- ½ cup chia seeds
- 2 cups almond milk
- ¼ cup almonds
- ¼ cup coconut, shredded
- 4 teaspoons sugar

Directions:
Put chia seeds in your instant pot. Add milk, almonds and coconut flakes, stir, cover and cook at High for 3 minutes. Release the pressure quick, divide the pudding between bowls, top each with a teaspoon of sugar and serve. Enjoy!

Nutrition: calories 130, fat 1, fiber 4, carbs 2, protein 14

Breakfast Sweet Potatoes

Preparation time: 5 minutes
Cooking time: 7 minutes
Servings: 2

Ingredients:

- 4 sweet potatoes
- 2 teaspoons Italian seasoning
- 1 tablespoon bacon fat
- 1 cup chives, chopped for serving.
- Water
- Salt and pepper to the taste

Directions:

Put potatoes in your instant pot, add water to cover them, cover the pot and cook at High for 10 minutes. Release the pressure naturally, transfer potatoes to a working surface and leave them to cool down. Peel potatoes, transfer them to a bowl and mash them a bit with a fork. Set your instant pot on sauté mode, add bacon fat and heat up. Add potatoes, seasoning, salt and pepper to the taste, stir, cover the pot and cook at High for 1 minute. Release the pressure quickly, stir potatoes again, divide them between plates and serve with chives sprinkled on top. Enjoy!

Nutrition: calories 90, fat 3, fiber 1, carbs 6, protein 7

Delicious Korean Eggs

Preparation time: 10 minutes
Cooking time: 5 minutes
Servings: 1

Ingredients:

- 1 and 1/3 cup water
- 1 egg
- A pinch of garlic powder
- A pinch of sea salt and black pepper
- A pinch of sesame seeds
- 1 teaspoon scallions, chopped

Directions:

Crack the egg into a bowl, add 1/3 cup water and whisk well. Strain this into a heat proof bowl, add garlic powder, salt, pepper, scallions and sesame seeds and whisk again. Put 1 cup water in your instant pot, add the steamer basket and place the bowl with the egg mixture inside. Cover, cook on High for 5 minutes. Transfer to a plate and serve. Enjoy!

Nutrition: calories 100, fat 1, fiber 2, carbs 2, protein 4

Great French Eggs

Preparation time: 10 minutes
Cooking time: 20 minutes
Servings: 6

Ingredients:
- 1
- yellow onion, chopped
- 6 eggs
- 1 cup bacon, cooked and crumbled
- 1 cup kale, chopped
- 1 teaspoon herbs de Provence
- 1 cup water
- A pinch of sea salt and black pepper

Directions:
In a bowl, mix eggs with onion, kale, bacon, salt, pepper and herbs, whisk really well and pour into a heat proof dish.Put the water in your instant pot, add the steamer basket and put the dish with the eggs inside. Cover, cook on High for 20 minutes, leave aside to cool down a bit, divide among plates and serve. Enjoy!

Nutrition: calories 132, fat 3, fiber 1, carbs 4, protein 7

Different Eggs Breakfast

Preparation time: 10 minutes
Cooking time: 10 minutes
Servings: 2

Ingredients:
- 2 tablespoons olive oil
- 1 cup water
- 1 cup sweet potatoes, cubed
- 2 eggs
- 1 jalapeno pepper, chopped
- ½ cup yellow onion, chopped
- 1 tablespoon cilantro, chopped
- A pinch of salt and black pepper

Directions:
Put 1 cup water in your instant pot, add the steamer basket, place cubed potatoes inside, cover, cook on High for 3 minutes and transfer to a bowl. Take the steamer basket out, clean instant pot, add the oil and set the pot on Sauté mode. Add onion, jalapeno and return potato cubes, stir and sauté for a couple of minutes. Crack eggs, season with a pinch of salt, black pepper and sprinkle cilantro. Stir gently, cover and cook on High for 2 minutes. Divide this breakfast mix between plates and serve. Enjoy!

Nutrition: calories 142, fat 2, fiber 1, carbs 3, protein 6

Delicious Breakfast Casserole

Preparation time: 10 minutes
Cooking time: 30 minutes
Servings: 6

Ingredients:

- 1 and 1/3 cups leek, chopped
- 2 tablespoons coconut oil
- 2 teaspoons garlic, minced
- 8 eggs
- 1 cup kale, chopped
- 2/3 cup sweet potato, grated
- 1 and ½ cups sausage, cooked and sliced
- 1 and ½ cups water

Directions:

Set your instant pot on sauté mode, add oil and heat it up. Add kale, leeks and garlic, stir, cook for 3 minutes, transfer to a bowl and clean the pot. Meanwhile, in a bowl, mix eggs with sausage, sautéed veggies and sweet potato, whisk really well and pour into a heat proof dish. Add the water to your instant pot, add the steamer basket, place the dish with the eggs mix inside, cover and cook on Manual for 25 minutes. Divide among plates and serve for breakfast. Enjoy!

Nutrition: calories 254, fat 4, fiber 1, carbs 4, protein 20

Hearty Breakfast

Preparation time: 10 minutes
Cooking time: 20 minutes
Servings: 6

Ingredients:

- 3 pounds pork roast, boneless
- 2 teaspoons cumin, ground
- 1 teaspoon red pepper flakes, crushed
- A pinch of sea salt and black pepper
- 1 teaspoon oregano, dried
- Juice from 1 orange
- Orange peel from 1 orange, grated
- 6 garlic cloves, minced
- 1 yellow onion, chopped
- 1 bay leaf
- 1 tablespoon avocado oil
- 2 teaspoons cilantro, chopped
- 1 butter lettuce head, torn
- 2 radishes, sliced
- 2 avocados, pitted, peeled and sliced
- 1 cup Paleo salsa
- 2 jalapenos, chopped
- 3 limes, quartered

Directions:

Put roast in your instant pot. Add cumin, pepper flakes, salt, pepper, oregano, orange juice, orange peel, garlic, yellow onion, bay leaf and oil and rub roast well. Cover instant pot and cook on High for 20 minutes. Transfer roast to a cutting board, leave aside to cool down a bit, shred and divide among plates. Also divide lettuce leaves, radishes, avocado slices, jalapenos and lime wedges. Sprinkle cilantro, divide salsa on top and serve for breakfast. Enjoy!

Nutrition: calories 275, fat 4, fiber 1, carbs 5, protein 14

Great Egg Casserole

Preparation time: 10 minutes
Cooking time: 3 hours
Servings: 6

Ingredients:
- 32 ounces sweet potatoes, cubed
- 1 cup coconut milk
- 2 cups ham, chopped
- 1 yellow onion, chopped
- 12 eggs
- A pinch of salt and black pepper
- Cooking spray

Directions:
In a bowl, mix eggs with salt, pepper, onion, ham, sweet potatoes and milk and whisk well. Spray your instant pot with some cooking spray, add eggs mix, cover and cook on Low for 3 hours. Divide among plates and serve hot.
Enjoy!

Nutrition: calories 253, fat 3, fiber 1, carbs 5, protein 12

Breakfast Quiche

Preparation time: 10 minutes
Cooking time: 30 minutes
Servings: 4

Ingredients:
- 1 cup water
- 6 eggs, whisked
- A pinch of black pepper
- ½ cup coconut milk
- 4 bacon slices, cooked and crumbled
- 1 cup sausage, cooked and ground
- ½ cup ham, chopped
- 2 green onions, chopped

Directions:
Put the water in your instant pot and add the steamer basket inside. Put bacon, sausage and ham in a bowl, mix and spread on the bottom of a quiche dish. In a bowl, mix eggs with black pepper, coconut milk and green onions and whisk well. Pour this over meat, spread, place inside the pot, cover and cook on High for 30 minutes. Slice, divide among plates and serve. Enjoy!

Nutrition: calories 243, fat 3, fiber 1, carbs 6, protein 12

Wonderful Frittata

Preparation time: 10 minutes
Cooking time: 18 minutes
Servings: 4

Ingredients:

- 4 ounces sweet potatoes, cut into medium fries
- 6 eggs
- A pinch of sea salt and black pepper
- 1 tablespoon olive oil
- ¼ cup scallions, chopped
- 1 garlic clove, minced
- ¼ cup coconut milk
- 1 teaspoon Paleo tomato paste
- 1 and ½ cups water
- 1 green bell pepper, chopped

Directions:

Grease a heat proof dish with the oil and spread sweet potato fries on the bottom. In a bowl, mix eggs with salt, pepper, scallions, garlic and bell pepper and whisk well. In another bowl, mix coconut milk with tomato paste and stir. Pour this over eggs mix, stir well and spread everything on top of sweet potato fries. Put the water in your instant pot, add the steamer basket inside and place the eggs mix in the basket. Cover, cook on High for 18 minutes, slice, divide among plates and serve hot. Enjoy!

Nutrition: calories 153, fat 7, fiber 2, carbs 5, protein 15

Pumpkin and Apple Butter

Preparation time: 10 minutes
Cooking time: 10 minutes
Servings: 8

Ingredients:

- 3 apples, peeled, cored and chopped
- 30 ounces pumpkin puree
- 1 tablespoon pumpkin pie spice
- 1 cup honey
- 12 ounces apple cider

Directions:

Put pumpkin puree in your instant pot. Add apples, pumpkin pie spice, cider and honey, stir well, cover and cook on High for 10 minutes. Divide into jars, seal them and serve for breakfast when ever you want. Enjoy!

Nutrition: calories 100, fat 3, fiber 1, carbs 4, protein 6

Breakfast Spinach Delight

Preparation time: 10 minutes
Cooking time: 20 minutes
Servings: 4

Ingredients:

- 1 pound mustard leaves
- 1 pound spinach, torn
- 2 tablespoons olive oil
- A small ginger piece, grated
- 2 yellow onions, chopped
- 4 garlic cloves, minced
- 1 teaspoon cumin, ground
- 1 teaspoon coriander, ground
- 1 teaspoon garam masala
- A pinch of cayenne pepper
- ½ teaspoon turmeric
- A pinch of black pepper
- A pinch of fenugreek leaves, dried

Directions:

Set your instant pot on Sauté mode, add oil and heat it up. Add onion, garlic, ginger, coriander, cumin, garam masala, turmeric, cayenne pepper, black pepper and fenugreek, stir and cook for 5 minutes. Add spinach and mustard leaves, stir gently, cover and cook on High for 15 minutes. Divide into bowls and serve for breakfast. Enjoy!

Nutrition: calories 200, fat 3, fiber 2, carbs 5, protein 7

Delicious Breakfast Cobbler

Preparation time: 10 minutes
Cooking time: 10 minutes
Servings: 4

Ingredients:

- 1 apple, cored and chopped
- 1 pear, chopped
- 2 tablespoons honey
- 1 plum, chopped
- ½ teaspoon cinnamon, ground
- 3 tablespoons coconut oil
- ¼ cup coconut, unsweetened and shredded
- 2 tablespoons sunflower seeds
- 2 tablespoons pecans, chopped

Directions:

Put the oil in your instant pot and heat it up on Sauté mode. Add the apple, pear, plum and honey in your instant pot, stir, cover and cook on Steam mode for 10 minutes. Divide among plates, sprinkle sunflower seeds, pecans coconut, and serve. Enjoy!

Nutrition: calories 154, fat 2, fiber 2, carbs 5, protein 3

Amazing Bacon And Sweet Potato Breakfast

Preparation time: 10 minutes
Cooking time: 10 minutes
Servings: 4

Ingredients:

- 2 pounds sweet potatoes, cubed
- A pinch of salt and black pepper
- 3 bacon strips
- 2 tablespoons water
- 2 teaspoons parsley, dried
- 1 teaspoon garlic powder
- 4 eggs, fried for serving

Directions:

In your instant pot, mix sweet potatoes with bacon, salt, pepper, water, parsley and garlic powder, stir, cover and cook on High for 10 minutes. Divide among plates next to fried eggs and serve. Enjoy!

Nutrition: calories 200, fat 2, fiber 2, carbs 6, protein 8

Great Veggie Quiche

Preparation time: 10 minutes
Cooking time: 30 minutes
Servings: 8

Ingredients:

- ½ cup almond milk
- ½ cup almond flour
- 8 eggs
- A pinch of sea salt and black pepper
- 1 red bell pepper, chopped
- 2 green onions, chopped
- 1 cup tomatoes, chopped
- ½ cup zucchinis, chopped
- 1 cup water

Directions:

In a bowl, mix eggs with almond flour, almond milk, salt, pepper, red bell pepper, green onions, zucchinis and tomatoes, whisk well, pour this into a round baking dish. Put the water in your instant pot, add the steamer basket, add the baking dish inside, cover and cook on High for 30 minutes. Leave quiche to cool down a bit, slice, divide among plates and serve. Enjoy!

Nutrition: calories 200, fat 3, fiber 2, carbs 5, protein 7

Tomato And Spinach Breakfast Mix

Preparation time: 10 minutes
Cooking time: 20 minutes
Servings: 6

Ingredients:
- 12 eggs
- A pinch of salt and black pepper
- ½ cup coconut milk
- 3 cups baby spinach, chopped
- 1 cup tomato, chopped
- 1 and ½ cups water
- 3 green onions, chopped

Directions:
In a bowl, mix eggs with salt, pepper, milk, spinach, tomato and green onions and whisk well. Pour this into a round baking dish. Put the water in your instant pot, add the steamer basket, place the dish inside, cover and cook on High for 20 minutes. Divide among plates and serve for breakfast. Enjoy!

Nutrition: calories 210, fat 3, fiber 3, carbs 4, protein 4

Special Breakfast Egg Muffins

Preparation time: 10 minutes
Cooking time: 10 minutes
Servings: 4

Ingredients:
- 1 green onion, chopped
- 4 eggs
- ¼ teaspoon lemon pepper
- 4 bacon slices, cooked and crumbled
- 1 and ½ cups water

Directions:
In a bowl, mix eggs with green onion, bacon and lemon pepper, whisk well and divide this into 4 muffin cups. Put the water in your instant pot, add the steamer basket, place muffin cups inside, cover and cook on High for 8 minutes. Divide egg muffins between plates and serve. Enjoy!

Nutrition: calories 172, fat 4, fiber 2, carbs 6, protein 7

Breakfast Scotch Eggs

Preparation time: 10 minutes
Cooking time: 12 minutes
Servings: 4

Ingredients:

- 1 pound sausage, ground
- 4 eggs
- 1 tablespoon olive oil
- 2 cups water

Directions:

Put 1 cup water in your instant pot, add the steamer basket and put the eggs inside. Cover, cook on High for 6 minutes, transfer eggs to a cutting board, cool them down and peel. Divide sausage mix into 4 pieces, flatten each, add an egg in the center of each and wrap well. Put the oil in your instant pot and set it on Sauté mode. Add scotch eggs, brown them on all sides and transfer to a plate. Add 1 cup water to the pot, add the steamer basket, add scotch eggs, cover and cook on High for 6 minutes. Divide eggs between plates and serve. Enjoy!

Nutrition: calories 210, fat 3, fiber 5, carbs 6, protein 6

Wonderful Breakfast Omelet

Preparation time: 10 minutes
Cooking time: 30 minutes
Servings: 6

Ingredients:

- 1 and ½ cups water
- 4 spring onions, chopped
- 6 ounces bacon, chopped
- ½ cup red, green and orange bell peppers, chopped
- A pinch of black pepper
- 6 eggs
- ½ cup coconut milk
- Olive oil spray

Directions:

In a bowl, mix eggs with a pinch of black pepper and coconut milk and whisk well. Add mixed bell peppers, bacon and spring onions and whisk again. Spray a round dish with olive oil spray, pour eggs mix and spread. Put the water in your instant pot, add the steamer basket and the baking dish inside, cover and cook on High for 30 minutes. Leave your omelet to cool down a bit, slice, divide among plates and serve. Enjoy!

Nutrition: calories 182, fat 2, fiber 2, carbs 6, protein 12

Superb Zucchini Breakfast

Preparation time: 10 minutes
Cooking time: 5 minutes
Servings: 6

Ingredients:

- 1 and ½ cups yellow onion, chopped
- 1 tablespoon olive oil
- 2 garlic cloves, minced
- 12 ounces mushrooms, chopped
- 1 basil spring, chopped
- A pinch of sea salt and black pepper
- 8 cups zucchinis, sliced
- 15 ounces canned tomatoes, crushed

Directions:

Put the oil in your instant pot and heat it up on Sauté mode. Add onion and garlic, stir and cook for 2 minutes. Add mushrooms, basil, salt and pepper, stir and cook for 1 minute more. Add zucchinis and tomatoes, stir, cover and cook on High for 2 minutes. Divide among plates and serve for breakfast. Enjoy!

Nutrition: calories 176, fat 2, fiber 3, carbs 5, protein 6

Poached Eggs

Preparation time: 10 minutes
Cooking time: 2 minutes
Servings: 3

Ingredients:

- A drizzle of olive oil
- 3 tablespoons coconut cream
- 1 tablespoons chives, chopped
- 3 eggs
- 1 cup water
- A pinch of sea salt and black pepper

Directions:

Grease 3 ramekins with some olive oil and divide coconut cream in each. Crack an egg into each ramekin, season with a pinch of salt and pepper and sprinkle chives all over. Put the water in your instant pot, add the steamer basket and place all 3 ramekins inside. Cover instant pot and cook on High for 2 minutes. Divide poached eggs between plates and serve. Enjoy!

Nutrition: calories 200, fat 2, fiber 1, carbs 2, protein 6

Delicious Breakfast Eggs And Sauce

Preparation time: 10 minutes
Cooking time: 12 minutes
Servings: 4

Ingredients:

- 2 garlic cloves, minced
- 1 tablespoon coconut oil
- 1 red bell pepper, chopped
- 1 small yellow onion, chopped
- 1 teaspoon chili powder
- ½ teaspoon cumin, ground
- ½ teaspoon paprika
- A pinch of salt and black pepper
- 1 and ½ cups Paleo and sugar free marinara sauce
- A handful parsley, chopped
- 4 eggs

Directions:

Set your instant pot on Sauté mode, add the oil and heat it up. Add onion, bell pepper, garlic, paprika, cumin and chili powder, stir and sauté for 5 minutes. Add sauce, stir and cook for 1 minute more. Crack eggs into the sauce, cover the pot and cook on Low for 1 minute. Season with a pinch of salt and black pepper, sprinkle parsley, divide among plates and serve. Enjoy!

Nutrition: calories 200, fat 2, fiber 1, carbs 3, protein 7

Light Breakfast

Preparation time: 10 minutes
Cooking time: 10 minutes
Servings: 4

Ingredients:

- 1 tablespoon olive oil
- 2 yellow onions, chopped
- 6 zucchinis, chopped
- 1 pound cherry tomatoes, halved
- 1 cup water
- 2 garlic cloves, minced
- A pinch of sea salt and black pepper
- 1 bunch basil, chopped

Directions:

Set your instant pot on Sauté mode, add the oil and heat it up. Add onions, tomatoes, water, zucchini, garlic, salt and pepper, stir, cover and cook on High for 5 minutes. Sprinkle basil, toss gently, divide among plates and serve for breakfast. Enjoy!

Nutrition: calories 120, fat 2, fiber 1, carbs 3, protein 6

Great Zucchini Spread

Preparation time: 20 minutes
Cooking time: 8 minutes
Servings: 4

Ingredients:

- 2 tablespoons olive oil
- 3 pounds zucchinis, peeled and roughly chopped
- 3 garlic cloves, minced
- 2 yellow onions, chopped
- 2 carrots, chopped
- ½ cup water
- 1/3 cup tomatoes, crushed
- 2 bay leaves
- A pinch of cayenne pepper
- A pinch of salt and black pepper

Directions:

Put zucchinis in a bowl, add some salt, toss, leave aside for 20 minutes and drain excess water. Put the oil in your instant pot, set on sauté mode and heat it up. Add carrots, zucchinis and onions, stir and sauté for 5 minutes. Add bay leaves, a pinch of salt, pepper, cayenne, tomatoes and water, stir, cover and cook on High for 3 minutes. Transfer to your blender, leave aside to cool down a bit and pulse until you obtain a paste. Transfer to a bowl and serve for breakfast. Enjoy!

Nutrition: calories 100, fat 2, fiber 1, carbs 3, protein 4

Great Butternut Squash Breakfast

Preparation time: 10 minutes
Cooking time: 8 minutes
Servings: 7

Ingredients:

- 6 pounds butternut squash, peeled and cut into chunks
- 1 cup water
- 1 cup apple cider
- 2 cinnamon sticks
- 1 teaspoon ginger, grated
- ½ cup honey
- A pinch of nutmeg, ground
- 1 tablespoon apple cider vinegar
- A pinch of cloves, ground

Directions:

Put the water in your instant pot, add the steamer basket and put butternut squash inside. Cover, cook on High for 5 minutes, transfer squash to a bowl and leave aside to cool down. Clean instant pot, add squash, apple cider, cinnamon sticks, ginger, cloves, vinegar, nutmeg and honey, stir, cover and cook on High for 3 minutes more. Discard cinnamon sticks, blend using an immersion blender, transfer to jars and serve cold for breakfast. Enjoy!

Nutrition: calories 153, fat 3, fiber 1, carbs 5, protein 7

Special Onion And Bacon Jam

Preparation time: 10 minutes
Cooking time: 25 minutes
Servings: 6

Ingredients:

- 3 tablespoons bacon fat
- 2 tablespoons garlic olive oil
- 4 pounds yellow onions, sliced
- ½ teaspoon baking soda
- ½ package bacon, cooked and cut into thin strips
- 5 garlic cloves, minced
- ½ cup water
- ¼ cup balsamic vinegar
- 1 teaspoon thyme, dried
- Black pepper to the taste
- 1 teaspoon red pepper flakes
- 2 tablespoons stevia

Directions:

Put the bacon fat in your instant pot, set on Sauté mode and heat it up. Add onions, stir and sauté for 3 minutes. Add garlic olive oil, baking soda, bacon, garlic, water, vinegar, thyme, black pepper, red pepper flakes and stevia, stir, cover and cook on High for 20 minutes. Uncover the pot, set it on Sauté mode again and cook for 2 minutes more. Stir well, divide into jars and serve for breakfast. Enjoy!

Nutrition: calories 254, fat 3, fiber 2, carbs 5, protein 7

Breakfast Apple Spread

Preparation time: 10 minutes
Cooking time: 4 minutes
Servings: 10

Ingredients:

- Juice from 1 lemon
- 1 teaspoon allspice
- 1 teaspoon clove, ground
- 3 pounds apples, peeled, cored and chopped
- 1 tablespoon cinnamon, ground
- 1 and ½ cups water
- ¼ teaspoon nutmeg, ground
- 1 cup maple syrup

Directions:

In your slow cooker, mix apples with water, lemon juice, allspice, clove, cinnamon, maple syrup and nutmeg. Stir, cover and cook on High for 4 minutes Blend using an immersion blender, pour into small jars and serve for breakfast! Enjoy!

Nutrition: calories 180, fat 3, fiber 1, carbs 4, protein 3

Simple Breakfast Meatloaf

Preparation time: 10 minutes
Cooking time: 50 minutes
Servings: 4

Ingredients:

- 1 onion, chopped
- 1 and ½ cups water
- 2 pounds pork, minced
- 1 teaspoon red pepper flakes
- 1 teaspoon olive oil
- 3 garlic cloves, minced
- ¼ cup almond flour
- 1 teaspoon oregano, chopped
- 1 tablespoon sage, minced
- A pinch of sea salt and black pepper
- 1 tablespoon paprika
- 1 teaspoon marjoram, dried
- 2 eggs

Directions:

Set your instant pot on sauté mode, add the oil and heat it up. Add onion and garlic, stir and sauté for 3 minutes. Transfer these to a bowl, leave aside to cool down and mix with the meat. Add a pinch of salt, black pepper, pepper flakes, almond flour, sage, oregano, eggs, paprika and marjoram, stir really well and transfer this to a greased meatloaf pan. Add the water to your instant pot, add the steamer basket, add the meatloaf inside, cover and cook on High for 50 minutes. Leave meatball to cool down, slice, divide among plates and serve for breakfast. Enjoy!

Nutrition: calories 210, fat 3, fiber 1, carbs 5, protein 12

Summer Veggie Breakfast

Preparation time: 10 minutes
Cooking time: 10 minutes
Servings: 4

Ingredients:

- 1 and ½ cups red onion, roughly chopped
- 1 cup cherry tomatoes, halved
- 2 cups okra, sliced
- 1 cup water
- 1 cup mushrooms, sliced
- 2 and ½ cups zucchini, roughly chopped
- 2 cups yellow bell pepper, chopped
- Black pepper to the taste
- 2 tablespoons basil, chopped
- 1 tablespoon thyme, chopped
- ½ cup olive oil
- ½ cup balsamic vinegar

Directions:

In a large bowl, mix onion with tomatoes, okra, zucchini, bell pepper, mushrooms, basil, thyme, black pepper, oil and vinegar and toss well. Transfer to your instant pot, add 1 cup water, cover and cook on High for 10 minutes. Divide among plates and serve for breakfast. Enjoy!

Nutrition: calories 120, fat 2, fiber 2, carbs 3, protein 6

Special Breakfast Butter

Preparation time: 10 minutes
Cooking time: 6 minutes
Servings: 12

Ingredients:

- 5 cups blueberries puree
- 2 teaspoons cinnamon powder
- Zest from 1 lemon
- 1 cup coconut sugar
- ½ teaspoon nutmeg, ground
- ¼ teaspoon ginger, ground

Directions:

Put blueberries puree in your instant pot, cover and cook on High for 3 minutes. Add coconut sugar, ginger, nutmeg and lemon zest, stir, cover and cook on High for 3 minutes more. Stir, transfer to jars, cover and serve for breakfast.
Enjoy!

Nutrition: calories 123, fat 2, fiber 3, carbs 3, protein 4

Zucchini And Carrots Delightful Breakfast

Preparation time: 10 minutes
Cooking time: 4
Servings: 4

Ingredients:

- 1 and ½ cups almond milk
- A pinch of nutmeg, ground
- 1 small zucchini, grated
- 1 carrot, grated
- A pinch of cloves, ground
- 2 tablespoons agave nectar
- ½ teaspoon cinnamon powder
- ¼ cup pecans, chopped

Directions:

Put the milk, zucchini, carrots, nutmeg, cloves, cinnamon and agave nectar in your instant pot, cover and cook on High for 4 minutes. Add pecans, stir gently, divide into bowls and serve for breakfast.Enjoy!

Nutrition: calories 100, fat 1, fiber 2, carbs 5, protein 5

Bacon and Sweet Potatoes

Preparation time: 10 minutes
Cooking time: 10 minutes
Servings: 4

Ingredients:
- ½ cup orange juice
- 4 bacon slices, cooked and crumbled
- 4 pounds sweet potatoes, sliced
- 3 tablespoons agave nectar
- ½ teaspoon thyme, dried
- ½ teaspoon sage, crushed
- A pinch of sea salt and black pepper
- 2 tablespoons olive oil

Directions:
Put sweet potato slices, orange juice, agave nectar, thyme, sage, sea salt, black pepper, olive oil and bacon in your instant pot, cover and cook on High for 10 minutes. Transfer to plates and serve for breakfast. Enjoy!

Nutrition: calories 159, fat 4, fiber 4, carbs 5, protein 4

Acorn Squash Breakfast Surprise

Preparation time: 10 minutes
Cooking time: 7 minutes
Servings: 4

Ingredients:
- ¼ cup raisins
- ¼ teaspoon cinnamon powder
- 14 ounces cranberry sauce, unsweetened
- 2 acorn squash, peeled and cut into medium chunks
- A pinch of sea salt
- Black pepper to the taste

Directions:
In your instant pot, mix squash pieces with sauce, raisins, cinnamon, salt and pepper, stir, cover and cook on High for 7 minutes Divide into medium bowls and serve for breakfast. Enjoy!

Nutrition: calories 160, fat 3, fiber 2, carbs 7, protein 5

Tasty Zucchini And Squash

Preparation time: 10 minutes
Cooking time: 10 minutes
Servings: 6

Ingredients:

- 2 cups zucchinis, sliced
- 2 tablespoons olive oil
- 1 teaspoon Italian seasoning
- Black pepper to the taste
- 2 cups yellow squash, peeled and cut into wedges
- 1 teaspoon garlic powder
- A pinch of sea salt

Directions:

Set your instant pot on sauté mode, add the oil and heat it up. Add squash and zucchinis, stir and sauté for 3 minutes. Add seasoning, garlic powder, salt and black pepper, toss, cover and cook on High for 7 minutes. Divide among plates and serve as a quick breakfast. Enjoy!

Nutrition: calories 132, fat 2, fiber 4, carbs 3, protein 4

Breakfast Balls

Preparation time: 10 minutes
Cooking time: 12 minutes
Servings: 8

Ingredients:

- 2 eggs
- 1 teaspoon baking soda
- 1 pound sausage, casings removed and chopped
- ¼ cup almond flour
- 1 cup water
- Black pepper to the taste
- 1 teaspoon smoked paprika

Directions:

In your food processor, mix sausage with eggs, baking soda, flour, pepper and paprika, pulse well and shape medium balls from this mix. Put the water in your instant pot, add the steamer basket, place meatballs inside, cover and cook on High for 12 minutes. Divide among plates and serve for breakfast. Enjoy!

Nutrition: calories 150, fat 3, fiber 3, carbs 6, protein 5

Breakfast Muffins

Preparation time: 10 minutes
Cooking time: 20 minutes
Servings: 10

Ingredients:
- 1 cup water
- ½ teaspoon baking soda
- 2 and ½ cups almond flour
- 1 tablespoon vanilla extract
- ¼ cup coconut oil
- ¼ cup coconut milk
- 2 eggs
- ¼ cup maple syrup
- 3 tablespoons cinnamon, ground
- 1 cup blueberries

Directions:
In a bowl, mix almond flour with baking soda, eggs, oil, coconut milk, cinnamon, maple syrup, vanilla and blueberries, stir everything using your mixer and divide this into silicone muffin cups. Put the water in your instant pot, add the steamer basket, add muffin cups, cover and cook on High for 20 minutes. Divide muffins between plates and serve them for breakfast. Enjoy!

Nutrition: calories 170, fat 3, fiber 1, carbs 3, protein 5

Avocado Muffins

Preparation time: 10 minutes
Cooking time: 30 minutes
Servings: 12

Ingredients:
- 1 cup water
- 6 bacon slices, chopped
- A drizzle of olive oil
- 1 yellow onion, chopped
- 4 avocados, pitted, peeled and chopped
- 4 eggs
- ½ cup almond flour
- ½ teaspoon baking soda
- 1 cup almond milk
- A pinch of sea salt
- Black pepper to the taste

Directions:
Set your instant pot on Sauté mode, add a drizzle of oil and heat it up. Add onion and bacon, stir, sauté for 3 minutes and transfer to a bowl. Add avocados and mash everything using a fork. Add a pinch of salt, pepper, eggs, baking soda, milk and flour, whisk everything well and divide into silicon muffin tins. Put the water in your instant pot, add the steamer basket, add the muffins inside, cover and cook on High for 25 minutes. Divide among plates and serve for breakfast. Enjoy!

Nutrition: calories 180, fat 4, fiber 3, carbs 5, protein 7

Chorizo Breakfast

Preparation time: 10 minutes
Cooking time: 15 minutes
Servings: 2

Ingredients:
- 1 small avocado, peeled, pitted and chopped
- ½ cup beef stock
- 1 pound chorizo, chopped
- 2 poblano peppers, chopped
- 1 cup kale, chopped
- 8 mushrooms, chopped
- ½ yellow onion, chopped
- 3 garlic cloves, minced
- ½ cup cilantro, chopped
- 4 bacon slices, chopped
- 4 eggs

Directions:
Set your instant pot on Brown mode, add bacon and chorizo and cook for a couple of minutes. Add onions, poblano peppers and garlic, stir and sauté for a few more minutes. Add stock, mushrooms and kale and stir. Make holes in this mix, crack an egg in each, cover and cook on High for 3 minutes Divide this mix on plates, sprinkle cilantro and avocado on top and serve for breakfast. Enjoy!

Nutrition: calories 170, fat 5, fiber 3, carbs 6, protein 6

Eggs, Ham And Mushroom Mix

Preparation time: 10 minutes
Cooking time: 10 minutes
Servings: 1

Ingredients:
- 2 tablespoons ghee
- ¼ cup coconut milk
- 3 eggs
- 3.5 ounces smoked ham, chopped
- 3 ounces mushrooms, sliced
- 1 cup arugula, torn
- A pinch of black pepper

Directions:
Set your instant pot on Sauté mode, add the ghee and heat it up. Add mushrooms and ham, stir and cook for 3 minutes. Meanwhile, in a bowl, mix eggs with milk and some black pepper and whisk well. Spread this mix over mushrooms and ham, stir gently, cover and cook on Low for 6 minutes. Divide among plates and serve with arugula on top. Enjoy!

Nutrition: calories 156, fat 2, fiber 2, carbs 6, protein 14

Delicious Nuts And Fruits Breakfast

Preparation time: 10 minutes
Cooking time: 10 minutes
Servings: 4

Ingredients:
- ½ cup almonds, soaked for 12 hours and drained
- ½ cup walnuts, soaked for 12 hours and drained
- 2 apples, peeled, cored and cubed
- 1 butternut squash, peeled and cubed
- 1 teaspoon cinnamon powder
- 1 tablespoon honey
- ½ teaspoon nutmeg, ground
- 1 cup coconut milk

Directions:
Put almonds and walnuts in your blender, add some of the soaking water, blend well, transfer to your instant pot, add apples, squash, cinnamon, honey, nutmeg and coconut milk, stir, cover and cook on High for 10 minutes Mash everything, divide into bowls and serve for breakfast. Enjoy!

Nutrition: calories 140, fat 1, fiber 2, carbs 2, protein 4

Leek and Kale Breakfast

Preparation time: 10 minutes
Cooking time: 10 minutes
Servings: 4

Ingredients:
- 1 and 1/3 cups leek, chopped
- ½ cup water
- 2 tablespoons coconut oil
- 1 cup kale, chopped
- 2 teaspoons garlic, minced
- 8 eggs
- 2/3 cup sweet potato, grated
- 1 and ½ cups beef sausage, casings removed and chopped

Directions:
Put the oil in your instant pot, set on Sauté mode and heat it up. Add leeks, stir and cook for 1 minute. Add garlic, sweet potatoes and kale, stir and sauté for 2 minutes more. Add eggs and sausage meat, stir everything, cover and cook on High for 6 minutes. Divide among plates and serve for breakfast. Enjoy!

Nutrition: calories 170, fat 2, fiber 2, carbs 6, protein 6

Nuts Porridge

Preparation time: 10 minutes
Cooking time: 7 minutes
Servings: 2

Ingredients:
- ½ cup pecans, soaked overnight and drained
- ½ banana, mashed
- 1 cup hot water
- 2 tablespoons coconut butter
- ½ teaspoon cinnamon
- 2 teaspoons honey

Directions:
In a blender, mix pecans, with water, banana, coconut butter, cinnamon and honey, pulse really well, transfer to your instant pot, cover and cook on High for 7 minutes. Divide into bowls and serve for breakfast. Enjoy!

Nutrition: calories 130, fat 4, fiber 2, carbs 6, protein 5

Simple Cherry Breakfast

Preparation time: 10 minutes
Cooking time: 20 minutes
Servings: 4

Ingredients:
- 2 cups almond milk
- 2 cups water
- 2 tablespoons flax meal
- 2 tablespoons cocoa powder
- 1/3 cup cherries, pitted
- 3 tablespoons honey
- ½ teaspoon almond extract

For the sauce:
- 2 tablespoons water
- 1 and ½ cups cherries, pitted and chopped
- ¼ teaspoon almond extract

Directions:
Put the almond milk, 2 cups water, flax meal, cocoa powder, 1/3 cup cherries, honey and ½ teaspoon almond extract, stir, cover and cook on High for 10 minutes. In a small pan, mix 2 tablespoons water with 1 and ½ cups cherries and ¼ teaspoon almond extract, stir well, bring to a simmer over medium heat and cook for 10 minutes until it thickens. Divide cherries mix into bowls, top with the sauce you've just made and serve for breakfast. Enjoy!

Nutrition: calories 143, fat 1, fiber 2, carbs 5, protein 4

Carrot Breakfast Dish

Preparation time: 10 minutes
Cooking time: 6 minutes
Servings: 3

Ingredients:

- 2 cups coconut milk
- 3 tablespoons flax meal
- 1 cup carrots, chopped
- 2 tablespoons agave nectar
- 1 teaspoon cardamom, ground
- A pinch of saffron
- Some chopped pistachios for serving

Directions:

Put coconut milk in your instant pot, add flax meal, carrots, agave nectar, saffron and cardamom, stir, cover and cook on High for 6 minutes. Divide into bowls and serve for breakfast with chopped pistachios sprinkled all over. Enjoy!

Nutrition: calories 160, fat 2, fiber 2, carbs 4, protein 5

Cauliflower Rice Pudding

Preparation time: 10 minutes
Cooking time: 35 minutes
Servings: 4

Ingredients:

- 6 and ½ cups water
- ¾ cup stevia
- 2 cups cauliflower rice
- 2 cinnamon sticks
- A pinch of salt
- 5 cardamom pods, crushed
- 3 cloves
- ½ cup coconut, grated

Directions:

Put the cauliflower rice your instant pot, add a pinch of salt and the water. In a cheesecloth, mix cardamom with cinnamon and cloves, tie, add to the pot, cover and cook on Low for 12 minutes. Add coconut and stevia, set your pot to sauté mode, cook pudding for 10 minutes more, discard spices, divide into bowls and serve for breakfast.
Enjoy!

Nutrition: calories 118, fat 1, fiber 1, carbs 6, protein 8

Breakfast Cauliflower Rice

Preparation time: 10 minutes
Cooking time: 12 minutes
Servings: 4

Ingredients:

- 1 and ½ cups cauliflower rice
- 1 and ½ teaspoons cinnamon powder
- 1/3 cup stevia
- A pinch of salt
- 2 tablespoons ghee, melted
- 2 apples, peeled, cored and sliced
- 1 cup natural apple juice
- 3 cups almond milk
- ½ cup cherries, dried

Directions:

Set your instant pot on Sauté mode, add ghee and heat it up Add rice, stir, sauté for 5 minutes and mix with stevia, apples, apple juice, milk, a pinch of salt and cinnamon, stir, cover and cook on High for 6 minutes. Add cherries, stir, cover, leave aside for 5 more minutes, divide into bowls and serve for breakfast Enjoy!

Nutrition: calories 160, fat 3, fiber 3, carbs 7, protein 5

Strawberries Breakfast

Preparation time: 10 minutes
Cooking time: 10 minutes
Servings: 2

Ingredients:

- 3 tablespoons flax meal
- 2 tablespoon strawberries, dried
- A pinch of salt
- 2 cups water
- 2/3 cup almond milk
- ½ teaspoon honey

Directions:

Put the water in your instant pot and mix with strawberries, flax meal, almond milk and honey Cover, cook on High for 10 minutes, divide into bowls and serve for breakfast. Enjoy!

Nutrition: calories 150, fat 5, fiber 3, carbs 6, protein 8

Conclusion

A Paleo diet will change your life! It will make you look good and feel good about yourself!
Millions of people all over the world have already made this amazing choice! Maybe it's time you became a part of this community of happy and healthy people!
Chose the Paleo diet and start your new life!

In order to help you, we've gathered the best Paleo diet recipes collection ever: an instant pot Paleo recipes collection!
Is this great or what?

So, do not wait anymore! Start your Paleo life today and make some of the most wonderful Paleo recipes using your instant pot!
Have a lot of fun and enjoy!

Recipe Index

A

Almond and Chia Breakfast, 130
Almond Cake, 104
Almond Cauliflower Rice, 76
Almond Cream Cheese Cake, 215
Almond Porridge, 130
Almonds Surprise, 176
Amazing Bacon And Sweet Potato Breakfast, 243
Amazing Carrots Side Dish, 196
Amazing Chocolate Dessert, 217
Appetizer Meatballs, 171
Appetizer Salad, 181
Apple Cake, 103
Apple Cake, 227
Apple Cobbler, 109
Apple Mash, 202
Artichoke Dip, 46
Artichokes and Sauce, 35
Artichokes Delight, 204
Asian Brussels Sprouts, 66
Asian Shrimp Appetizer, 51
Asian Style Salmon, 145
Asparagus and Cheese Side Dish, 72
Asparagus and Prosciutto Appetizer, 46
Asparagus Cream, 37
Avocado Dip, 58
Avocado Muffins, 254
Avocado Pudding, 93
Avocado Side Salad, 74

B

Baby Mushrooms Sauté, 71
Bacon and Sweet Potatoes, 252
Bacon Muffins, 132
Banana Cake, 102
Banana Dessert, 227
Beef and Cabbage Stew, 32
Beef and Mushroom Stew, 29
Beef and Radish Hash, 136
Beef Breakfast Pie, 128
Beef Meatloaf, 21
Beef Soup, 160
Beef Stew, 149
Beet and Arugula Side Salad, 87
Beet and Garlic, 85
Beets and Capers, 87
Beets and Squash Dip, 42
Beets Side Dish, 205
Berry Compote, 224
Berry Cream, 97
Berry Marmalade, 225
Blueberries and Strawberries Cream, 91
Blueberry and Yogurt Bowl, 123

Bok Choy and Garlic, 86
Breakfast Apple Spread, 249
Breakfast Avocado Cups, 127
Breakfast Balls, 253
Breakfast Blueberry Cake, 119
Breakfast Cauliflower Pudding, 124
Breakfast Cauliflower Rice, 259
Breakfast Chia Pudding, 236
Breakfast Frittata, 121
Breakfast Muffins, 254
Breakfast Oatmeal, 122
Breakfast Omelet, 137
Breakfast Pancake, 120
Breakfast Quiche, 240
Breakfast Scotch Eggs, 245
Breakfast Spinach Delight, 242
Breakfast Sweet Potatoes, 237
Broccoli and Garlic, 88
Broccoli Side Dish, 206
Broccoli Soup, 19
Broiled Lobster Tails, 178
Brussels Sprouts and Dill, 89
Brussels Sprouts Delight, 194
Burrito Casserole, 122
Butternut And Chard Soup, 144

C

Cabbage and Carrot Soup, 37
Cajun Breakfast Hash Browns, 117
Cajun Shrimp, 53
Caramel Pudding, 98
Carrot and Chia Seed Pudding, 115
Carrot And Ginger Soup, 146
Carrot Appetizer, 182
Carrot Breakfast Dish, 258
Carrot Cake, 218
Carrot Mash, 82
Carrot Puree, 202
Carrot Snack, 170
Carrot Snack, 174
Carrot, Pecans and Raisins Cake, 112
Carrots Dessert, 219
Carrots with Thyme and Dill, 83
Cauliflower and Eggs Salad, 71
Cauliflower And Leeks, 213
Cauliflower And Mushroom Risotto, 192
Cauliflower and Parmesan, 67
Cauliflower and Pineapple Risotto, 80
Cauliflower Congee, 126
Cauliflower Dip, 44
Cauliflower Dip, 188
Cauliflower Mash, 81
Cauliflower Rice Bowl, 140

261

Cauliflower Rice Pudding, 258
Cauliflower Risotto And Artichokes, 192
Cauliflower Soup, 16
Cauliflower Soup, 152
Celeriac and Bacon Breakfast, 125
Celeriac Fries, 79
Celery and Rosemary Side Dish, 77
Cheddar and Parmesan Muffins, 132
Cheese and Sausage Dip, 43
Cheesecake, 102
Cherry Tomatoes and Parmesan Mix, 75
Chestnut Cream, 101
Chia Jam, 99
Chia Pudding, 133
Chicken and Delicious Sauce, 16
Chicken and Mushrooms, 26
Chicken and Salsa, 26
Chicken and Squash Spaghetti, 18
Chicken and Tasty Cauliflower Rice, 22
Chicken Appetizer, 171
Chicken Curry, 22
Chicken Liver Breakfast Spread, 235
Chicken Stew, 38
Chicken Stew, 148
Chili Bowl, 18
Chili Dip, 41
Chinese Squid Appetizer, 52
Chocolate Cake, 221
Chocolate Cream, 96
Chocolate Oatmeal, 123
Chocolate Pudding, 111
Chorizo and Veggies Mix, 139
Chorizo Breakfast, 255
Cinnamon and Pumpkin Muffins, 57
Cinnamon Oatmeal, 126
Cinnamon Rice Pudding, 115
Clams and Mussels, 50
Clams And Mussels Appetizer, 179
Classic Indian Side Dish, 211
Cocoa Pudding, 93
Coconut and Pomegranate Oatmeal, 140
Coconut Cream and Sausage Gravy, 70
Coconut Pudding, 94
Cod Fillets And Orange Sauce, 153
Cod Puddings, 47
Cold Veggie Delight, 150
Collard Greens and Tomato Sauce, 90
Colored Cauliflower and Eggs Breakfast, 116
Colored Tomato And Zucchini, 165
Cool Pudding, 223
Crab and Cheese Dip, 60
Crab Appetizer, 171
Crab Legs, 40
Cranberries Jam, 228

Cranberry Dip, 41
Crazy And Unique Appetizer, 175
Crazy Carrots Casserole, 163
Crazy Delicious Pudding, 232
Cream Cheese Bars, 92
Creamy Carrot Soup, 152
Creamy Mushroom Dip, 43
Creamy Soup, 145

D

Delicious Apples And Cinnamon, 231
Delicious Breakfast Casserole, 239
Delicious Breakfast Cobbler, 242
Delicious Breakfast Eggs And Sauce, 247
Delicious Breakfast Meatloaf, 117
Delicious Breakfast Skillet, 128
Delicious Carrot Dessert, 220
Delicious Cauliflower Rice, 201
Delicious Fish Stew, 147
Delicious Korean Eggs, 237
Delicious Nuts And Fruits Breakfast, 256
Delicious Okra, 210
Delicious Oysters, 64
Delicious Pork Chops, 17
Delicious Pumpkin Side Dish, 212
Delicious Vanilla and Espresso Oatmeal, 139
Delightful Herring Appetizer, 178
Delightful Peaches Surprise, 219
Dessert Stew, 231
Different And Special Stew, 151
Different Dessert, 233
Different Eggs Breakfast, 238
Different Lasagna, 17
Divine Pears, 225

E

Easy And Delicious Salad, 166
Easy And Delicious Zucchini Pasta, 165
Easy Artichoke Soup, 157
Easy Asparagus And Prosciutto Dish, 167
Easy Leeks Platter, 56
Easy Pork Roast, 19
Easy Tomato Soup, 146
Egg Casserole, 119
Eggplant Breakfast Spread, 235
Eggplant Spread, 55
Eggs and Cheese Breakfast, 118
Eggs and Chives, 118
Eggs and Turkey, 133
Eggs, Ham And Mushroom Mix, 255
Elegant Dessert, 220
Elegant Duck Appetizer, 190
Elegant Scallops Salad, 184
Endives and Ham Appetizer, 54
Exotic Anchovies, 181

F

Fast Dessert, 222
Fast Mussels, 156
Fast Side Dish Delight, 209
Fish and Carrot Soup, 23
Fish Delight, 173
Flavored And Delicious Chicken, 159
Flavored Chicken And Veggies, 163
Flavored Pears, 105
French Coconut Cream, 105
French Endives, 54
French Endives Side Dish, 209
Fresh Fennel and Leek Soup, 38
Fresh Figs, 112

G

Great Broccoli Dish, 194
Great Butternut Squash Breakfast, 248
Great Egg Casserole, 240
Great French Eggs, 238
Great Green Dip, 173
Great Pears Dessert, 216
Great Pumpkin Dessert, 234
Great Veggie Appetizer, 191
Great Veggie Quiche, 243
Great Zucchini Spread, 248
Green Beans and Tomatoes, 85
Green Beans Side Dish, 80
Green Beans Side Dish, 197
Green Cabbage and Paprika, 69

H

Haddock and Mayonnaise, 25
Healthy Broccoli Side Dish, 212
Healthy Mackerel, 155
Healthy Mushrooms and Green Beans, 201
Hearty Breakfast, 239
Hearty Eggplants Appetizer, 183
Hot Beef Stew, 27
Hot Cauliflower Rice and Avocado, 77
Hot Radishes with Bacon and Cheese, 73

I

Incredible Beet Soup, 157
Incredible Chicken Appetizer, 185
Incredible Scallops, 178
Italian Chicken Wings, 62
Italian Dip, 58
Italian Mussels Appetizer, 48
Italian Side Dish, 204

K

Kale and Almonds, 69
Kale And Carrots Side Dish, 210
Kale and Prosciutto Muffins, 131

L

Lamb Shanks and Carrots, 32
Lamb Stew, 28

Leek and Beef Breakfast Mix, 138
Leek and Kale Breakfast, 256
Leg of Lamb and Spinach Salad, 28
Lemon and Garlic Shrimp, 25
Lemon Broccoli, 83
Lemon Cauliflower Rice, 78
Lemon Cream, 92
Lemon Cream, 96
Lemon Jam, 229
Light Breakfast, 247
Light Brussels Sprouts Side Dish, 206
Light Salmon, 154
Lovely Mash, 201

M

Mashed Sweet Potatoes, 199
Meat Quiche, 125
Meatballs and Sauce, 33
Mediterranean Octopus Appetizer, 52
Melon Cream, 100
Mexican Breakfast Casserole, 121
Mexican Chicken Soup, 31
Mexican Chicken Soup, 151
Mint Dip, 177
Minty Shrimp Appetizer, 59
Mixed Bell Peppers Side Dish, 84
Mixed Veggies, 203
Mushroom and Arugula Side Dish, 68
Mushroom Appetizer, 174
Mushroom Spread, 236
Mushroom Stew, 39
Mushroom Stew, 150
Mushroom, Tomatoes and Zucchini Mix, 134
Mussels Appetizer, 48
Mussels Bowls, 49
Mustard and Mushrooms Dip, 45

N

Napa Cabbage Side Salad, 66
Nutritious Side Dish, 214
Nuts Bowl, 131
Nuts Porridge, 257
Nuts, Squash and Apples Breakfast, 137

O

Okra and Beef Stew, 31
Okra and Zucchinis Breakfast, 135
Okra Bowls, 55
Onions Delight, 170
Orange Cake, 95
Orange Delight, 225
Orange Dessert, 234
Original Fruits Dessert, 231

P

Parsnips Mash, 81
Peach Cream, 100

Peach Marmalade, 107
Peaches and Sweet Sauce, 101
Peanut and Chia Pudding, 98
Pear Marmalade, 107
Pear Pudding, 113
Pears And Special Sauce, 216
Peppermint Pudding, 94
Perfect Chicken Stew, 161
Perfect Side Dish, 207
Pineapple and Cauliflower Pudding, 110
Plum Delight, 230
Poached Eggs, 246
Poached Fennel, 84
Pomegranate and Walnuts Chicken, 29
Popular Shrimp Appetizer, 177
Pork and Veggies, 21
Pork Bowls, 20
Pork Chops and Gravy, 20
Pork Sausage Quiche, 129
Pork with Lemon Sauce, 33
Pumpkin and Apple Butter, 241
Pumpkin And Cauliflower Rice, 193
Pumpkin Cake, 103
Pumpkin Cream, 99
Pumpkin Granola, 114
Pumpkin Pudding, 106
Pumpkin Spread, 134

R
Radish Snack, 191
Radishes and Chives, 73
Raspberry Dessert, 91
Red Cabbage and Applesauce, 86
Red Chard and Olives, 68
Red Chard Wonder, 186
Red Pepper Spread, 169
Red Peppers Soup, 147
Refreshing Curd, 224
Refreshing Fennel Soup, 158
Refreshing Fruits Dish, 230
Refreshing Zucchini Snack, 189
Rhubarb Dessert, 230
Rich Beef Stew, 161
Rich Beets Side Dish, 197
Rich Cabbage Salad, 164

S
Saffron Cauliflower Rice, 76
Salmon and Veggies, 34
Salmon Balls, 64
Salmon Cakes, 182
Salmon Patties, 47
Salmon Patties, 179
Salsa Chicken Soup, 27
Sausage, Leeks and Eggs Casserole, 129
Sausages and Mashed Celeriac, 30

Savoy Cabbage and Bacon, 89
Scotch Eggs, 124
Seafood Summer Mix, 30
Shrimp and Mushrooms, 24
Shrimp and Sausage Appetizer Bowls, 51
Shrimp and Turnips, 34
Shrimp and Zucchini Spaghetti, 23
Shrimp Delight, 166
Shrimp Surprise, 168
Simple And Delicious Cake, 217
Simple And Delicious Compote, 219
Simple And Delicious Compote, 221
Simple And Fast Side Dish, 203
Simple Artichoke Dish, 168
Simple Artichokes, 53
Simple Beef Party Patties, 183
Simple Breakfast Hash Browns, 116
Simple Breakfast Meatloaf, 250
Simple Cherry Breakfast, 257
Simple Cobbler, 218
Simple Fennel Side Dish, 202
Simple Glazed Carrots, 194
Simple Octopus, 156
Simple Peach Compote, 109
Simple Squash Pie, 226
Smoked Salmon and Shrimp Breakfast, 127
Southern Side Dish, 208
Special And Delicious Snack, 170
Special Artichokes, 167
Special Bell Peppers Appetizer, 186
Special Breakfast Butter, 251
Special Breakfast Egg Muffins, 244
Special Carrots Side Dish, 214
Special Cod Dish, 153
Special Collard Greens, 196
Special Dessert, 229
Special Flavored Side Dish, 208
Special Lemon Cream, 220
Special Olives Snack, 187
Special Onion And Bacon Jam, 249
Special Party Spread, 169
Special Pork And Sauce, 149
Special Pudding, 222
Special Shrimp Appetizer, 180
Special Spinach Appetizer Salad, 184
Special Sweet Potatoes, 195
Special Turkey Wings, 162
Special Vanilla Dessert, 228
Special Veggie Side Dish, 193
Spicy Chili Balls, 57
Spicy Mango Dip, 44
Spicy Mussels, 49
Spicy Salsa, 63
Spinach And Chard Appetizer Salad, 191

Spinach and Chard Mix, 75
Spinach Cauliflower Rice, 78
Spinach Cauliflower Rice, 200
Spinach Dip, 61
Sprouts and Apple Side Dish, 72
Squash and Chicken Cream, 36
Squash and Cranberry Sauce, 135
Squash Puree, 79
Squash Puree, 200
Squid and Veggies, 35
Strawberries and Coconut Breakfast, 138
Strawberries and Cranberries Marmalade, 106
Strawberries Breakfast, 259
Strawberries Compote, 108
Strawberries Compote, 111
Strawberry Cream, 97
Stuffed Bell Peppers, 40
Stuffed Clams, 50
Stuffed Mushrooms, 61
Stuffed Squid, 180
Summer Lamb Appetizer, 190
Summer Veggie Breakfast, 250
Superb Banana Dessert, 229
Superb Stuffed Tomatoes, 159
Superb Zucchini Breakfast, 246
Sweet Apples, 217
Sweet Cabbage, 90
Sweet Carrots, 113
Sweet Carrots Breakfast, 136
Sweet Cauliflower Rice Pudding, 215
Sweet Peaches, 108
Sweet Potato Salad, 160
Sweet Potato Spread, 176
Sweet Potatoes, 211
Sweet Potatoes Side Dish, 198
Swiss Chard and Garlic, 67
Swiss Chard and Pine Nuts, 74

T

Tapioca Pudding, 216
Tasty And Amazing Pear Dessert, 228
Tasty Cauliflower And Mint Rice, 195
Tasty Side Dish, 199
Tasty Squash Side Dish, 213
Tasty Turnip Sticks, 187
Tasty Zucchini And Squash, 253
Tender Pork Chops, 144
Textured Appetizer Salad, 185
The Best Jam Ever, 224
Tomato and Beet Side Salad, 88

Tomato And Spinach Breakfast Mix, 244
Tomato and Spinach Eggs, 120
Tomato Dip, 45
Tomato Side Salad, 205
Tomato Stew, 164
Tomatoes Appetizer, 56
Trout Fillet and Sauce, 24
Tuna Patties, 65
Tuna Patties, 189
Turkey Appetizer Meatballs, 189
Turkey Meatballs, 62
Turkey Stew, 39
Turkey Stew, 162
Turnips Puree, 82

U

Unbelievable Cabbage Side Dish, 207
Unbelievable Chicken, 158
Upside Down Cake, 104

V

Veggie Soup, 36
Veggie Stew, 148
Vietnamese Eggplant Side Dish, 70

W

Walnuts Cream, 95
White Fish Delight, 155
Winter Fruit Cobbler, 114
Winter Fruits Dessert, 233
Winter Pudding, 226
Wonderful And Special Side Dish, 198
Wonderful Berry Pudding, 232
Wonderful Breakfast Omelet, 245
Wonderful Frittata, 241
Wonderful Salmon And Veggies, 154
Worcestershire Shrimp, 65
Wrapped Shrimp, 188

Y

Yummy Mushrooms Snack, 188

Z

Zucchini And Carrots Delightful Breakfast, 251
Zucchini Appetizer, 175
Zucchini Appetizer Salad, 59
Zucchini Cake, 110
Zucchini Dessert, 223
Zucchini Dip, 42
Zucchini Hummus, 60
Zucchini Rolls, 63
Zucchini Side Dish, 214

Copyright 2017 by Vincent Brian All rights reserved.

All rights Reserved. No part of this publication or the information in it may be quoted from or reproduced in any form by means such as printing, scanning, photocopying or otherwise without prior written permission of the copyright holder.

Disclaimer and Terms of Use: Effort has been made to ensure that the information in this book is accurate and complete, however, the author and the publisher do not warrant the accuracy of the information, text and graphics contained within the book due to the rapidly changing nature of science, research, known and unknown facts and internet. The Author and the publisher do not hold any responsibility for errors, omissions or contrary interpretation of the subject matter herein. This book is presented solely for motivational and informational purposes only.

Made in the USA
Lexington, KY
21 November 2017